Communications in Computer and Information Science 2162

Rationale

The CCIS series is devoted to the publication of proceedings of computer science conferences. Its aim is to efficiently disseminate original research results in informatics in printed and electronic form. While the focus is on publication of peer-reviewed full papers presenting mature work, inclusion of reviewed short papers reporting on work in progress is welcome, too. Besides globally relevant meetings with internationally representative program committees guaranteeing a strict peer-reviewing and paper selection process, conferences run by societies or of high regional or national relevance are also considered for publication.

Topics

The topical scope of CCIS spans the entire spectrum of informatics ranging from foundational topics in the theory of computing to information and communications science and technology and a broad variety of interdisciplinary application fields.

Information for Volume Editors and Authors

Publication in CCIS is free of charge. No royalties are paid, however, we offer registered conference participants temporary free access to the online version of the conference proceedings on SpringerLink (http://link.springer.com) by means of an http referrer from the conference website and/or a number of complimentary printed copies, as specified in the official acceptance email of the event.

CCIS proceedings can be published in time for distribution at conferences or as post-proceedings, and delivered in the form of printed books and/or electronically as USBs and/or e-content licenses for accessing proceedings at SpringerLink. Furthermore, CCIS proceedings are included in the CCIS electronic book series hosted in the SpringerLink digital library at http://link.springer.com/bookseries/7899 Conferences publishing in CCIS are allowed to use Online Conference Service (OCS) for managing the whole proceedings lifecycle (from submission and reviewing to preparing for publication) free of charge.

Publication process

The language of publication is exclusively English. Authors publishing in CCIS have to sign the Springer CCIS copyright transfer form, however, they are free to use their material published in CCIS for substantially changed, more elaborate subsequent publications elsewhere. For the preparation of the camera-ready papers/files, authors have to strictly adhere to the Springer CCIS Authors' Instructions and are strongly encouraged to use the CCIS LaTeX style files or templates.

Abstracting/Indexing

CCIS is abstracted/indexed in DBLP, Google Scholar, EI-Compendex, Mathematical Reviews, SCImago, Scopus. CCIS volumes are also submitted for the inclusion in ISI Proceedings.

How to start

To start the evaluation of your proposal for inclusion in the CCIS series, please send an e-mail to ccis@springer.com.

Azza Basiouni · Claude Frasson
Editors

Breaking Barriers with Generative Intelligence

Using GI to Improve Human Education and Well-Being

First International Workshop, BBGI 2024
Thessaloniki, Greece, June 10, 2024
Proceedings

Springer

Editors
Azza Basiouni
Liwa College
Al Ain, United Arab Emirates

Claude Frasson
University of Montreal
Montréal, QC, Canada

ISSN 1865-0929 ISSN 1865-0937 (electronic)
Communications in Computer and Information Science
ISBN 978-3-031-65995-9 ISBN 978-3-031-65996-6 (eBook)
https://doi.org/10.1007/978-3-031-65996-6

This Springer imprint is published by the registered company Springer Nature Switzerland AG
The registered company address is: Gewerbestrasse 11, 6330 Cham, Switzerland

Preface

These proceedings contains the papers of the Workshop on Breaking Barriers with Generative Intelligence (BBGI 2024) which was held on June 10, 2024 in Thessaloniki, Greece. This workshop was part of the 20th International Conference on Intelligent Tutoring Systems (ITS 2024) which was held in Thessaloniki on June 10–13, 2024.

Research is evolving to a new concept of Artificial Intelligence (AI) which can be found in various disciplines and can serve human education and wellbeing. This new concept is named Generative Intelligence (GI). This concerns various AI systems, techniques, architectures, methods, or tools based on machine learning, in particular deep learning, which can be used to generate texts, images, solutions, and environments, and to enhance Human Intelligence, cognitive capacities, memory, and learning. Instead of trying to reproduce human behavior or recognize human traits using artificial intelligence techniques or learning analytics, Generative Intelligence provides a means to increase human cognitive potential.

Breaking Barriers with Generative Intelligence delves into how GI in AI improves human education and wellbeing. This interdisciplinary event brought together professionals from academia, industry, and government to address AI ethics, human–AI interaction, and the societal implications of GI. Participants learned to tackle social concerns and promote diversity in research and development through keynote presentations, panel discussions, and interactive workshops.

The topics of the workshop were GI in Tutoring Systems; Teachers and AI Collaborations; GI for Adaptive Learning; AI in Special Needs Education; Games and Virtual Reality Technology in Education; GI and Metaverse Technology in Education; GI for Autonomous Robots and Learning; and Changing Skills Sets and Learning Paradigms.

The international Program Committee of the workshop consisted of 7 leading members and 3 senior members of the Intelligent Tutoring Systems and AI communities, assisted by additional external reviewers.

Research papers came from Canada, Malaysia, Greece, and the United Arab Emirates and were reviewed by two reviewers through a double-blind process. The workshop applied the strict, high standards in the review process that have been established over the years for the main colocated event ITS, and which have made it a top-flight, selective conference. From the 24 submitted papers, 19 papers were accepted as full papers, whereas 1 paper was accepted as a short paper. We believe that these describe very significant research and new ideas.

The review process and the preparation of the proceedings was handled through the EasyChair platform.

Complementing the BBGI 2024 Workshop, the ITS 2024 program also included a panel on Potential Ways to Creatively Use Gen AI (e.g., ChatGPT) in Computer Science departments. Together these events provided a platform for experts and participants to explore innovative solutions and share insights on the evolving role of AI in education and beyond. They fostered collaborative discussions, highlighted the latest research, and set the stage for future advancements in the application of generative intelligence and digital transformation in educational settings.

In addition to the contributors mentioned above, we would like to thank all the authors, the members of the Program Committees, the external reviewers, and the Steering Committee members, as well as the hosting institution of the conference, the University of Macedonia, in Thessaloniki, Greece.

We finally would like to acknowledge that BBGI 2024 was held under the auspices of the Institute of Intelligent Systems (IIS) and was organized by Neoanalysis Ltd., under the guidance of Kitty Panourgia, the Organization Chair, and her team.

May 2024

Azza Basiouni
Claude Frasson

Organization

Workshop Chair

Azza Basiouni	Liwa College, UAE

Senior Program Committee

Claude Frasson	University of Montreal, Canada
Oscar Lin	Athabasca University, Canada
Kinshuk Kinshuk	University of North Texas, USA

Organization Chair

Kitty Panourgia	Neoanalysis Ltd., Greece

Program Committee

Michael Lin	Mount Saint Vincent University, Canada
Xiaokun Zhang	Athabasca University, Canada
Khaled Shaalan	British University, UAE
Ahmed Al Gindy	Canadian University, UAE
Ray Al Barazie	Liwa College, UAE
Beenu Mago	Skyline University College, UAE
Rasha Hasan	Liwa College, UAE
Said Salloum	University of Salford, UK
Usman Butt	British University, UAE

Contents

Applications, Challenges and Early Assessment of AI and ChatGPT in Education

Dimitrios Sidiropoulos(✉) and Christos-Nikolaos Anagnostopoulos

Social Science School, Cultural Technology and Communication Department, University of Aegean, Mytilene, Greece
dsidir@gmail.com

Abstract. Artificial Intelligence (AI) in recent years has shown an unprecedentedly impressive development, tending to play a catalytic role in all aspects of life. The interest of the academic community, but also of governments, is huge in the dynamics of AI and is reflected by the truly explosive amount of investment and research that is underway. Enthusiastic opinions and statements about AI are made every day, but at the same time they also bring to the fore alarming predictions about its effects. This paper aims to describe the opportunities emerging from the use of artificial intelligence and ChatGPT to improve education, but also to provide an early assessment of ChatGPT in education.

Keywords: Artificial Intelligence · ChatGPT · Assessment

1 Introduction

The rapid technological developments that have taken place in recent decades play a decisive role in various areas of human life and affect almost every aspect of daily life [1, 2]. Of course, education could not remain untouched by this technological revolution [3].

The evolution of the educational process over time has been dynamically transformed. The traditional model of learning as we know it is now considered obsolete, and teaching has undergone sweeping changes both in its structure and in the way information and knowledge are transmitted, creating a new landscape on the educational map. The addition of technology, interactive media, distance education, new approaches to implement personalized learning and recently Artificial Intelligence (AI), tend to shape a new reality in education [4].

The application of AI in education began to make its appearance dynamically in recent years, signaling a new revolution in the educational process [1] with the ultimate goal of the smooth integration of new proposals and technologies into the educational process. This new technology (AI) can theoretically offer a multitude of tools and benefits in the field of education, but first of all it should be tested in many ways while taking care of the concerns, doubts and ethical barriers of the educational community, resulting from its application.

A. Basiouni and C. Frasson (Eds.): BBGI 2024, CCIS 2162, pp. 1–12, 2024.
https://doi.org/10.1007/978-3-031-65996-6_1

The uniqueness of the nature of people, the diversity of characters but also the diversity of cognitive level, experiences and the way and pace of learning, demonstrate the need to adapt the educational process in a way that promotes and applies personalized learning techniques. Over the years, various algorithms, methods, and techniques have been proposed by researchers in order to integrate personalized learning capabilities into the educational process. However, given the complexity of human nature, the possible factors influencing how a learner learns can be so numerous that they are difficult to capture. However, certain factors have been proven to play a very important role in the way a student learns. Various machine learning algorithms, having a wealth of data at their disposal, can offer personalized learning options, creating almost unique learning paths for each learner. A catalytic role at this point promises to be offered by AI, which is expected to be an important addition, taking over part of the work of a teacher [5]. AI can create customized training materials, assessment sheets, provide feedback, be a personalized assistant - Intelligence Tutoring System [6], but also contribute to the evaluation of the learner.

Understandably, all of these new developments, especially since the advent of ChatGPT, have upset much of the educational community. Many trainers feel they will lose their jobs and AI will replace their role. Educators are also aware that they will likely face new risks related to privacy, plagiarism and data security. The role of the teacher can be transformed, to be the supervisor of the whole process, who will use AI in support [6], but in any case he should determine the goals and intended results of the educational process.

It is very important and should be an absolute priority of researchers as well as governments, the in-depth investigation of the possibilities, disadvantages and ethical barriers resulting from the integration of AI in various areas of everyday life and especially education. The educational community needs to act quickly, wisely and efficiently in order to smoothly absorb the positives that AI can offer in the education sector, while ensuring the quality and reliability of the education provided. The educational staff should join forces with AI, and governments should draw up a modern educational policy, in order to upgrade the education provided for the benefit of the learners.

All actors in the field of education should act collectively, in order to obtain the greatest possible benefits from the use of artificial intelligence in education, but at the same time to be properly protected from the risks it entails. It is imperative to properly use AI in education, to realize and exploit the key opportunities, but also to prevent or mitigate the extraordinary risks, as well as to deal with the unintended consequences in a timely manner.

2 Description of ChatGPT

ChatGPT, developed by Open Artificial Intelligence (OpenAI), is an advanced conversational AI, a large language model (LLM) that uses Deep Learning and allows humans to interact with a computer in a more natural way with the dialogue form [7, 8]. GPT, short for "Generative Pre-trained Transformer," refers to a series of natural language processing models developed by OpenAI, and was made available to the general public on November 30, 2022 [9]. At its core, ChatGPT uses machine learning techniques to generate human-like text based on the input prompts it receives. It is also known as a form of genetic artificial intelligence due to its capacity to generate unique outcomes. ChatGPT employs natural language processing to train with data from the web, providing users with answers to questions or prompts. It can understand the context of a conversation, answer questions, provide explanations and even produce creative content such as stories or poems. Generative corresponds to the model's ability to generate text rather than simply understand or classify it. Pretrained indicates that the model has undergone an initial training phase where it was learned from a large amount of Internet information. Transformer refers to the type of model architecture used, which helps understand the input text.

Models of this kind are trained on large text data sets including books, articles, web pages, so that they can predict the next word in a sentence and generate complete sentences in response to a question [10, 11]. In the case of ChatGPT, 570 GB of data were required, representing 300 billion words, while approximately 175 billion parameters have been provided to the system. This combination of technologies allows ChatGPT to generate meaningful responses that closely mimic natural human conversation [7, 12–14].

ChatGPT is a "large language model" (LLM), an artificial intelligence system or tool endowed with the ability to read, summarize, solve mathematical problems, produce learning materials, design syllabi, guide students, explain terms and abstract concepts and theories, find and correct errors in the source code of computer programs, write various types of essays, create advisory reports, identify scientific debates in various fields of study through access to relevant literature, translate texts into different languages, create a bibliographic list, and create complete sentences comparable to those of humans [12, 15].

ChatGPT utilizes machine learning, which presently stands as the leading method in the field of Artificial Intelligence (AI). Because of its ability to generate and evaluate information, ChatGPT can play an important role in teaching and learning processes. In addition to various types of AI, ChatGPT has the potential to enhance the educational process and experience for learners. It can function as an independent tool or be incorporated into different systems and platforms [13].

Educators can utilize ChatGPT to offer tailored educational assistance to their students. Based on the individual requirements and learning preferences of each student, ChatGPT is capable of suggesting specialized learning materials and activities. For example, an educator can employ ChatGPT to evaluate student performance data and pinpoint areas where learners are having difficulties with particular concepts. Teachers can take the help of ChatGPT to answer students' questions and provide feedback to them. In addition, teachers can request clarifications and examples from ChatGPT on a specific topic to further increase the effectiveness of their teaching. Educators can also harness the capabilities of ChatGPT to evaluate student assignments and quizzes. ChatGPT can be used to check submitted work for plagiarism. It is also very interesting that the model can generate questions/quizzes based on different levels of difficulty (e.g., high, medium, easy) for a variety of topics [16]. ChatGPT has the potential to produce impressive results for writing stories, poetry, songs, essays and other subjects, but it also has some limitations. Users can ask the Chatbot questions and it will answer persuasively and with arguments. ChatGPT's proficiency in grasping context and offering insightful analysis renders it an effective instrument for collecting, assessing, and comprehending market trends. This technology can enhance existing procedures and gather qualitative data via informal surveys, analyze data and extract features from massive amounts of unstructured data, and save researchers time and effort. ChatGPT differs from previous AI models in that it can write software in multiple languages, debug code, break down a complex topic into manageable chunks, prepare candidates for interviews, and write reports [9].

According to research by Firat [17], AI and ChatGPT can improve the performance of learners in different learning environments and also motivate them in this direction. The learning experience in educational environments can be enhanced using ChatGPT and increase learner engagement in e-courses by offering personalized suggestions for study according to the learning goals and needs of each learner. At the same time, self-learning is effectively promoted through personalized support, easy access to resources, real-time feedback and guidance, enhanced use of open educational resources, and self-assessment.

OpenAI has achieved considerable advancements in enhancing deep learning through the introduction of GPT-4. The release of GPT-4 in March 2023 has already generated widespread discussion, as the tool appears to be more accurate, reliable and adaptable than its predecessor [18]. This new multifunctional language model has the ability to accept not only text but also images and produce relevant results. It may not currently be as capable as a human in real-world scenarios, but it has performed very well in many professional and academic metrics. It clearly outperforms ChatGPT, which is promising for future releases [12]. GPT-4 is OpenAI's most advanced model, promising safer, more accurate and more useful answers. According to the company, GPT-4 can solve difficult problems more accurately thanks to its broader general knowledge and problem-solving abilities.

3 Applications of ChatGPT

AI and ChatGPT can find application in many everyday tasks and in many aspects of human life. One of the most obvious application of ChatGPT in business is customer service, offering 24-h support as a digital assistant and minimizing the requirement for human involvement. Users can engage with ChatGPT for tasks like organizing meetings, setting reminders, catching up on news, managing smart home devices, or sending messages, essentially through a new user-friendly communication experience. AI and ChatGPT can also be used as a mental health consultant, offering a wide range of support services, but also as a rich source of medical information for the provision of medical help and care. The multi-faceted role of ChatGPT allows it to act as a virtual legal assistant to offer legal advice [19].

For education in particular, the advantages of AI applications and ChatGPT can be varied and truly impressive. Enhancing learners' motivation for autonomous learning [2], automated assessment and grading of exercises and assignments [20], feedback and specific suggestions for improvement, virtual assistants – Intelligence Tutoring Systems (ITS), the possibility of personalized learning with adapted content, learning pace and teaching approach, the prevention of cheating and plagiarism as well as the preparation of adapted teaching materials and assessment sheets, are just some of the positives that we have to attribute to AI [3, 21]. ChatGPT's ability to understand human language, to be able to converse with a human, its flexibility to respond to various situations, its speed of response, its relatively low cost of use, its ability to be used as a 24/7 personal training assistant, are some more of its strong points [7]. As a study assistant, ChatGPT can support learners beyond conventional textbooks to understand difficult topics by providing additional explanations and step-by-step advice [19].

AI appears to have the potential to make a positive contribution to education, increasing personalized learning for all learners [12]. Intelligent instructional support systems are currently the most promising field of artificial intelligence for the transformation of education, and are perhaps the most effective tools for personalizing instruction [20]. Several training platforms have integrated ChatGPT as a virtual instructor in order to adapt the learning pace and preferences of the learners making the learning experience more engaging and interesting [19]. The growth of this personalization is currently in full development as researchers experiment with new learning models and as a result new opportunities are created in the educational field [7].

Using ChatGPT, instructors can develop unique assessment sheets and instructional content [18]. Instructors can use AI to reduce their workload, gain insights into learners, and promote innovation in the classroom. AI systems are designed to assist instructors by automating assessment, plagiarism detection, classroom management, and providing feedback [7]. Also, instructors can benefit from creating lesson plans, activities and exercises, providing tailored support and answers to learners' questions, immediate assessment and feedback [16].

A major advantage of ChatGPT is that it allows learners to learn through experimentation and experiences. ChatGPT can aid students in enhancing their reading and writing abilities by offering recommendations, such as for syntax and grammar. Additionally, the model is capable of creating practice exercises and quizzes across diverse subjects, including mathematics, physics, and language arts. It can also generate explanations and step-by-step solutions to a given problem and help develop problem-solving and analytical thinking skills [16]. Using ChatGPT, learners can evaluate different strategies and approaches to solving problems and achieving goals through play. It is therefore imperative for educators to turn challenges into opportunities [7].

Storytelling and creative writing suit ChatGPT, which as a creative partner can promote brainstorming. ChatGPT's ability to understand and correctly render content and suggestions makes it a vital resource for content creators. The model excels at writing reports [22], writing emails, creating marketing materials, and even managing social media. Also, ChatGPT as a virtual translator has shown promising results in various languages. ChatGPT is also proving to be a significantly promising tool for code generation in programming as well as a debugging aid in software development [16, 19].

ChatGPT offers both students and educators the chance to obtain precise responses to theoretical queries, particularly in the fields of communication, business writing, and music courses. The answers provided by ChatGPT are usually accurate. Learners, if they want instant answers on a topic, can consider ChatGPT as a reliable option. In contrast to search engines that deliver countless results which may sometimes lack precision and relevance, ChatGPT furnishes responses tailored to the user-defined criteria, within the confines of the answer's word limit. These responses can provide users with sufficient information, eliminating the need to sift through an extensive array of sources to assess their accuracy and reliability. ChatGPT also has the ability to provide students with customized answers for case study analysis, writing business correspondence and reports. These responses can provide learners with information on how to approach the case study and create appropriate relevant reports [23].

Each learner has a unique cognitive profile based on their own prior knowledge of a subject, their personal social background, their own financial, aesthetic and emotional situation. Teaching is most effective when it adapts to these changing contexts. AI can help identify learning gaps in each learner, offer tailored recommendations and content as well as step-by-step solutions to complex problems [21].

Several studies have shown that one of the functions pursued by the use of AI is the automated assessment of learners. [20]. Assessment in the educational context refers to any control or judgment of a task or a learner's performance. Assessment has been identified as one of the three pillars of school education along with curriculum, learning and teaching. The purpose of contemporary assessment is to measure what students know, what they have understood and what they can apply. Optimally, evaluations should encompass the entire spectrum of learners' skills and offer valuable insights into learning achievements. However, every student is unique and so are their learning paths. How standardized assessment can be used to assess each student, with unique abilities, skills, and preferences, is a question that requires much investigation [20].

4 Challenges of ChatGPT

Despite the advantages that AI and ChatGPT may have, there are limitations, challenges and disadvantages associated with its use that we should consider. Some of them are found in the unreliability of the information that produces when it does not have sufficient data and references resulting in providing wrong answers [7], it cannot use idioms intelligently, it is not able to correctly and accurately cite the sources or to evaluate their quality, there is an absence of ethical criteria, it shows occasional logical errors and grammatical errors, there is a possible bias in technology, it has a weakness in calculating complex and difficult mathematical expressions, and it ignores its lack of knowledge [15, 24].

ChatGPT has demonstrated remarkable capabilities regarding text production, however it has presented cases with incorrect or misleading information [7]. Guaranteeing the precision and reliability of information generated by AI is of immense importance in order to maintain the integrity of any work or research [19]. ChatGPT has been trained on a huge amount of data, which may contain bias and affect the actual results. ChatGPT has the potential to produce detrimental material, including hate speech or misinformation. Implementing safeguards to avert the creation of such content is crucial. Additionally, ChatGPT might exhibit biases towards specific cultural and linguistic groups, potentially resulting in skewed or unsuitable responses. Ensuring reliable results requires constant control, feedback and updating [12].

Although ChatGPT possesses a broad awareness and comprehension of many subjects, its depth of knowledge might be insufficient for certain specialized niche topics.

A differential performance is also observed in different subject areas, including finance, programming, mathematics and general public questions [18]. Lack of quality and diversity in training data can lead to biased results with negative consequences. The decline in critical thinking, independence in problem solving, and skill development seem quite close to the increasing reliance on AI [12].

ChatGPT has access to the data of a huge number of users, which raises privacy and data protection concerns. Developing policies and regulations is crucial to guarantee the protection and responsible use of user data. Also, models like ChatGPT are quite complex and require huge computing resources and perhaps we should also consider the environmental footprint they leave in terms of energy consumption [12].

ChatGPT has the ability to exhibit critical thinking abilities and produce highly authentic text with limited data input, posing a potential risk to the credibility of online examinations. This is especially pertinent in higher education environments where such testing is increasingly prevalent. It is important for both educators and institutions to be aware of the possibility of using ChatGPT for cheating and to explore countermeasures in order to maintain the fairness and validity of online testing for all learners [11].

In general, ChatGPT has several limitations and disadvantages, including: i) Inaccurate or Misleading Information ii) Sensitivity to prompts iii) Overuse of certain phrases iv) Inability to control sources or access information in real time v) Difficulty handling ambiguous queries vi) Lack of contextual association vii) Ethically ambiguous content viii) Long chat texts ix) Inability to create visual content x) Addressing requests that are unsuitable or damaging xi) Challenges in identifying and adjusting to the user's level of expertise xii) Restricted capacity for emotional understanding xiii) Absence of individualized feedback xiv) Constrained expertise in specific fields xv) Incapacity to engage with external systems xvi) Difficulty in processing queries in multiple languages xvii) Struggles with interpreting figurative language xviii) Restricted creative abilities xix) Tendency to make overly broad generalizations xx) Variability in output quality xxi) Significant energy use and environmental impact during training xxii) Challenges in comprehending human intuition xxiii) Absence of self-awareness xxiv) Significant resources needed for training and development [7, 12, 18, 19, 25, 26].

5 Early Assessment of ChatGPT

The launch of ChatGPT for widespread public use in November 2022 has sparked a multitude of inquiries among educators, scholars, and policy makers. A crucial issue to address is determining whether AI models like ChatGPT represent a beneficial opportunity for the educational sector or pose challenges that could lead to adverse outcomes.

In 2023, Anagnostopoulos [27] conducted a study on evaluating AI and ChatGPT-generated content in computer science programming and programming education. The focus was on examining the primary uses, benefits, drawbacks, and future ethical and practical considerations of AI in the educational sphere. The study involved posing specific queries to ChatGPT version 3.5, seeking insights into ChatGPT's most significant applications, key advantages, notable limitations, and prospective impact in programming and developer training. The findings indicated that while AI and ChatGPT can significantly aid beginners in computer programming and researchers, it's crucial to verify the information they provide for accuracy. Additionally, the research highlighted the need to be mindful of potential negative effects on the critical thinking and expressive abilities of both learners and educators.

In 2023, Wardat [28] conducted a qualitative case study using interviews to explore the viewpoints on the use of AI and ChatGPT in mathematics education, considering both learners' and teachers' perspectives. The initial phase of the research acknowledged ChatGPT's fundamental capabilities in mathematics, particularly as a helpful tool in teaching geometry. However, insights from actual educational settings revealed that ChatGPT lacks an in-depth understanding of geometric concepts and is not fully capable of rectifying misconceptions. The effectiveness and precision of ChatGPT's responses are largely contingent on the complexity of the problems being addressed and the quality of the data and prompts it receives.

The study by Frieder [29] revealed that while ChatGPT is effective as a tool for retrieving mathematical facts, akin to a search engine for math topics, its performance in mathematics using open-source datasets like miniGHOSTS and GHOSTS was underwhelming. ChatGPT, particularly in its GPT-4 version, shows promise in assisting with undergraduate mathematics but falls short in producing dependable results for more complex, advanced mathematical problems. Its capability in solving mathematical problems, especially those found in exam questions, does not reach the proficiency level of a graduate student. Similarly, Shakarian [30] found that ChatGPT's effectiveness in solving mathematical problems significantly deteriorates as the difficulty level of the subject matter and the complexity of the calculations increase.

In 2023, Tian [31] and colleagues undertook a comprehensive empirical study to assess the viability of ChatGPT as a fully automated programming assistant. This study concentrated on typical, essential, and routine tasks performed by programmers, such as writing code, debugging, and code explanation. ChatGPT demonstrated the ability to create accurate code for a range of problem types and difficulty levels on the LeetCode platform. However, like previous large language models (LLMs), ChatGPT faces challenges in generating satisfactory code for novel and unfamiliar problems without pre-existing data, with its effectiveness significantly decreasing for high-difficulty challenges. In terms of code correction, ChatGPT achieved relatively competitive results compared to other tools, though its average efficiency remained around 60%. The study found that ChatGPT can effectively explain the intended purpose of a code, even when the code includes errors. The conclusion drawn from this research is that developers can utilize ChatGPT as a supportive tool for generating solutions to relatively straightforward and repetitive programming tasks, but caution is advised when tackling new problems of high complexity.

In 2023, Qureshi [32] conducted a study on the performance of Computer Science students in algorithmic programming and problem-solving skills, dividing them into two groups, with one group having access to ChatGPT for support. The results indicate that ChatGPT is capable of generating well-structured code and proposing optimized solutions. The model shows promise in providing useful results and explanations for students tackling problems. With the right prompts, ChatGPT offers step-by-step guidance and explains the algorithms to be used. However, there were instances where the generated code was not entirely correct, contained inaccuracies, or was not executable by the compiler, particularly as the problem's difficulty level rose. The study emphasizes the significance of users having the training and experience to give precise commands and instructions to ChatGPT in order to yield more effective and relevant outcomes.

A comparative study by Laskar [33] noted that ChatGPT, as a general-purpose model, performs less effectively on known datasets but often matches human-level performance in algorithmic tasks. Different versions of ChatGPT can yield varying results for the same prompt, and its performance may decline with an increase in the number of questions. While ChatGPT excels in multilingual capabilities, its performance in less common languages is weaker. ChatGPT also outperforms other LLMs in math and coding, demonstrating more ethical, less biased, and truthful characteristics.

In 2023, Antaki [34] conducted a study to evaluate the performance of ChatGPT and GPT-4 in a test focused on Ophthalmology. They utilized 260 random questions from a non-public Ophthalmology database, ensuring these questions were not previously indexed by any search engine like Google or included in ChatGPT's training data. The study uncovered notable performance disparities between the two AI models, with the updated version of ChatGPT demonstrating significantly better results. Additionally, the research pointed out variations in the models' effectiveness, which depended not only on the difficulty level of the questions but also on the specific educational content of each teaching unit.

In a survey by Das [35] involving 96 microbiology questions and evaluated by three expert microbiologists, ChatGPT displayed excellent performance, achieving around 80% accuracy. This suggests its potential as a useful tool in microbiology, although continual improvements are necessary for academic applications. Nasution [36] from the University of East Java's Department of Educational Sciences conducted qualitative research to test the reliability and validity of ChatGPT-created biology assessment questions. Following specific instructions, ChatGPT produced 21 multiple-choice questions, with 20 being positively evaluated. Over 70% of learners found the questions relevant, acceptable, and accurate.

ChatGPT's advanced natural language processing capabilities have made it a notable tool in various fields like health, finance, law, information, sales, and marketing. In education, it assists in developing personalized teaching materials, real-time feedback, guiding learners, creating interactive exercises and presentations, evaluating trainees, and grading their work, as well as fostering an adaptive learning environment. In computer programming, ChatGPT can generate, debug, improve, and explain code, as noted by Ray [12].

6 Conclusion

It is clear from the evidence presented in this research that AI technology has reached extraordinary levels and is now capable not only of retrieving and providing simple information, but also of critical thinking to an extent. Among ChatGPT's most remarkable capabilities is its aptitude for critical thinking, coupled with its skill in articulating thoughts and ideas in flawlessly written language. It has demonstrated exceptional ability and results in various fields, to the point of simulating the abilities of humans [11].

While ChatGPT has made significant strides in creating comprehensive responses, there is room for improvement in handling extended conversations. Prompting methods and techniques can allow users to actively contribute to managing ChatGPT responses [18]. Future research should focus on bias prevention and equity enhancement to reduce bias. Research should provide advanced solutions for maintaining privacy, confidentiality, and personal data protection [19].

The implementation of AI and ChatGPT in education also requires a number of immediate changes in order for this transition to be smooth and with minimal negative effects. Teachers should improve the structure of assignments and exams to students, using more interactive tools in order to reduce the possibility of plagiarism. Instructors should be informed and trained in order to detect plagiarism, but also to incorporate AI into their teaching preparation. It is of utmost importance to educate students about the disadvantages of ChatGPT, including its reliance on faulty data, lack of current knowledge, and the potential to produce false or misleading findings [18].

References

1. Xue, Y., Wang, Y.: Artificial intelligence for education and teaching. Wirel. Commun. Mob. Comput. **2022**, 10 (2022). Article ID 4750018. https://doi.org/10.1155/2022/4750018
2. Ali, J., Shamsan, M., Hezam, T., Majeed, A.: Impact of ChatGPT on learning motivation: teachers and students' voices. J. Engl. Stud. Arabia Felix **2**, 41–49 (2023). https://doi.org/10.56540/jesaf.v2i1.51
3. Owoc, M.L., Sawicka, A., Weichbroth, P.: Artificial intelligence technologies in education: benefits, challenges and strategies of implementation. In: Owoc, M.L., Pondel, M. (eds.) Artificial Intelligence for Knowledge Management. IAICT, vol. 599, pp. 37–58. Springer, Cham (2021). https://doi.org/10.1007/978-3-030-85001-2_4
4. Reiss, M.J.: The use of AI in education: practicalities and ethical considerations. London Rev. Educ. **19**(1), 5, 1–14 (2021). https://doi.org/10.14324/LRE.19.1.05
5. Minn, S.: I-assisted knowledge assessment techniques for adaptive learning environments. Comput. Educ. Artif. Intell. **3** (2022). https://doi.org/10.1016/j.caeai.2022.100050. ISSN 2666-920X
6. Schiff, D.: Out of the laboratory and into the classroom: the future of artificial intelligence in education. AI Soc. **36**, 331–348 (2021). https://doi.org/10.1007/s00146-020-01033-8
7. Jürgen, R., Samson, T., Shannon, T.: ChatGPT: bullshit spewer or the end of traditional assessments in higher education? J. Appl. Learn. Teach. (2023). https://doi.org/10.37074/jalt.2023.6.1.9
8. Damian, E.: ChatGPT and the rise of generative AI: threat to academic integrity? (2023). https://doi.org/10.1016/j.jrt.2023.100060
9. Haleem, A., Javaid, M., Singh, R.: An era of ChatGPT as a significant futuristic support tool: a study on features, abilities, and challenges. BenchCouncil Trans. Benchmarks Stand. Eval. **2**(4) (2022). https://doi.org/10.1016/j.tbench.2023.100089. ISSN 2772-4859
10. Giray, L.: Prompt engineering with ChatGPT: a guide for academic writers. Ann. Biomed. Eng. (2023). https://doi.org/10.1007/s10439-023-03272-4. Epub 2023
11. Susnjak, T.: ChatGPT: the end of online exam integrity? arXiv:2212.09292 (2022). https://doi.org/10.48550/arXiv.2212.09292
12. Ray, P.: ChatGPT: a comprehensive review on background, applications, key challenges, bias, ethics, limitations and future scope. Internet Things Cyber-Phys. Syst. **3**, 121–154 (2023). https://doi.org/10.1016/j.iotcps.2023.04.003. ISSN 2667-3452
13. Emma, S., Arianna, V.: ChatGPT and artificial intelligence in higher education: quick start guide. UNESCO International Institute for Higher Education in Latin America and the Caribbean (2023)

14. Heston, T.F., Khun, C.: Prompt engineering in medical education. Int. Med. Educ. **2**(3), 198–205 (2023). https://doi.org/10.3390/ime2030019
15. Zhang, B.: Preparing educators and students for ChatGPT and AI Technology in higher education: benefits, limitations, strategies, and implications of ChatGPT & AI technologies (2023). https://doi.org/10.13140/RG.2.2.32105.98404
16. Rahman, M.M., Watanobe, Y.: ChatGPT for education and research: opportunities, threats, and strategies. Appl. Sci. **13**(9), 5783 (2023). https://doi.org/10.3390/app13095783
17. Firat, M.: How chat GPT can transform autodidactic experiences and open education? OSF Preprints, 12 January 2023. https://doi.org/10.31219/osf.io/9ge8m
18. Gill, S.S., et al.: Transformative effects of ChatGPT on modern education: emerging era of AI Chatbots. Internet Things Cyber-Phys. Syst. (2023). https://doi.org/10.1016/j.iotcps.2023.06.002
19. Nazir, A., Wang, Z.: A comprehensive survey of ChatGPT: advancements, applications, prospects, and challenges. Meta Radiol. **1**(2), 100022 (2023). https://doi.org/10.1016/j.metrad.2023.100022. PMID: 37901715; PMCID: PMC10611551
20. Calatayud Gonzalez, V., Prendes, P., Roig-Vila, R.: Artificial intelligence for student assessment: a systematic review. Appl. Sci. **11**, 5467 (2021). https://doi.org/10.3390/app11125467
21. Chaudhry, M., Kazim, E.: Artificial Intelligence in Education (AIEd): a high-level academic and industry note 2021. AI Ethics **2**, 1–9 (2022). https://doi.org/10.1007/s43681-021-00074-z
22. Shoufan, A.: Exploring students' perceptions of ChatGPT: thematic analysis and follow-up survey (2023). https://doi.org/10.1109/ACCESS.2023.3268224
23. Alafnan, M., Dishari, S., Jovic, M., Lomidze, K.: ChatGPT as an educational tool: opportunities, challenges, and recommendations for communication, business writing, and composition courses **3**, 60–68 (2023). https://doi.org/10.37965/jait.2023.0184
24. Azaria, A.: ChatGPT usage and limitations (2022). https://doi.org/10.13140/RG.2.2.26616.11526
25. Bender, E., Gebru, T., McMillan-Major, A., Shmitchell, S.: On the dangers of stochastic parrots: can language models be too big? In: Proceedings of the 2021 ACM Conference on Fairness, Accountability, and Transparency (FAccT 2021), pp. 610–623. Association for Computing Machinery, New York, NY, USA (2021). https://doi.org/10.1145/3442188.3445922
26. Navigli, R., Conia, S., Ross, B.: Biases in large language models: origins, inventory and discussion. J. Data Inf. Q. **15** (2023). https://doi.org/10.1145/3597307
27. Anagnostopoulos, C.: ChatGPT impacts in programming education: a short list of input questions and output answers from ChatGTP. Zenodo (2023). https://doi.org/10.5281/zenodo.8375014
28. Wardat, Y., Tashtoush, M.A., AlAli, R., Jarrah, A.M.: ChatGPT: a revolutionary tool for teaching and learning mathematics. Eurasia J. Math. Sci. Technol. Educ. **19**(7), em2286 (2023). https://doi.org/10.29333/ejmste/13272
29. Frieder, S., et al.: Mathematical capabilities of ChatGPT. arXiv:2301.13867 [cs.LG] (2023). https://doi.org/10.48550/arXiv.2301.13867
30. Shakarian, P., Koyyalamudi, A., Ngu, N., Mareedu, L.: An independent evaluation of ChatGPT on mathematical word problems (MWP). (2023). arXiv:2302.13814. https://doi.org/10.48550/arXiv.2302.13814
31. Tian H., et al.: Is ChatGPT the ultimate programming assistant - how far is it? (2023). https://doi.org/10.48550/arXiv.2304.11938
32. Qureshi, B.: Exploring the use of ChatGPT as a tool for learning and assessment in undergraduate computer science curriculum: opportunities and challenges (2023). arXiv:2304.11214. https://doi.org/10.48550/arXiv.2304.11214

33. Laskar, R., Bari, S., Rahman, M., Bhuiyan, H., Joty, S., Huang, J.: A systematic study and comprehensive evaluation of ChatGPT on benchmark datasets. In: Findings of the Association for Computational Linguistics: ACL 2023, pp. 431–469. Association for Computational Linguistics, Toronto, Canada (2023)
34. Antaki, F., Touma, S., Milad, D., El-Khoury, J., Duval, R.: Evaluating the performance of ChatGPT in ophthalmology: an analysis of its successes and shortcomings (2023). https://doi.org/10.1101/2023.01.22.23284882
35. Das, D., et al.: Assessing the capability of ChatGPT in answering first- and second-order knowledge questions on microbiology as per competency-based medical education curriculum (2023). https://doi.org/10.7759/cureus.36034. PMID: 37056538, PMCID: PMC10086829
36. Nasution, N.: Using artificial intelligence to create biology multiple choice questions for higher education. Agricult. Environ. Educ. **2**, em002 (2023). https://doi.org/10.29333/agrenvedu/13071

Empowering the Metaverse in Education: ChatGPT's Role in Transforming Learning Experiences

Raghad Alfaisal(✉), Haslinda Hashim, and Ummu Husna Azizan

Faculty of Computing and Meta-Technology, Universiti Pendidikan Sultan Idris, Tanjung Malim, Perak, Malaysia
raghad.alfaisal81@gmail.com, {haslinda, ummuhusna}@meta.upsi.edu.my

Abstract. As the concept of the Metaverse gains traction, its potential to revolutionize education has become increasingly evident. This abstract explores the role of ChatGPT, an advanced AI-powered language model, in enhancing the Metaverse's impact on education. The Metaverse represents a digital convergence of physical and virtual realities, fostering immersive and interactive environments. ChatGPT's integration into this space introduces a novel dimension to education, redefining how students and educators engage with content and each other. This abstract delves into ChatGPT's contributions to the educational landscape within the Metaverse. By harnessing natural language processing capabilities, ChatGPT enables real-time, contextually rich interactions. It acts as an intelligent conversational agent, offering personalized guidance, answering queries, and facilitating discussions. This interactivity engenders a dynamic learning experience, transcending the boundaries of traditional classrooms. Additionally, ChatGPT's language versatility ensures inclusivity in education. It bridges linguistic gaps, enabling multilingual interactions and content delivery. The AI's role as a virtual tutor and content creator further strengthens its significance. From explaining complex concepts to generating tailored learning materials, ChatGPT facilitates adaptive learning experiences. Furthermore, ChatGPT's continuous learning analytics furnish educators with insights into student behaviors, informing data-driven instructional strategies. Collaborative learning is promoted through the AI's mediation of discussions and group projects. As a virtual companion, ChatGPT nurtures personalized, immersive, and collaborative learning environments, empowering learners within the Metaverse.

Keywords: AI Integration · ChatGPT · Education · Metaverse · Learning Platforms

1 Introduction

The metaverse, a collective virtual shared space formed by the convergence of virtually augmented physical reality and persistent virtual space, has steadily garnered attention as the next frontier in digital evolution [1–3]. Emerging from the realms of science fiction to the dawn of tangible reality [4, 5], it promises to weave together the digital and

A. Basiouni and C. Frasson (Eds.): BBGI 2024, CCIS 2162, pp. 13–31, 2024.
https://doi.org/10.1007/978-3-031-65996-6_2

physical worlds, offering unparalleled immersion and interactivity [6, 7]. Education, an ever-evolving domain, hasn't remained untouched. The potential applications of the metaverse in educational contexts range from fully immersive virtual classrooms [8, 9], global collaborations without geographical constraints, to experiential learning in simulated environments [10, 11]. Parallel to the rise of the metaverse, ChatGPT, developed by OpenAI, stands as one of the prominent advancements in the field of artificial intelligence. It has demonstrated a wide array of applications, from simple conversational agents to more complex roles in content generation, problem-solving, and tutoring. Its natural language processing capabilities have positioned it as a relevant tool in the educational landscape, providing real-time feedback, answering queries, and assisting in personalized learning paths [12].

The metaverse, coupled with the capabilities of advanced AI models like ChatGPT, holds immense promise in redefining the educational landscape. However, while each has been individually studied to an extent, there remains a conspicuous research gap in understanding their combined implications, applications, and challenges in the context of education. Previous studies have primarily focused on the educational potential of the metaverse [9, 13] or the versatile applications of ChatGPT, but a comprehensive exploration of their confluence remains sparse. Despite the surge in interest around both the metaverse and ChatGPT, there is a limited body of work that holistically examines how these two domains intersect, particularly within the sphere of education. This presents an opportunity for a thorough investigation into the synergies they might create, the challenges they could introduce, and the transformative potential they hold for learners, educators, and institutions alike.

The aim of this review is to explore the intersection of the metaverse and ChatGPT within the sphere of education. In doing so, we endeavor to:

- Provide an overview of current practices, offering a synthesized perspective on how educators and institutions are leveraging these technologies.
- Highlight transformative learning experiences enabled by the metaverse and ChatGPT, detailing real-world case studies and theoretical possibilities.
- Shed light on potential challenges, from technical hurdles to pedagogical considerations that stakeholders might encounter.
- Offer avenues for future research, presenting questions and directions that have yet to be extensively explored.

2 Background

2.1 The Metaverse: A Historical Overview and Its Key Features

The concept of the metaverse finds its roots in science fiction. Coined by Neal Stephenson in his 1992 novel "Snow Crash," the term described a collective virtual space created by the convergence of physical and virtual reality [14]. This idea of an expansive, interconnected digital universe has since evolved beyond fiction and is gradually materializing in various forms. Historically, the evolution of the metaverse can be traced back to the early days of the internet and virtual worlds. Platforms like Second Life in the mid-2000s offered a glimpse into persistent, user-generated virtual spaces where individuals could interact using avatars [15]. Over the years, advancements in augmented reality (AR), virtual reality (VR), and 3D web technologies have furthered the development of the metaverse concept.

The metaverse, a rapidly evolving digital universe, is characterized by several distinct features that set it apart from traditional digital platforms. First and foremost, it exhibits persistence, meaning it exists continuously and does not reset or turn off, regardless of whether users are actively participating or not. This creates a living, evolving space that is always 'on' [16]. Secondly, the metaverse emphasizes interoperability, allowing for the seamless transfer of assets and experiences between various platforms and environments. This interoperability breaks down barriers and creates a more unified digital experience [17]. Thirdly, user-generated content is a cornerstone of the metaverse. It heavily relies on the creativity and input of its inhabitants, who contribute everything from digital assets to entire virtual spaces. This democratizes content creation and empowers users to shape their digital environment [15]. Figure 1 illustrates a virtual classroom, designed for digital learning environments. The room is rendered in bright colors with educational decorations on the walls, such as posters and children's artwork, creating an engaging atmosphere. Several desks are equipped with laptops, suggesting that this space facilitates technology-based learning. A large interactive whiteboard displaying a web browser is at the front, indicating a focus on interactive and web-based teaching methods. Lastly,

Fig. 1. Virtual spaces (Image generated using [19])

the metaverse is often underpinned by its own economy. Many platforms within the metaverse have established economic systems that enable users to buy, sell, and trade digital assets, adding a layer of complexity and realism to the virtual experience [18]. These features collectively define the metaverse, making it a unique and continuously evolving digital frontier.

2.2 ChatGPT: Origins, Capabilities, and Applications

Developed by OpenAI, ChatGPT is based on the GPT (Generative Pre-trained Transformer) series of models, which are a part of a new wave of neural network architectures primarily used for tasks involving natural language processing [20]. The initial GPT model was groundbreaking, but subsequent iterations, especially GPT-3 and GPT-4, have been even more influential, showcasing a vast range of capabilities beyond what was previously thought possible for machine learning models. ChatGPT's primary capability is its advanced natural language processing, which allows it to understand and generate human-like text based on the patterns it learned during its training [21]. The versatility of ChatGPT has led to its integration into a variety of applications, each demonstrating its capacity to revolutionize different facets of digital interaction and productivity. Firstly, as a conversational agent, ChatGPT is adept at engaging in meaningful interactions with users. This capability makes it an ideal choice for chatbots or virtual assistants, where it can provide immediate, intelligent responses to a wide array of queries [22]. Secondly, in the realm of content generation, ChatGPT exhibits remarkable versatility. From crafting well-structured essays to generating imaginative and creative content, it can either assist in or completely automate the content creation process, thereby streamlining tasks that traditionally require significant human effort [23]. Thirdly, ChatGPT's application in tutoring and education showcases its educational potential. It can assist students with homework, answer complex questions, or guide learners through intricate topics, making it a valuable educational tool that complements traditional teaching methods [24]. Lastly, in the field of programming, tools like GitHub Copilot leverage ChatGPT's capabilities to aid developers. ChatGPT can suggest code snippets or even generate entire functions, thereby enhancing productivity and providing valuable support to programmers [25]. These diverse applications highlight ChatGPT's transformative impact across multiple domains, from enhancing user experience in digital interactions to supporting complex educational and professional tasks.

3 The Current Landscape of the Metaverse in Education

The integration of the metaverse into educational settings is an evolving frontier, reflecting the growing trend of digital transformation in learning environments. Educational institutions and educators are increasingly recognizing the metaverse's potential as an immersive, interactive platform that can enhance student learning and engagement (See Fig. 2) [19]. This section outlines the current usage, benefits, and challenges of the metaverse in education, drawing upon recent studies and experiences.

Fig. 2. Metaverse in education (Image generated using [19])

3.1 Usage in Educational Institutions

The metaverse's adoption in education varies from simple virtual reality (VR) experiences to complex, fully-integrated educational platforms. The integration of the metaverse into educational institutions is reshaping the landscape of learning and teaching, providing innovative ways to engage with educational content. One significant application is the development of virtual campuses and classrooms. Leading universities, such as Stanford and the Massachusetts Institute of Technology (MIT), are pioneering the use of virtual spaces that mirror their real-world campuses. In these digital environments, students and faculty interact as avatars, participating in classes, office hours, and social events. This approach not only bridges geographical barriers but also enriches the learning experience by leveraging the unique capabilities of virtual interaction [26]. Another key application is the creation of simulated experiences and virtual field trips. Through VR simulations, students are able to explore otherwise inaccessible locations, such as Mars or ancient historical sites, and engage with complex phenomena like molecular structures or historical events. These immersive experiences provide a deeper understanding of subjects by allowing students to 'experience' them in a controlled and interactive manner [27].

Additionally, the metaverse is being utilized for skill training and practical workshops, especially in fields that require a high degree of practical skill, such as medicine, architecture, and engineering. The metaverse offers platforms where students can practice and refine their skills in a safe and reproducible environment. This not only enhances the learning experience but also reduces the risks and costs associated with physical training [28]. Through these varied applications, educational institutions are leveraging the metaverse to create a more dynamic, immersive, and effective learning environment.

3.2 Benefits of Metaverse-Based Learning

The metaverse significantly enriches educational outcomes through several key mechanisms. First, it enhances student engagement and motivation. The interactive and immersive nature of the metaverse captivates learners, fostering a more dynamic learning environment. Students learn through exploration and experience, which can lead to higher levels of engagement and a deeper understanding of the subject matter. This experiential form of learning often proves more effective than traditional lecture-based approaches [29]. Secondly, the metaverse contributes to greater accessibility and inclusivity in education. Virtual spaces remove many of the barriers associated with physical classrooms. Students from any geographical location can access high-quality education, and those with physical disabilities can participate in a learning environment tailored to their needs. This democratization of education ensures that more students have the opportunity to learn and succeed, irrespective of their physical or geographical limitations [30]. Lastly, the metaverse fosters collaborative learning environments. It connects students from diverse backgrounds, allowing them to work together, share perspectives, and learn from each other. This level of collaboration and cross-cultural exchange is often challenging to achieve in traditional classrooms. The metaverse's global reach facilitates teamwork and understanding among students from various parts of the world, thus enriching the educational experience and preparing students for a globalized workforce [31]. Collectively, these factors highlight how the metaverse can transform and enhance educational practices, leading to more engaging, accessible, and collaborative learning experiences.

3.3 Limitations and Challenges

While the metaverse presents numerous benefits for educational purposes, there are notable challenges that hinder its widespread adoption in this sector. One of the primary challenges is the technical barriers associated with the implementation of metaverse technologies. The high cost of VR equipment and the necessity for strong, reliable internet connectivity can be significant hurdles, particularly in regions with limited technological infrastructure. This issue may exacerbate existing digital divides, as students without access to necessary technology or internet services are unable to participate in metaverse-based education [32]. Another challenge lies in the pedagogical integration of the metaverse into education. Educators may find it difficult to effectively incorporate metaverse technologies into existing curricula. There is a need to ensure that these tools are used to supplement traditional, evidence-based teaching methods rather than replace them. This requires careful planning, training, and a deep understanding of how virtual environments can enhance learning outcomes without diminishing the value of conventional educational approaches [33].

Additionally, privacy and security concerns within the metaverse are critical issues that educational institutions must address. As with any digital platform, the metaverse poses risks related to data privacy and cybersecurity. The safety of users, particularly younger students, in virtual spaces is of paramount importance. Ensuring the security of personal information and protecting users from potential cyber threats is a complex challenge that requires robust security measures and continuous monitoring [33].

Overall, while the metaverse has the potential to revolutionize the educational landscape, addressing these challenges is crucial for its successful and equitable integration into educational practices. Institutions must navigate these obstacles thoughtfully to fully leverage the benefits of the metaverse in education.

4 ChatGPT's Role in Metaverse-Based Learning

As metaverse platforms continue to integrate cutting-edge technologies to improve learning experiences, artificial intelligence and, specifically, conversational AI models like ChatGPT have found a significant niche in enhancing interactive educational environments. ChatGPT's advanced natural language processing capabilities enable rich interactions, tailored learning experiences, and instant feedback. This section delves into the integration, successful deployments, and benefits of ChatGPT in the educational metaverse landscape.

4.1 Integration in Metaverse Platforms

The integration of AI conversational models like ChatGPT into educational metaverse platforms is enhancing the learning experience through various innovative applications. One such application is in virtual classrooms. Instructors within metaverse-based virtual classrooms are employing ChatGPT to manage frequently asked questions and provide supplementary information during lessons. This integration creates a more interactive and informative learning environment. ChatGPT's ability to understand and respond to a wide range of queries in real-time allows instructors to offer more personalized and immediate feedback to students, thereby enriching the learning experience [34]. Another significant application is the development of learning bots in these virtual environments. These virtual learning assistants, powered by ChatGPT, are becoming a valuable resource in some educational metaverse platforms. They assist students by explaining topics, providing resources, and resolving queries instantly. The instantaneity and accessibility of these AI-driven bots make them an effective tool for enhancing understanding and engagement among students. They can offer individualized assistance, adapting their responses to the specific needs and learning pace of each student [35].

The seamless integration of conversational AI like ChatGPT into the metaverse signifies a step forward in creating more dynamic, responsive, and student-centered educational platforms. These innovations not only make learning more accessible and engaging but also open up new possibilities for personalized education in a virtual setting.

4.2 Case Studies and Successful Deployments

The integration of ChatGPT into metaverse platforms for educational purposes has seen some successful deployments, as evidenced by various case studies. One notable case study involves the use of virtual labs in a university setting. In this scenario, a virtual science lab was created within the metaverse, where ChatGPT was utilized to guide students through their experiments. The AI model played a crucial role in explaining scientific concepts and providing feedback. This interactive, AI-assisted approach resulted in an improved understanding of the subject matter and higher levels of engagement among the students. The study indicated that the combination of a virtual lab environment with the conversational capabilities of ChatGPT significantly enhanced the learning experience, making it more immersive and interactive [36].

Another successful deployment of ChatGPT in the educational metaverse can be seen in language learning platforms. In this context, ChatGPT was used as a conversation partner for learners. The AI model's ability to adjust to the learner's proficiency level allowed for a more tailored learning experience. Students could practice real-time language skills with the AI, receiving immediate feedback and guidance. This approach provided learners with a safe and responsive environment to practice language skills, significantly improving their ability to communicate in the target language [37]. These case studies demonstrate the potential of ChatGPT and similar AI models in transforming educational experiences within the metaverse. By providing interactive, personalized, and engaging learning opportunities, these technologies are paving the way for innovative and effective educational practices.

4.3 Benefits for Learners

The integration of ChatGPT into metaverse educational environments brings a multitude of benefits that enhance the learning experience. One of the primary advantages is personalized learning. ChatGPT can adapt to the unique learning profile of each student, offering explanations and guidance that are tailored to their individual pace and level of understanding. This personalized approach fosters a more effective and enjoyable learning journey, as students receive support that aligns with their specific educational needs [38]. Another significant benefit is the provision of instant feedback. In traditional learning environments, students often have to wait for responses to their queries or for feedback on their exercises. ChatGPT, however, offers immediate responses, which can greatly improve comprehension and retention of information. This real-time interaction ensures that students can quickly clarify misunderstandings and solidify their grasp on complex concepts [39]. The 24/7 availability of ChatGPT-powered assistants is another crucial advantage. Unlike human educators who are bound by time constraints and availability, AI-powered educational tools in the metaverse are accessible at any time. This constant availability ensures that learners have uninterrupted access to information and guidance, making learning more flexible and accommodating to the individual schedules of students [40]. Lastly, the integration of ChatGPT in the metaverse enhances learner engagement. The interactive nature of conversing with an AI model, combined with the visually rich and immersive environment of the metaverse, creates a more engaging and motivating learning experience. Students are more likely to participate actively and consistently when they are immersed in a dynamic and interactive educational platform [41]. This heightened engagement can lead to better learning outcomes and a more positive attitude towards learning. Overall, these advantages illustrate how the incorporation of ChatGPT into metaverse educational platforms can transform traditional learning paradigms, making education more personalized, accessible, and engaging.

5 Challenges and Limitations of ChatGPT in Metaverse-Based Learning

The integration of ChatGPT in the metaverse's educational platforms brings forth a range of transformative opportunities. However, alongside these opportunities are challenges and limitations that stakeholders must address to ensure effective and responsible use. This section explores the ethical, technical, and data-related challenges of using ChatGPT in the metaverse.

5.1 Ethical Considerations

One of the primary ethical concerns is the potential for bias in AI models. ChatGPT and similar systems are trained on large datasets that may contain inherent biases. In an educational context, there is a risk that these biases could be reinforced or perpetuated. This can influence learners' perceptions and understandings in subtle but significant ways. For instance, biases in language or content representation might lead to a skewed view of certain topics or groups. It is crucial for educational institutions to acknowledge this risk and work towards implementing measures to identify and mitigate biases in AI-driven content [42]. Another concern is the potential over-reliance on ChatGPT for educational content and insights. While AI can be a powerful tool for enhancing learning, there is a risk that it might diminish the role and value of human educators. Additionally, excessive dependence on AI may hinder learners from seeking and valuing diverse perspectives, which are essential for a well-rounded education. It is important to strike a balance where AI complements, rather than replaces, human teaching and encourages students to engage with a variety of sources and viewpoints [43]. The capability of AI to generate content, including essays and answers, poses a challenge to authentic learning. There is a potential for misuse, where students might rely on AI to complete assignments, thus bypassing genuine engagement with the learning material. This raises concerns about academic integrity and the quality of learning. Educational institutions may need to develop new frameworks and guidelines to ensure that while AI tools are used to aid learning, they do not replace the critical thinking and engagement that are essential for educational growth [44].

These ethical considerations require careful deliberation and the development of guidelines and policies that ensure AI tools like ChatGPT are used responsibly and effectively in educational settings, enhancing rather than undermining the quality and integrity of education.

5.2 Technical Limitations

The integration of ChatGPT into metaverse educational platforms, while promising, faces several technical limitations that must be considered:

One of the challenges with ChatGPT is its ability to fully grasp and maintain context over extended interactions. In learning scenarios, where continuity and understanding of context are crucial, this limitation can lead to misunderstandings or inadequate responses. For instance, if a student is engaged in a complex discussion or working through a series of related problems, ChatGPT might not always accurately track the conversation's progression or the interconnections between concepts. This can be a significant hurdle in ensuring that AI-driven interactions are as effective and meaningful as those with human educators [21].

Metaverse platforms are inherently three-dimensional and interactive, which poses unique challenges for the integration of ChatGPT. Ensuring that ChatGPT can function effectively in these 3D environments requires advanced capabilities, such as recognizing virtual objects or responding to non-verbal cues. The AI's ability to interact with and respond to the dynamic elements of a 3D space is crucial for creating an immersive and effective learning experience. This requires not just advanced AI programming but also seamless integration with the metaverse's virtual environment [45]. Deploying ChatGPT effectively in metaverse platforms demands significant computational power and robust internet bandwidth. This requirement can be a barrier to accessibility, particularly for learners in regions with limited technological infrastructure. The need for advanced hardware and high-speed internet to access AI-enhanced metaverse educational platforms could exacerbate existing digital divides, limiting the reach and benefits of such innovative educational tools [46]. Addressing these technical limitations is essential for the successful and equitable integration of ChatGPT into metaverse educational platforms. This involves not only advancements in AI technology and metaverse design but also considerations of accessibility and inclusivity to ensure that these educational innovations are available to all learners.

5.3 Data Privacy and Security Concerns

Data privacy and security are critical concerns in the integration of ChatGPT and similar AI models into metaverse educational platforms:

One of the primary concerns with ChatGPT's use in an educational setting is the potential inadvertent collection of personal or sensitive information from students. Since ChatGPT interactions are based on free-form dialogue, there's a risk that students might share information that could be sensitive or private. This raises questions about how this data is stored, used, and protected. Ensuring that data collection complies with privacy laws and ethical standards is crucial. Educational institutions and developers must implement robust protocols for data management to safeguard students' privacy [47].

As with any online platform, AI models like ChatGPT are susceptible to cybersecurity threats. These could include hacking, unauthorized access, or other forms of malicious attacks. Such exploits could compromise the integrity of the educational system and the privacy and security of user data. Protecting these platforms from cyber threats requires continuous vigilance, advanced security measures, and regular updates to counteract evolving threats [48].

It's essential to ensure that users, particularly minors, are fully informed about the data collection and processing practices associated with the use of ChatGPT in education. This includes obtaining consent where necessary and providing transparent information about how data is used, stored, and protected. This is not only a legal requirement in many jurisdictions but also an ethical imperative. It's particularly challenging with younger learners who might not fully understand the implications of data privacy and security [49].

Addressing these data privacy and security concerns is crucial for maintaining the trust and safety of students and educators in metaverse educational environments. It requires a concerted effort from technology developers, educational institutions, policy makers, and guardians to create a secure and privacy-conscious learning environment.

6 Future Trends and Predictions in Metaverse-Based Education with ChatGPT

The metaverse, with its promise of an immersive, interconnected digital universe, has profound implications for education. When coupled with AI systems like ChatGPT, the potential transformations become even more pronounced. Let's explore the emerging trends in this realm, predict the trajectory of ChatGPT's integration, and highlight other technologies that could influence this landscape.

6.1 Emerging Trends in Metaverse-Based Education

The field of metaverse-based education is rapidly evolving, with several emerging trends that promise to transform the learning experience:

One of the most exciting trends is the development of hyper-realistic simulations, driven by advancements in virtual reality (VR) and augmented reality (AR) technologies. These technologies are enabling educational simulations in the metaverse to become increasingly lifelike and immersive. This enhancement in realism greatly benefits areas such as virtual labs, where students can conduct experiments in a simulated environment that closely mimics the real world. Similarly, historical recreations can provide a vivid and accurate representation of past events, offering students a unique and engaging way to learn history. This level of realism in educational simulations can significantly enhance learning by providing experiences that are as close to real-life as possible [50]. The metaverse is also setting the stage for more globally connected classrooms. Students from different parts of the world can interact and collaborate in real-time within these virtual spaces. This facilitates joint projects and cultural exchanges that were previously limited by geographical boundaries. Such global collaboration not only enriches the learning experience but also fosters cross-cultural understanding and prepares students for a more interconnected world [51]. Another emerging trend is the creation of digital twins of physical campuses within the metaverse. Educational institutions are starting to replicate their physical campuses in virtual environments. This allows for a range of new possibilities, such as hybrid events that combine physical and virtual attendance, virtual campus tours for prospective students, and alternative learning environments for remote students. Digital twins can also be used for emergency preparedness training, architectural planning, and a host of other applications that blend the physical and virtual worlds of education [52].

These trends highlight the dynamic and rapidly evolving nature of metaverse-based education. They promise to make learning more immersive, collaborative, and accessible, thereby shaping the future of education in profound and exciting ways.

6.2 Evolution of ChatGPT's Role in the Metaverse

As the metaverse continues to expand its role in education, ChatGPT is also evolving to play more integral and sophisticated roles within this virtual learning environment:

One of the key evolutions of ChatGPT in the metaverse is its potential role as a virtual teaching assistant. In this capacity, ChatGPT can answer student queries, provide relevant educational resources, and offer personalized learning recommendations, all in real-time. This functionality can greatly enhance the learning experience by providing immediate, tailored support to students, thereby complementing the efforts of human educators. These AI teaching assistants can adapt to the individual learning styles and needs of each student, making education more personalized and effective [40]. Utilizing its generative capabilities, ChatGPT could assist educators in dynamically crafting curriculum content. It can generate problem-solving scenarios, quizzes, and educational materials that are tailored to the learners' current needs and progression. This adaptability ensures that the curriculum remains relevant and challenging for students at different learning stages, offering a more customized and responsive educational experience [21]. Language Translation and Cultural Mediation: As metaverse classrooms become increasingly global, ChatGPT's role may expand to include real-time language translation and cultural mediation. This functionality will be particularly useful in breaking down language barriers, allowing students from different linguistic backgrounds to participate in a shared learning environment. Additionally, ChatGPT could provide insights into cultural nuances, fostering a deeper understanding and respect for global diversity among students. This not only enhances communication and collaboration in a multicultural classroom but also prepares students for the globalized nature of the modern world [53].

These evolving roles of ChatGPT in the metaverse signify a shift towards more interactive, personalized, and globally inclusive educational experiences. By leveraging AI capabilities, the metaverse is poised to offer a more enriched, adaptable, and accessible learning environment.

6.3 Evolution Influential Technologies and Tools

The evolution of the metaverse in education is closely tied to the development and integration of several influential technologies and tools:

Brain-Computer Interfaces (BCIs) represent a groundbreaking advancement in how learners could interact with the metaverse and AI systems like ChatGPT. By translating brain activity into commands, BCIs could allow users to control and navigate the metaverse using their thought processes. This technology promises to make the learning experience more intuitive and personalized. For instance, a student's level of understanding or interest could potentially be gauged in real-time, allowing AI systems like ChatGPT to tailor the content and pace of learning accordingly. This direct brain-to-computer interaction could revolutionize how educational content is accessed and consumed, making it far more aligned with the individual learner's cognitive and emotional state [54]. Blockchain technology and decentralized systems could underpin the next generation of educational platforms in the metaverse. They offer the potential for creating transparent, secure, and tamper-proof systems for credentialing and record-keeping.

This could revolutionize how educational achievements are recorded and shared, allowing for greater learner autonomy and portability of credentials. Decentralized platforms could also facilitate more democratic and equitable access to educational resources, breaking down traditional barriers and centralizations in the education sector [55]. The integration of haptic feedback systems in the metaverse will enhance the tactile aspect of virtual interactions. When combined with AI-driven tools like ChatGPT, these systems could enable multi-sensory learning experiences. Haptic technology simulates the sense of touch, allowing users to 'feel' virtual objects and environments. This could significantly enrich the learning experience, especially in fields where tactile skills are crucial, such as medicine, engineering, or art. The addition of haptic feedback would make the virtual learning environment more immersive and realistic, thereby enhancing the overall effectiveness of metaverse-based education [56].

These technologies and tools represent the forefront of innovation in metaverse-based education. Their integration promises to create more immersive, personalized, and interactive learning environments, fundamentally transforming how education is delivered and experienced.

7 Implications for Stakeholders in Metaverse-Based Education with ChatGPT

The metaverse, particularly when complemented with AI tools like ChatGPT, stands to reshape the landscape of education. Understanding the implications for various stakeholders – educators, learners, institutions, and policymakers – is crucial for harnessing the benefits and navigating the challenges.

7.1 Implications for Educators

The integration of the metaverse and AI tools like ChatGPT into education has significant implications for educators, necessitating a reevaluation and adaptation of their roles and teaching methodologies:

Educators are required to embrace a paradigm shift from traditional teaching methods to approaches that are better suited to the immersive and interactive nature of the metaverse. This transition involves adopting and mastering pedagogies that leverage the unique capabilities of the metaverse. Methods such as collaborative learning, problem-based learning, and experiential learning can be greatly enhanced in a metaverse environment. In this new setting, educators will need to become facilitators of learning rather than just providers of knowledge, guiding students through interactive, virtual experiences that foster deeper understanding and engagement [29]. The integration of AI technologies like ChatGPT into the educational process necessitates continuous professional development for educators. They need to stay informed about the latest advancements in AI, understanding both its capabilities and limitations within an educational context. This knowledge is essential for effectively integrating AI tools into the curriculum, ensuring that these technologies are used to enhance learning outcomes rather than detract from them. Educators must also be adept at using these tools to complement their teaching, rather than relying on them as replacements for traditional methods [57]. ChatGPT and similar AI tools have the ability to provide detailed insights into individual learner progress. This data can be invaluable for educators, enabling them to tailor their instruction to meet the specific needs and learning styles of each student. By understanding where a student excels or struggles, educators can provide more personalized support, addressing learning gaps and reinforcing strengths. This data-driven approach to education allows for more targeted and effective teaching strategies, ultimately improving educational outcomes [58].

7.2 Implications for Learners

The integration of the metaverse and AI tools like ChatGPT into education also has significant implications for learners, shaping how they engage with and benefit from the learning process:

In a metaverse-enhanced educational environment, learners need to develop strong digital literacy skills. This encompasses not just the ability to navigate digital platforms but also an understanding of how to effectively utilize tools like ChatGPT. Digital literacy in this context goes beyond basic computer skills; it involves a deeper comprehension of how to interact with advanced technologies, discern reliable information, and use these tools to enhance their learning experience. As the metaverse and AI become more prevalent in education, digital literacy will be a crucial skill for academic success and lifelong learning [59].

The immersive and engaging nature of the metaverse brings with it the challenge of self-regulation. Learners will need to exercise greater self-discipline and time management skills to ensure that they remain focused on educational goals. The risk of over-immersion or distractions is higher in such an engaging environment, so students must learn to balance the time spent in virtual learning spaces with other educational activities and personal responsibilities. Developing these self-regulation skills will be essential for learners to fully benefit from the metaverse without compromising other aspects of their lives [60].

The use of tools like ChatGPT in education allows learners to receive instant, personalized feedback. This can transform them into more active participants in their learning journey. Instant feedback from AI like ChatGPT encourages reflective practices and helps learners to quickly identify and address areas of misunderstanding. This interactive and responsive learning environment can significantly enhance the learning process, making it more adaptive to individual needs and promoting a deeper engagement with the material [61].

These implications highlight the evolving role of learners in an education landscape increasingly influenced by advanced technologies. Learners will need to adapt to these changes by developing new skills and approaches to learning, enabling them to thrive in this dynamic and technology-enhanced educational environment.

7.3 Implications for Educational Institutions

The advent of metaverse-based education and the integration of AI tools like ChatGPT bring several important implications for educational institutions, necessitating changes in infrastructure, curriculum, and data protection policies:

To facilitate metaverse learning environments, educational institutions will need to make significant investments in both hardware and software. This includes acquiring advanced computing systems, VR/AR equipment, and robust network infrastructure to support immersive virtual learning experiences. Ensuring that these resources are accessible to all students is crucial to prevent exacerbating digital divides. Institutions may also need to consider providing support or alternatives for students who lack access to necessary technology at home, ensuring equitable access to these advanced learning tools [62].

The traditional curriculum may require substantial redesign to align with the dynamics of the metaverse. This involves not only incorporating new technologies into the learning process but also rethinking pedagogical approaches to leverage the unique capabilities of these environments. Curriculum redesign should focus on maximizing the interactive and immersive aspects of the metaverse, ensuring that learning objectives are effectively met in this novel context. This might include developing new types of assignments, interactive learning modules, and assessment methods suited to a virtual learning environment [63].

With the implementation of AI tools like ChatGPT, which handle and process vast amounts of user data, educational institutions must place a high priority on privacy and security. This involves establishing robust data protection policies and secure IT infrastructures to safeguard student information. Institutions must be compliant with relevant data protection laws and ethical guidelines, ensuring that student data is used responsibly and securely. Additionally, they should implement measures to educate students and staff about data privacy and security best practices within these platforms [64]. The implications for educational institutions are profound and multifaceted. Adapting to these changes will be critical for these institutions to provide effective, equitable, and secure metaverse-based educational experiences. The successful implementation of these changes will likely shape the future of education, making it more immersive, interactive, and aligned with the digital age.

7.4 Implications for Policymakers

The integration of the metaverse and AI tools like ChatGPT in education also presents crucial considerations for policymakers. These considerations revolve around ensuring ethical use, accessibility, and the development of effective educational technologies:

Policymakers play a pivotal role in setting up frameworks and regulations that guide the ethical use of AI in education. This includes addressing potential biases in algorithms and ensuring that AI tools align with educational standards and values. Regulation and oversight are essential to ensure that AI-driven education benefits all learners and does not inadvertently perpetuate existing inequalities or ethical issues. Policymakers need to work closely with technology experts, educators, and ethicists to develop comprehensive guidelines and standards for AI in education [65]. It is imperative for policies to emphasize the accessibility and equity of educational technologies. Policymakers should ensure that the benefits of metaverse platforms and AI tools like ChatGPT are available to all learners, regardless of their socioeconomic status. This involves addressing issues such as the digital divide, providing support for under-resourced schools, and ensuring that these technologies are not just luxury additions but integral parts of the educational system that enhance learning for everyone. Policies should aim to create an education landscape where every student has the opportunity to benefit from these advanced learning tools [66]. Policymakers should also foster interdisciplinary collaboration to develop education technologies that are both technologically advanced and pedagogically sound. This involves encouraging partnerships between tech developers, educators, cognitive scientists, and other relevant stakeholders. Such collaborations can ensure that the development of educational tools in the metaverse is guided by a deep understanding of learning theories, cognitive development, and effective teaching practices. This interdisciplinary approach can lead to the creation of more effective and meaningful educational experiences that are grounded in sound educational principles [67]. By addressing these areas, policymakers can help shape an educational landscape that is innovative, equitable, and conducive to high-quality learning experiences. These policies will play a crucial role in ensuring that the integration of emerging technologies in education is beneficial, responsible, and aligned with broader educational goals.

8 Conclusion

The dawn of the metaverse in education presents a revolutionary paradigm shift, reshaping traditional pedagogical structures into immersive, interactive, and globally connected environments. When juxtaposed with the capabilities of AI-driven tools like ChatGPT, the transformative potential becomes even more profound. Throughout this review, we've navigated the historical context of the metaverse, delved into the pivotal role of ChatGPT in enhancing metaverse learning experiences, and critically examined the challenges and ethical implications. The confluence of these technologies holds the promise to not just reimagine but to actively redefine what education can achieve in the digital age. For the seamless integration of ChatGPT into metaverse-based learning, institutions and educators should prioritize continuous professional development to stay abreast with AI's evolving capabilities. The design of learning modules should leverage ChatGPT's strength in providing instant, personalized feedback, thereby promoting active and reflective learning. Researchers are encouraged to engage in longitudinal studies to understand long-term effects and potential unforeseen challenges of this amalgamation. Developers should focus on fostering interoperability between the metaverse platforms and AI tools, ensuring a harmonious interaction. Educators, on the other hand, must be provided with a repository of best practices, case studies, and resources to transition smoothly. Collectively, a collaborative effort from all stakeholders will ensure that the union of the metaverse and ChatGPT truly realizes its transformative potential in education.

References

1. Bell, M.W.: Toward a Definition of. J. Virtual Worlds Res. **1** (2008)
2. Akour, I.A., Al-Maroof, R.S., Alfaisal, R., Salloum, S.A.: A conceptual framework for determining metaverse adoption in higher institutions of gulf area: an empirical study using hybrid SEM-ANN approach. Comput. Educ. Artif. Intell. **3**, 100052 (2022)
3. Almarzouqi, A., Aburayya, A., Salloum, S.A.: Prediction of user's intention to use metaverse system in medical education: a hybrid SEM-ML learning approach. IEEE Access (2022)

4. Alawadhi, M., et al.: Factors affecting medical students' acceptance of the metaverse system in medical training in the United Arab Emirates. SEEJPH (2022). https://doi.org/10.11576/seejph-5759
5. AlHamad, A.Q., Alomari, K.M., Alshurideh, M., et al.: The adoption of metaverse systems: a hybrid SEM-ML method. In: 2022 International Conference on Electrical, Computer, Communications and Mechatronics Engineering (ICECCME), pp. 1–5. IEEE (2022)
6. Schroeder, R.: The Social Life of Avatars: Presence and Interaction in Shared Virtual Environments. Springer, London (2001). https://doi.org/10.1007/978-1-4471-0277-9
7. Salloum, S., Al Marzouqi, A., Alderbashi, K.Y., et al.: Sustainability model for the continuous intention to use metaverse technology in higher education: a case study from Oman. Sustainability **15**, 5257 (2023)
8. Salloum, S.A., Bettayeb, A., Salloum, A., et al.: Novel machine learning based approach for analysing the adoption of metaverse in medical training: a UAE case study. Inform. Med. Unlocked, 101354 (2023)
9. Alfaisal, R., Hashim, H., Azizan, U.H.: Metaverse system adoption in education: a systematic literature review. J. Comput. Educ., 1–45 (2022)
10. De Freitas, S., Griffiths, M.: Online gaming as an educational tool in learning and training. Br. J. Educ. Technol. **38**, 535–537 (2007)
11. Aburayya, A., Salloum, S., Alderbashi, K., et al.: SEM-machine learning-based model for perusing the adoption of metaverse in higher education in UAE. Int. J. Data Netw. Sci. **7**, 667–676 (2023)
12. Okonkwo, C.W., Ade-Ibijola, A.: Chatbots applications in education: a systematic review. Comput. Educ. Artif. Intell. **2**, 100033 (2021)
13. Alfaisal, R.M., Zare, A., Alfaisal, A.M., et al.: The acceptance of metaverse system: a hybrid SEM-ML approach. Int. J. Adv. Appl. Comput. Intell. **1**, 34–44 (2022)
14. Stephenson, N.: Snowcrash. ROC, London (1992)
15. Castronova, E.: Synthetic worlds: the business and culture of online games. In: Synthetic Worlds. University of Chicago Press (2008)
16. Schroeder, R.: Being There Together: Social Interaction in Shared Virtual Environments. Oxford University Press (2010)
17. Han, S.: Exploring customer relationship management through technology-enabled experience in virtual environment (2021)
18. Brey, P.: The physical and social reality of virtual worlds. In: Oxford Handbook of Virtuality, pp. 42–54 (2014)
19. Openart AI (2024). https://openart.ai/home
20. Radford, A., Wu, J., Child, R., et al.: Language models are unsupervised multitask learners (2019)
21. Brown, T.B., Mann, B., Ryder, N., et al.: Language models are few-shot learners. arXiv (2020)
22. Gao, J., Galley, M., Li, L.: Neural approaches to conversational AI. In: The 41st International ACM SIGIR Conference on Research & Development in Information Retrieval, pp. 1371–1374 (2018)
23. Raffel, C., Shazeer, N., Roberts, A., et al.: Exploring the limits of transfer learning with a unified text-to-text transformer. J. Mach. Learn. Res. **21**, 5485–5551 (2020)
24. Fadel, C., Holmes, W., Bialik, M.: Artificial Intelligence in Education: Promises and Implications for Teaching and Learning. Center for Curriculum Redesign (2019)
25. Majestic. https://github.com/rlilojr/Detecting-Malicious-URL-Machine-Learning
26. Makransky, G., Lilleholt, L.: A structural equation modeling investigation of the emotional value of immersive virtual reality in education. Educ. Technol. Res. Dev. **66**, 1141–1164 (2018)
27. Fowler, C.: Virtual reality and learning: where is the pedagogy? Br. J. Educ. Technol. **46**, 412–422 (2015)

28. Jensen, L., Konradsen, F.: A review of the use of virtual reality head-mounted displays in education and training. Educ. Inf. Technol. **23**, 1515–1529 (2018)
29. Dede, C.: Immersive interfaces for engagement and learning. Science **323**, 66–69 (2009)
30. Freina, L., Ott, M.: A literature review on immersive virtual reality in education: state of the art and perspectives. In: Proceedings eLearning Software Education (eLSE), Bucharest, Rom, 23–24 April 2015, vol. 8 (2015). https://doi.org/10.12753/2066-026X-15-020
31. Allcoat, D., von Mühlenen, A.: Learning in virtual reality: effects on performance, emotion and engagement. Res. Learn. Technol. **26**, 1–13 (2018). https://doi.org/10.25304/rlt.v26.2140
32. Merchant, Z., Goetz, E.T., Cifuentes, L., et al.: Effectiveness of virtual reality-based instruction on students' learning outcomes in K-12 and higher education: a meta-analysis. Comput. Educ. **70**, 29–40 (2014)
33. Warburton, S.: Second Life in higher education: assessing the potential for and the barriers to deploying virtual worlds in learning and teaching. Br. J. Educ. Technol. **40**, 414–426 (2009)
34. Huang, W.D., Johnson, T.E., Han, S.-H.C.: Impact of online instructional game features on college students' perceived motivational support and cognitive investment: a structural equation modeling study. Internet High. Educ. **17**, 58–68 (2013)
35. Dahan, N.A., Al-Razgan, M., Al-Laith, A., et al.: Metaverse framework: a case study on E-learning environment (ELEM). Electronics **11**, 1616 (2022)
36. Penn, M., Ramnarain, U.: Current status and future perspectives on the integration of virtual and augmented reality in STEM education in African schools and universities. In: Information and Communications Technology in STEM Education an African Perspect, vol. 166 (2023)
37. Johnson-Glenberg, M.C., Birchfield, D.A., Tolentino, L., Koziupa, T.: Collaborative embodied learning in mixed reality motion-capture environments: two science studies. J. Educ. Psychol. **106**, 86 (2014)
38. Pedro, F., Subosa, M., Rivas, A., Valverde, P.: Artificial intelligence in education: challenges and opportunities for sustainable development (2019)
39. Winkler-Schwartz, A., Bissonnette, V., Mirchi, N., et al.: Artificial intelligence in medical education: best practices using machine learning to assess surgical expertise in virtual reality simulation. J. Surg. Educ. **76**, 1681–1690 (2019)
40. Fryer, L.K., Nakao, K., Thompson, A.: Chatbot learning partners: connecting learning experiences, interest and competence. Comput. Hum. Behav. **93**, 279–289 (2019)
41. Dunleavy, M., Dede, C., Mitchell, R.: Affordances and limitations of immersive participatory augmented reality simulations for teaching and learning. J. Sci. Educ. Technol. **18**, 7–22 (2009)
42. Bolukbasi, T., Chang, K.-W., Zou, J.Y., et al.: Man is to computer programmer as woman is to homemaker? debiasing word embeddings. In: Advances in Neural Information Processing Systems, vol. 29 (2016)
43. Selwyn. N.: Should Robots Replace Teachers? AI and the Future of Education. Wiley (2019)
44. Mallik, S., Gangopadhyay, A.: Proactive and reactive engagement of artificial intelligence methods for education: a review. Front. Artif. Intell. **6**, 1151391 (2023)
45. Bailenson, J.N.: Nonverbal overload: a theoretical argument for the causes of Zoom fatigue (2021)
46. Warschauer, M.: Technology and Social Inclusion: Rethinking the Digital Divide. MIT Press (2004)
47. Bietti, E.: From ethics washing to ethics bashing: a view on tech ethics from within moral philosophy. In: Proceedings of the 2020 Conference on Fairness, Accountability, and Transparency, pp. 210–219 (2020)
48. Biggio, B., Roli, F.: Wild patterns: ten years after the rise of adversarial machine learning. In: Proceedings of the 2018 ACM SIGSAC Conference on Computer and Communications Security, pp. 2154–2156 (2018)

49. Livingstone, S., Third, A.: Children and young people's rights in the digital age: an emerging agenda. New Media Soc. **19**, 657–670 (2017)
50. Bailenson, J.: Experience on Demand: What Virtual Reality is, How It Works, and What It Can Do. WW Norton & Company (2018)
51. Rojas-Sánchez, M.A., Palos-Sánchez, P.R., Folgado-Fernández, J.A.: Systematic literature review and bibliometric analysis on virtual reality and education. Educ. Inf. Technol. **28**, 155–192 (2023)
52. Kapp, K.M., O'Driscoll, T.: Learning in 3D: Adding a New Dimension to Enterprise Learning and Collaboration. Pfeiffer & Company (2010)
53. Vaswani, A., Shazeer, N., Parmar, N., et al.: Attention is all you need. In: Advances in Neural Information Processing Systems, vol. 30 (2017)
54. Lebedev, M.A., Nicolelis, M.A.L.: Brain–machine interfaces: past, present and future. TRENDS Neurosci. **29**, 536–546 (2006)
55. Sharples, M., Domingue, J.: The blockchain and kudos: a distributed system for educational record, reputation and reward. In: Verbert, K., Sharples, M., Klobučar, T. (eds.) Adaptive and Adaptable Learning. LNCS, vol. 9891, pp. 490–496. Springer, Cham (2016). https://doi.org/10.1007/978-3-319-45153-4_48
56. Culbertson, H., Schorr, S.B., Okamura, A.M.: Haptics: the present and future of artificial touch sensation. Annu. Rev. Control Robot. Auton. Syst. **1**, 385–409 (2018)
57. Graesser, A., McNamara, D.: Self-regulated learning in learning environments with pedagogical agents that interact in natural language. Educ. Psychol. **45**, 234–244 (2010)
58. Heffernan, N.T., Heffernan, C.L.: The ASSISTments ecosystem: building a platform that brings scientists and teachers together for minimally invasive research on human learning and teaching. Int. J. Artif. Intell. Educ. **24**, 470–497 (2014)
59. Gilster, P., Glister, P.: Digital Literacy. Wiley Computer Publication, New York (1997)
60. Zimmerman, B.J.: Becoming a self-regulated learner: an overview. Theory Pract. **41**, 64–70 (2002)
61. Shute, V.J.: Focus on formative feedback. Rev. Educ. Res. **78**, 153–189 (2008)
62. Oblinger, D.: The next generation of educational engagement. J. Interact. Media Educ. (2004)
63. Schacter, J., Fagnano, C.: Does computer technology improve student learning and achievement? How, when, and under what conditions? J. Educ. Comput. Res. **20**, 329–343 (1999)
64. Zeide, E.: The structural consequences of big data-driven education. Big Data **5**, 164–172 (2017)
65. Bostrom, N., Yudkowsky, E.: The ethics of artificial intelligence. In: Artificial Intelligence Safety and Security, pp. 57–69. Chapman and Hall/CRC (2018)
66. Crabtree, A., Mortier, R.: Personal data, privacy and the internet of things: the shifting locus of agency and control. In: Private Internet Things Shifting Locus Agency Control, 22 November 2016 (2016)
67. Hall, W., Pesenti, J.: Growing the artificial intelligence industry in the UK (2017)

Effectiveness of Logistic Regression for Sentiment Analysis of Tweets About the Metaverse

Said A. Salloum[1,2](✉), Raghad Alfaisal[3], Azza Basiouni[4], Khaled Shaalan[5], and Ayham Salloum[6]

[1] Health Economic and Financing Group, University of Sharjah, Sharjah, UAE
ssalloum@sharjah.ac.ae
[2] School of Science, Engineering, and Environment, University of Salford, Sharjah, UAE
[3] Faculty of Computing and Meta-Technology, Universiti Pendidikan Sultan Idris, Tanjung Malim, Perak, Malaysia
[4] Faculty of Information Technology, Liwa College, Abu Dhabi, UAE
azza.basiouni@lc.ac.ae
[5] Faculty of Engineering and IT, The British University in Dubai, Dubai, UAE
khaled.shaalan@buid.ac.ae
[6] College of Medicine, University of Sharjah, Sharjah, UAE

Abstract. In the evolving landscape of digital communication, sentiment analysis provides crucial insights into public opinions, particularly concerning emerging technologies like the Metaverse. While various models have been employed to perform sentiment analysis, there is a need to assess the effectiveness of traditional machine learning approaches, specifically Logistic Regression (LR), given its advantages in terms of simplicity and interpretability. This study employs LR to analyze a dataset of tweets related to the Metaverse, focusing on preprocessing techniques such as tokenization and vectorization to optimize model performance. The LR model demonstrated high efficacy, achieving an accuracy of 96% with precision, recall, and F1-scores of 0.93, 0.96, and 0.95 respectively for negative sentiments, and 0.97, 0.95, and 0.96 for positive sentiments. The findings suggest that Logistic Regression remains a robust tool for sentiment analysis in social media contexts, offering significant implications for businesses and developers interested in the public perception of new technologies such as the Metaverse.

Keywords: Sentiment Analysis · Logistic Regression · Metaverse · Social Media Analysis · Machine Learning · Public Opinion

1 Introduction

Sentiment analysis is a key field within natural language processing (NLP) and machine learning (ML) that focuses on interpreting and classifying emotions expressed in text data [1, 2]. It has become increasingly important in various applications, from monitoring brand perception on social media to analyzing public opinion on political issues [3, 4]. As digital platforms continue to explode in data volume, the need for effective sentiment analysis tools becomes paramount.

A. Basiouni and C. Frasson (Eds.): BBGI 2024, CCIS 2162, pp. 32–41, 2024.
https://doi.org/10.1007/978-3-031-65996-6_3

The concept of the Metaverse, a collective virtual shared space created by the convergence of virtually enhanced physical and digital reality, is gaining traction as technology advances [5]. With companies like Facebook (now Meta Platforms, Inc.) Meta Platforms [6] investing heavily in this area, public interest and debate around the Metaverse are burgeoning, manifested vividly across social media platforms.

In the digital era, Twitter serves as a pivotal platform for gauging public sentiment on emerging technologies, including the Metaverse. As a virtual space anticipated to revolutionize interactions within digital environments, the Metaverse has sparked widespread discussion among users worldwide. By analyzing tweets, researchers can capture diverse opinions ranging from enthusiastic support to skepticism and concern. These sentiments are not only reflective of individual expectations and doubts but also indicate broader societal readiness to embrace or challenge this technological frontier. Figure 1 illustrates the distribution of sentiment categories derived from a dataset of Metaverse-related tweets, showcasing the predominant emotions and topics that people associate with the Metaverse. This visual representation aids in understanding the complex public perceptions and the factors driving these views.

Fig. 1. People's opinion about the Metaverse (Image generated using [7])

While deep learning models have shown remarkable success in sentiment analysis, they often require substantial computational resources and large datasets to perform optimally [8, 9]. Logistic Regression (LR), by contrast, offers a more interpretable and less resource-intensive alternative. However, its efficacy in processing complex and nuanced sentiments typical of social media data needs more exploration, especially in new and rapidly evolving topics like the Metaverse [10, 11].

This study aims to evaluate the effectiveness of Logistic Regression for sentiment analysis specifically within the context of Metaverse-related discussions on Twitter. The novelty of this research lies in its focus on a traditional ML model within the framework of an emerging digital phenomenon, providing insights into the model's resilience and adaptability to new content domains. The contributions of this paper are twofold: (1) It provides empirical evidence of the applicability of Logistic Regression in sentiment analysis under the lens of an emerging technology. (2) It offers a comparative analysis of Logistic Regression's performance against standard metrics like accuracy, precision, recall, and F1-score.

The paper is structured as follows: Sect. 2 reviews the literature on sentiment analysis techniques and their applications. Section 3 describes the methodology, including data collection, preprocessing, and model configuration. Section 4 presents the results and discusses their implications. Finally, Sect. 5 concludes the study with a summary of findings, limitations, and future research directions.

2 Literature Review

Logistic Regression (LR) has been a staple method in the field of statistical modeling and machine learning, valued for its simplicity, efficiency, and interpretability [12]. In sentiment analysis, LR has been effectively utilized to classify text into predefined sentiment categories based on feature vectors derived from the text data [10]. The application of LR in sentiment analysis has spanned various domains from analyzing consumer reviews [4] to monitoring social media for public health communications [13]. For example, Agarwal et al. [10] demonstrated how features like unigrams and bigrams could be leveraged in LR to provide baseline accuracy in classifying tweets into positive, negative, and neutral categories. While traditional approaches such as LR have shown considerable success, they are often outperformed by more complex models like deep neural networks when vast amounts of labeled data are available [14]. Additionally, LR's linear nature means it may not capture more complex patterns and interactions in text data as effectively as non-linear models [15].

Recent studies have explored hybrid approaches, combining LR with other machine learning techniques to enhance performance without compromising the model's interpretability. For instance, Wang et al. [16] incorporated LR into a decision-making framework with support vector machines, showing improved sentiment classification in online forums. Despite its extensive application, the potential of LR in analyzing sentiments specifically related to emerging technological concepts like the Metaverse has not been extensively explored. Most existing studies focus on general or domain-specific contexts, such as product reviews or movie reviews. There is a research gap in understanding how traditional models like LR perform when applied to novel and rapidly evolving topics, where data may exhibit different linguistic features and sentiment distributions than more traditional datasets.

3 Methodology

3.1 Data Source

The dataset comprises tweets extracted using the Twitter API, focusing specifically on keywords related to the Metaverse, such as "Metaverse," "virtual reality," and "augmented reality." This approach ensures that the dataset is relevant and targeted, capturing a wide range of opinions and discussions about the Metaverse [17]. The dataset contains 50,003 entries and 13 columns. Here's a brief overview of some key columns:

- **user_name**: The name of the Twitter user.
- **user_location**: Location of the user, often not provided.
- **user_description**: A brief description provided by the user.
- **user_created**: The creation date of the user's Twitter account.
- **user_followers**: Number of followers the user has.
- **user_friends**: Number of people the user follows.
- **user_favourites**: Number of tweets the user has liked.
- **user_verified**: Whether the user is verified on Twitter.
- **date**: Date and time the tweet was posted.
- **text**: The actual tweet text.
- **hashtags**: Hashtags used in the tweet.
- **source**: Device/app used to post the tweet.
- **is_retweet**: Whether the tweet is a retweet.

3.2 Data Preprocessing

Data preprocessing is a critical step in ensuring the quality and effectiveness of machine learning models [18]. The preprocessing of the dataset involved several key steps:

- **Text Cleaning**: Tweets were cleaned to remove noise that is typical in social media texts, such as hashtags, mentions, URLs, emojis, and special characters. This step used regular expressions to strip unwanted text elements that could distort the analysis.
- **Tokenization**: The cleaned text data was tokenized, breaking text into individual words or tokens, which simplifies the modeling of language data.
- **Vectorization**: We employed the **CountVectorizer** from the **scikit-learn** library, converting the text data into a numerical format. This transformation creates a document-term matrix that quantifies the frequency of each word present in the dataset, serving as input for the Logistic Regression model.
- **Feature Engineering**: In addition to basic token counts, we explored n-grams (up to bi-grams) to capture context within the data that single words might miss.

3.3 Model Training

The Logistic Regression model was implemented using the **LogisticRegression** class from **scikit-learn**. This model choice was due to its efficiency and interpretability, suitable for a dataset with high-dimensional features. The model was configured with the following settings:

- **Solver**: The 'liblinear' solver was used, optimal for smaller datasets and binary classification problems.
- **Regularization**: L2 regularization was applied to prevent model overfitting, ensuring that the model generalizes well to new, unseen data.

3.4 Model Evaluation

The performance of the Logistic Regression model was evaluated using several metrics:

- **Accuracy**: Measures the overall correctness of the model across all classes.
- **Precision, Recall, and F1-Score**: These metrics provide insight into the model's performance across individual classes (positive and negative sentiments), assessing both the precision and recall to compute the harmonic mean (F1-score).
- **Confusion Matrix**: Helps in visualizing the performance of the algorithm where the rows represent the actual classes and the columns represent the predicted classes.

3.5 Validation Technique

To ensure the robustness of the model, we utilized a train-test split approach, where 80% of the data was used for training the model, and the remaining 20% was used for testing. This technique helps in assessing how the trained model performs on new, unseen data, which is crucial for validating the model's predictive power. The source code utilized in this study is publicly available to ensure transparency and facilitate further research. Interested parties can access and review the code at the following Kaggle link [19]. We encourage researchers and practitioners to explore and utilize the code in their own studies and applications.

4 Results

The application of Logistic Regression for sentiment analysis on Metaverse-related tweets has yielded insightful results. Logistic Regression, a tried and tested statistical method, proved to be both effective and efficient in classifying the sentiment of tweets as either positive or negative.

The Logistic Regression model demonstrated a high degree of accuracy, with an overall accuracy rate of 96%. The precision, recall, and F1-scores were particularly impressive for both negative and positive classes, as seen in the classification report below:

- Negative Tweets: Precision of 0.93, recall of 0.96, and an F1-score of 0.95.
- Positive Tweets: Precision of 0.97, recall of 0.95, and an F1-score of 0.96.

The weighted averages of these metrics were consistent with the individual class scores, indicating a balanced performance across both sentiment classes. This suggests that the Logistic Regression model was able to handle the nuances of sentiment in the Metaverse-related tweets with a high degree of reliability.

The confusion matrix further substantiates the model's performance (Fig. 2). The matrix shows a substantial number of true positives and true negatives, with the model correctly identifying 3816 negative tweets and 5755 positive tweets. While there were instances of false negatives and false positives (275 and 155, respectively), these were relatively low compared to the correct predictions, thus reinforcing the model's robustness in classification tasks.

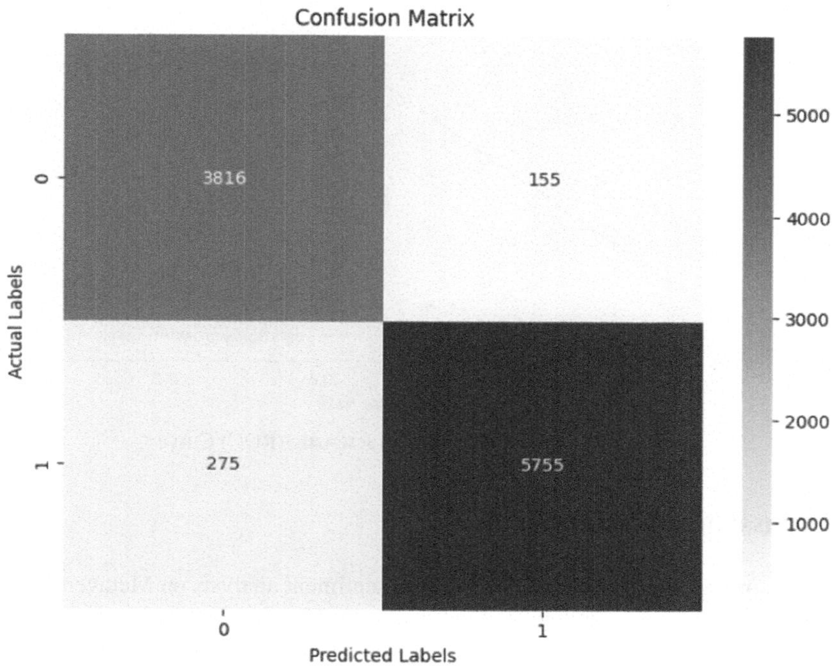

Fig. 2. The confusion matrix

The ROC curve analysis yielded an area under the curve (AUC) of 0.99 (Fig. 3), indicating an excellent level of separability. This high AUC value means that the Logistic Regression model has a high chance of correctly distinguishing between positive and negative sentiment tweets.

The near-perfect AUC value is indicative of the model's strong discriminative ability, despite Logistic Regression's simplicity compared to more complex algorithms. This is in line with the findings of Hosmer Jr, Lemeshow, & Sturdivant (2013) who highlighted the effectiveness of Logistic Regression in various classification scenarios, particularly when interpretability is of essence.

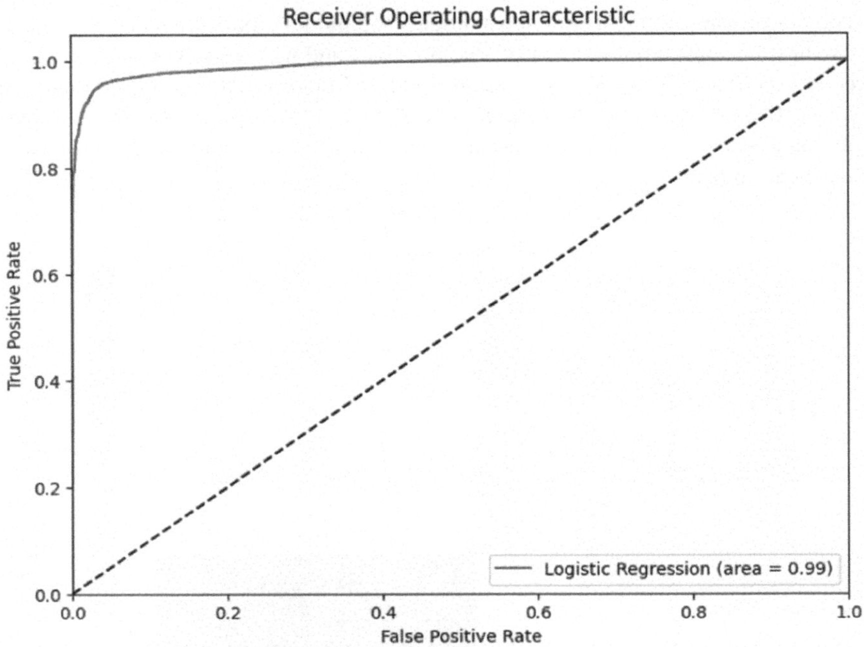

Fig. 3. Receiver Operating Characteristic (ROC) Curve

5 Discussion of Results

The results of applying Logistic Regression to sentiment analysis on Metaverse-related tweets not only affirm its standalone effectiveness but also stand up well when compared to similar studies. James et al. highlight the strength of Logistic Regression in predictive accuracy for binary outcomes, which is consistent with the precision and recall rates observed in our study. The model's ability to distinguish between positive and negative sentiments with high confidence underscores the robustness of linear classifiers in scenarios where complex relationships in data are not predominant. Agarwal et al. [10] found that simple features such as unigrams could effectively support sentiment classification tasks in Twitter data, reinforcing our findings that even fundamental models can yield significant results. This complements studies by Thelwall et al. [20], which concluded that Logistic Regression could perform competitively in social media sentiment analysis, often rivaling more sophisticated algorithms when used with well-crafted feature sets. In terms of comparative performance, Logistic Regression has shown an impressive ability to generalize well across different domains, maintaining strong predictive power even in contexts that differ significantly from the training data [4]. Its applicability to real-world data, as demonstrated in our study, aligns with the findings of Go et al. [21], who used Logistic Regression for classifying sentiment polarity on a large dataset of tweets, achieving noteworthy accuracy. Our findings also bear resemblance to the conclusions drawn by Munro [22], who suggested that when computational resources are limited,

Logistic Regression serves as an excellent baseline model due to its efficiency and relatively low resource demands. This assertion is particularly relevant given the model's performance in our resource-constrained study, which may not have been feasible with more computationally intensive deep learning methods. For the academic community, the demonstrated capability of Logistic Regression in the dynamically evolving topic of the Metaverse adds to the evidence that traditional machine learning models are not only relevant but can also be critical benchmarks for the development of new algorithms. This is particularly noteworthy in light of research by Bhalerao [23], who advocate for the continuous evaluation of baseline models such as Logistic Regression to understand progress in machine learning methodologies. From a practical standpoint, for social media analytics practitioners, the effectiveness of Logistic Regression indicates a viable path for sentiment analysis tasks, especially when interpretability and computational efficiency are prioritized. This echoes the practices seen in industry, as reported by Ravi and Ravi [24], where Logistic Regression remains a popular choice for sentiment analysis, credit scoring, and medical diagnosis due to its transparency and ease of implementation.

6 Conclusion

This study aimed to evaluate the efficacy of Logistic Regression (LR) for sentiment analysis of tweets pertaining to the burgeoning domain of the Metaverse. Our results demonstrate that LR not only holds its ground as a robust classifier but also excels in the specific context of social media sentiment analysis. The model showcased high accuracy, with substantial precision, recall, and F1-scores, thereby affirming its suitability for classifying sentiments in textual data, even within the nuanced and dynamic realm of Twitter discussions about emerging technologies. The implications of this study are multifold. Academically, it reinforces the merit of traditional machine learning models, illustrating that they can serve as reliable, efficient, and interpretable tools for sentiment analysis. Practically, for businesses and developers invested in the Metaverse, these findings suggest that leveraging such models could be instrumental in understanding and navigating public sentiment, informing marketing strategies, and enhancing user engagement. While the results are promising, the study is not without its limitations. The analysis was confined to English-language tweets, potentially overlooking a broader spectrum of global sentiments expressed in other languages. Additionally, the inherent biases present in any social media-derived dataset could affect the generalizability of the findings. Future research should aim to address these limitations by incorporating multilingual datasets and employing more sophisticated preprocessing techniques to mitigate biases. Exploring the integration of LR with other machine learning algorithms or feature sets could also unveil insights into its performance. Further, comparative studies with advanced neural network models could better delineate the trade-offs between complexity and interpretability in sentiment analysis. As the concept of the Metaverse continues to evolve, so too should the methodologies employed to understand the sentiments it elicits.

References

1. Alshamsi, A., Bayari, R., Salloum, S.: Sentiment analysis in English texts. Adv. Sci. Technol. Eng. Syst. **5** (2020). https://doi.org/10.25046/AJ0506200
2. Al Mansoori, S., Salloum, S.A., Shaalan, K.: The impact of artificial intelligence and information technologies on the efficiency of knowledge management at modern organizations: a systematic review. Recent Adv. Intell. Syst. Smart Appl., 163–182 (2020)
3. Liu, B.: Sentiment Analysis and Opinion Mining. Springer, Cham (2022). https://doi.org/10.1007/978-3-031-02145-9
4. Pang, B., Lee, L.: Opinion mining and sentiment analysis. Found Trends® Inf. Retr. **2**, 1–135 (2008)
5. Dionisio, J.D.N., Iii, W.G.B., Gilbert, R.: 3D virtual worlds and the metaverse: current status and future possibilities. ACM Comput. Surv. **45**, 1–38 (2013)
6. Meta Platforms. https://investor.fb.com/home/default.aspx
7. Openart AI (2024). https://openart.ai/home
8. Almarzouqi, A., Aburayya, A., Salloum, S.A.: Determinants predicting the electronic medical record adoption in healthcare: a SEM-artificial neural network approach. PLoS ONE **17**, e0272735 (2022)
9. Wahdan, A., Hantoobi, S., Salloum, S.A., Shaalan, K.: A systematic review of text classification research based on deep learning models in Arabic language. Int. J. Electr. Comput. Eng. **10**, 6629–6643 (2020). https://doi.org/10.11591/ijece.v10i6.pp6629-6643
10. Agarwal, A., Xie, B., Vovsha, I., et al.: Sentiment analysis of twitter data. In: Proceedings of the Workshop on Language in Social Media (LSM 2011), pp. 30–38 (2011)
11. Tsur, O., Rappoport, A.: What's in a hashtag? Content based prediction of the spread of ideas in microblogging communities. In: Proceedings of the Fifth ACM International Conference on Web Search and Data Mining, pp. 643–652 (2012)
12. Hosmer, D.W., Jr., Lemeshow, S., Sturdivant, R.X.: Applied Logistic Regression. Wiley (2013)
13. Paul, M., Dredze, M.: You are what you tweet: analyzing twitter for public health. In: Proceedings of the International AAAI Conference on Web and Social Media, pp. 265–272 (2011)
14. Goodfellow, I., Bengio, Y., Courville, A., Bengio, Y.: Deep Learning. MIT Press, Cambridge (2016)
15. Goldberg, Y.: Neural Network Methods for Natural Language Processing. Springer, Cham (2022). https://doi.org/10.1007/978-3-031-02165-7
16. Wang, S.I., Manning, C.D.: Baselines and bigrams: simple, good sentiment and topic classification. In: Proceedings of the 50th Annual Meeting of the Association for Computational Linguistics (Volume 2: Short Papers), pp. 90–94 (2012)
17. Metaverse. Kaggle (2024). https://www.kaggle.com/datasets/fahaddevelops/metaverse
18. Famili, A., Shen, W.-M., Weber, R., Simoudis, E.: Data preprocessing and intelligent data analysis. Intell. Data Anal. **1**, 3–23 (1997)
19. Salloum, S.A.: Metaverse tweets. Kaggle (2024). https://www.kaggle.com/code/saidasalloum/metaverse-tweets?scriptVersionId=174638961
20. Thelwall, M., Buckley, K., Paltoglou, G.: Sentiment in Twitter events. J. Am. Soc. Inf. Sci. Technol. **62**, 406–418 (2011)
21. Go, A., Bhayani, R., Huang, L.: Twitter sentiment classification using distant supervision. CS224N Proj report, Stanford 1:2009 (2009)
22. Munro, R.: Subword and spatiotemporal models for identifying actionable information in Haitian Kreyol. In: Proceedings of the Fifteenth Conference on Computational Natural Language Learning, pp. 68–77 (2011)

23. Bhalerao, K.V.: Customer Reviews Sentiment Analysis: A hybrid technique of Lexicon and Machine Learning based Classification model (SVM, NB, Logistic Regression) (2021)
24. Ravi, K., Ravi, V.: A survey on opinion mining and sentiment analysis: tasks, approaches and applications. Knowl.-Based Syst. **89**, 14–46 (2015)

How Students Learn by Validating ChatGPT Responses

Chrysanthi Bekiari and Stavros Demetriadis(✉)

Aristotle University of Thessaloniki, Thessaloniki, Greece
{cmpekiari,sdemetri}@csd.auth.gr

Abstract. This study explores the hypothesis that students learn better when engaged in activities where they validate ChatGPT responses by contrasting them to reliable and valid human-generated content material. By applying an ecologically valid but not controlled experimental design we asked students to individually choose to work on an assignment either before (N = 80) or after (N = 42) a course written examination session. The assignment included four scenarios guiding students to interact with ChatGPT and evaluate afterwords the validity of the obtained responses. Available data indicate that students who worked on the assignment prior to examination were able to provide significantly improved answers to examination items that were conceptually relevant to the assignment tasks as compared to those irrelevant. This outcome, however, was valid only for open-ended questions included in the examination sheet and not for the closed-type ones. Overall, this study provides concrete research evidence that ChatGPT-like AI tools can provide the basis for designing beneficial learning activities, assuming the role of a "less competent partner" and offering to students the opportunity of critically reviewing their generated content. At theoretical level, we discuss how this perspective is in line with the proposed "AI as a black box" approach which bypasses the issues relevant to possible errors and misguidance generated by current level conversational AI technologies.

Keywords: Generative AI in Education · Conversational agents · Large language models (LLMs) · ChatGPT

1 Introduction

Current advances in the Natural Language Processing (NLP) domain have led to the development of Conversational Artificial Intelligence (shortly "AI-based") chat services able to provide responses to human user prompts by delivering human-like coherent text (e.g. [1, 2]). In the core of these chatting services lies some type of Large Language Model (LLM), which can stochastically produce word (or "token") sequences, that - under conditions- might be helpful to the human user of the chat service [3].

This affordance has attracted the attention of the educational community and several publications have already suggested possible educational uses of the AI-based chatbots (e.g. [2, 4, 5]), while numerous other studies have provided some initial results analyzing

A. Basiouni and C. Frasson (Eds.): BBGI 2024, CCIS 2162, pp. 42–52, 2024.
https://doi.org/10.1007/978-3-031-65996-6_4

the impact that this type of AI tools might have on student learning (e.g. [6–8]). At the same time, it is clearly recorded that this new technology comes with several risks that need to be carefully considered in education (e.g. [2, 9, 10]). Expecting that students gain important learning benefits by simply "consuming" AI-generated text, seems to be an inadequate perspective as there are already voices suggesting, for example, that "*it is therefore essential to critically analyse the results it* [ChatGPT] *provides and compare them with other sources of information.*" [1, p. 11] and "*students should be educated on effective questioning techniques and how to assess the generated responses*" [11, p. 45:1]. Theorists, additionally, suggest that we need further advanced theoretical models to deeper understand Human-AI interaction and build well-thought innovative learning designs that provide valuable AI-based learning experiences to our students (e.g. [12, 13]).

In this paper we explore the hypothesis that students who work to validate ChatGPT responses by critically contrasting them to reliable human-developed material may reach an improved understanding of the domain. Therefore, the AI generated text is not considered as a resource of possibly useful knowledge but as an opportunity for applying critical thinking to explore its degree of validity whatsoever. We argue that this view is in line with the proposed "AI as a black box" theoretical model [12, 13] suggesting that AI output need not necessarily be "explained" but instead approached as an opportunity for having students focused on the quality standards of their discipline through meaningful Human-AI interactions.

We operationalized this theoretical perspective by implementing a research design exploring the learning outcomes of two groups of students: 'Submitters' vs. 'Non-submitters'. Students in the former group worked and submitted a ChatGPT-based assignment before a course examination session while those in the latter did not. In this study we present quantitative data revealing benefits and limitations for the 'submitters' group and we also highlight opportunities for further exploration of key research questions within the same perspective. The rest of the paper is structured as follows:

In Sect. 2 (background) we provide key information regarding advances of conversational AI and ChatGPT in education and state our research questions. In Sect. 3 we present the method and in Sect. 4 the results of our experimentation. Finally, in Sect. 5 we discuss the outcomes of our study, and we conclude (Sect. 6) summarizing the key lessons learned and highlighting future research questions.

2 Background

2.1 Conversational AI

Artificial intelligence (AI) is "*the ability of a digital computer or computer-controlled robot to perform tasks commonly associated with intelligent beings*" [14] and the use of AI artifacts to perform various tasks can be conceptualized as an "augmentation" of human cognitive abilities [15]. Conversational AI is an "umbrella" term referring to AI software able to communicate with humans using natural language [16]. Conversational AI is expected to significantly facilitate human-machine interaction by enabling humans to interact with advanced technology applications using natural language. Although conversational AI is offered in various genres (for example "rule-based" or "retrieval-based" chatbots) it is the "generative conversational AI" genre (GC-AI) that mostly attracts the interest of researchers currently. By "generative" we refer to systems developing "from scratch" a textual response (that is, constructed "step by step" as opposed to retrieving ready-made text), which expectedly is a relevant and helpful reply to the human user's original prompt. ChatGPT and similar tools are currently "state-of-the-art" (SOTA) applications of GC-AI, based on various editions of LLMs [17].

A large language model is typically described as a probability distribution over language tokens that provides the basis for computer software to perform text predictive modelling tasks [3]. The rise of artificial neural networks (ANNs) led to the development of complex LLMs (for example, BERT and GPT families) making use of Transformer architecture enhanced with Attention mechanisms [18]. While LLMs provide an initial basis, other complementary forms of model training may significantly improve the performance of the GC-AI applications in generating human-like replies. A typical example of these methods is the "Reinforcement learning from human feedback" (RLHF) technique applied also in the case of ChatGPT [19].

How does ChatGPT work? ChatGPT operates as a web-based chat service built upon a customized iteration of the OpenAI GPT family of language models [20]. These models are specifically trained to emulate human-like conversations. The fundamental mechanism behind ChatGPT's text generation lies in its ability to generate a distribution of conditional probabilities for the next word in a given context [21]. Through the application of the attention mechanism [18], ChatGPT can capture contextual information beyond just the immediately preceding words. It considers words that may have appeared several steps earlier but still hold significance in modeling the meaning of the human prompt. By using attention-based techniques, ChatGPT generates word sequences that closely resemble human-like text and are appropriately tailored to the human prompt.

2.2 ChatGPT in Education

Ever since the ChatGPT was openly available (November 2022) several publications appeared exploring the possible uses of ChatGPT in education. Certain studies review the potential of ChatGPT in various educational tasks (for example, content generation, assessment, summarization, etc.), and conclude mostly by listing and commenting on opportunities offered and risks generated by ChatGPT and similar technologies [e.g., 2, 4]. Although such articles do not provide any concrete research evidence, they do provide an initial guidance to the educational community by highlighting critical opportunities and risks in an AI-populated educational space. The global perspective of these category of publications is that GC-AI software might serve humans as a valuable content provider, editor, annotator, summarizer, etc. but its use also entails non-trivial risks that should be carefully considered such as inconsistencies, bias, software "hallucinations" and plagiarism [e.g., 1, 2, 5].

Another group includes publications reporting concrete research evidence on the use of ChatGPT in educational settings. Some of these studies are early reviews of the domain [e.g., 22, 23], others explore teachers'/students' perspectives and acceptance of ChatGPT [e.g., 6, 24, 25], while still others focus on various aspects of ChatGPT learning impact; for example [26] explores the efficiency of LLMs in providing feedback to students. Interestingly, there are also studies which report on the capability of ChatGPT to successfully pass typical course exams in various domains (e.g. [6, 27]).

While all the above mentioned studies routinely highlight the duality of benefits vs risks/limitations when using ChatGPT for learning, theorists explore and suggest new perspectives for learning in the era of conversational AI. In their editorial article Dawson et al. [12] emphasize that AI revolutionizes traditional learning settings, raising doubts about the relevance of conventional learning theories, as these theories were primarily developed for educational contexts with minimal mediation by AI-based agents. Inspired by this viewpoint we consider highly promising-and employ it as a basis for this work also-the "*AI as a black box*" theoretical model proposed by Bearman and Ajjawi [13]. This model suggests that since judgements (responses) by AI agents cannot really be traced due to high complexity of technology we may as well fully abandon the requirement of precisely understanding the "reasoning" of the machine (therefore, treat AI as a "black box"). Relatedly, we abandon the expectation that AI agents provide responses to student prompts that qualify as high-quality learning material to be used "as is". Instead, we view the Human-AI interactions as an opportunity for engaging students in meaningful interactions that help them deepen their understanding of domain quality standards [13]. Obviously, this perspective bypasses the "AI agent validity" issue as now the learning focus is not on the AI agent per se but on the quality standards of the domain which are revisited and rediscovered through the opportunity generated by the Human-AI interaction.

In the next section we explain how we operationalized the "AI as a black box" model in our study, engaging students in activities of evaluating AI-synthesized content by comparing it to reliable content authored by human experts in the domain.

Research Questions: Against the above background the current study sets two interrelated research questions:

- How can we operationalize the "AI as a black box" perspective in the form of a specific learning scenario?
- Do students learn and perform better after being engaged in an "AI as a black box" scenario based on the aforementioned perspective?

3 Method

3.1 Participants and Research Design

Participants (N = 122) were students at the School of Informatics, Aristotle University of Thessaloniki, in their fourth year of studies. Students were given an assignment - as part of their course tasks-asking them to perform the following steps in four different but similarly structured ChatGPT-based scenarios:

- Step-1: Prompt ChatGPT efficiently to get an informative response on a profile-relevant question given by the scenario instructions. The profiles suggested to students were an informatics teacher, a learning technologies professional, a Python programmer, and a student focusing on "soft skills" development.

- Step-2: Using the ChatGPT response as a "starting" material, critically compare it to human-developed resources (for example, instructor generated course material, course books or reliable web resources).
- Step-3: Report the evaluation comments (by submitting a structured assignment form) relevant to the quality of ChatGPT reply (e.g. errors identified or lack of precise/useful information, etc.)

Students beforehand were offered guidance about "prompt engineering" techniques and how to construct effective prompts for ChatGPT. They were also asked to explicitly report the validation resources they used in each scenario, but they were not given any detailed evaluation criteria. This assignment was handed to students a few weeks before their course examination session and they were free to decide whether they would work on the assignment (and submit the form) before or after the course exams. There was no control whatsoever on who would submit before or after the exam session. The "AI as a black box" model was operationalized as presented in Table 1:

Table 1. Theoretical Model and Activity Design

Theoretical model	Activity Design
AI as a black box	ChatGPT was used "as is" meaning that there was no effort to explain its inner mechanism of text generation, nor trying to find ways to avoid or minimize possible errors. Instead, any reply provided by the ChatGPT was a priori considered as a valid opportunity for the subsequent comparative analysis against reliable resources
Quality standards	Human-produced resources. These resources are considered reliable and valid as they were developed by the course instructor or other University instructors and domain experts in general
Meaningful interactions	Students reflecting on the quality of AI-generated content. The task oriented students toward a concrete objective (validating the ChatGPT response), thus rendering more meaningful their interactions with ChatGPT. It also enhanced students' awareness about the quality of Human-AI interactions for learning purposes

3.2 Data Collection and Analysis

Instruments for data collection included a course examination sheet with two types of test items: a) closed-type, and b) open-ended questions. These assessment items were further carefully constructed in four types as follows:

- [Closed-Rel]: Closed-type question items relevant to the assignment scenarios.
- [Closed-Irr]: Closed-type question items irrelevant to the assignment scenarios.
- [Open-Rel]: Open-ended question items relevant to the assignment scenarios.
- [Open-Irr]: Open-ended question items irrelevant to the assignment scenarios.

The terms ‘relevant’ and ‘irrelevant’ refer to the degree of conceptual relationship between the assessment items and the content material that students were expected to review when validating the ChatGPT responses. So, the key hypothesis tested is whether the processing of reliable course material during students’ effort to validate ChatGPT replies would result in detectable performance differences regarding the above varied types of assessment items.

Data analysis was administered by the two authors who first used a common rubric to assess open-ended items in about 15% of available assessment answer sheets, independently and blindly (not knowing if students had submitted the assignment or not). Then, they collaborated to a) develop a common understanding of their grading approach, b) resolve problematic cases by reaching consensus and, finally, c) proceed to grade the rest of the students’ answer sheets. An anonymized version of data was imported in a Jupyter notebook, and statistical controls were applied to test for the hypotheses presented in the following section.

4 Results

Students were grouped in two cohorts:

1. ‘*Submitters*’ (those who submitted the assignment before the exams, N = 80),
2. ‘*Non-submitters*’ (those who selected not to submit the assignment, N = 42).

Following the instructions of the assignment, submitters prompted ChatGPT writing relevant prompts such as (for example):

For the first scenario: *I am an IT teacher, and I am presenting at a seminar for fellow teachers. First of all, I would like you to present how classical constructivism (Piaget’s theory) and socio-cultural theory (Vygotsky) differ. Then explain how this has implications for educational technology.*

For the second scenario: *I work for an IT company. We are currently developing a software project in which we are creating “smart” mechanisms to support learners in learning environments. Help me organize some information. First, write an explanation*

Table 2. Submitters vs. Non-Submitters: Descriptive statistics of overall assessment score

Submitters (N=80)	*Non-Submitters (N=42)*
Mean = 18.663, Std = 9.772 Min = 2.00, Max = 48.00	Mean = 13.071, Std = 9.345 Min = 3.00, Max = 43.00
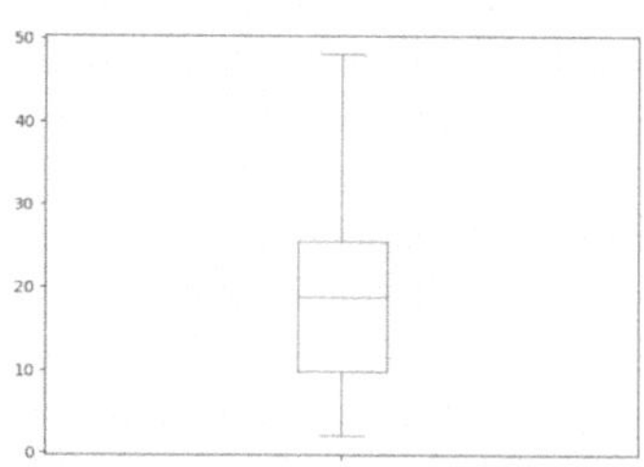 	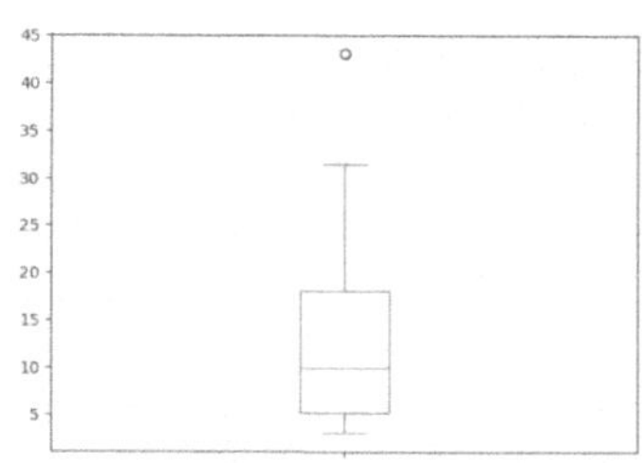

for my colleagues of what the "Zone of Proximal Development" is, and then how it affects the design of smart technology environments to support learning.

Table 2 presents basic descriptive statistics of the two groups. We further con-trolled for various hypotheses as presented in Table 3 and Table 4.

Table 3. "Within subjects" control considering the open-ended responses*

	Within Subjects	Open-Rel Mean (std)	Open-Irr Mean (std)	Control
1	*Submitters (N = 80)*	7.775 (5.908)	5.337 (5.001)	**Sig.** (paired t-test t = 3.473, $p < 0.001$) 95% CI [0.7 to 4.1], Cohen's d = 0.45
2	*Non-Submitters (N = 42)*	3.857 (5.215)	3.857 (4.693)	**Not Sig.** (paired t-test t = 0.0, p = 1.0)

Table 4. "Within subjects" control considering the answers to closed-type questions*

	Within Subjects	Closed-Rel Mean (std)	Closed-Irr Mean (std)	Control
1	*Submitters (N = 80)*	2.850 (1.223)	2.700 (0.999)	**Not Sig.** (paired t-test t = 1.070, p = 0.288)
2	*Non-Submitters (N = 42)*	2.643 (1.411)	2.714 (0.995)	**Not Sig.** (paired t-test t = -0.334, p = 0.740)

*Although the normality criterion is violated (the distributions appear positively skewed) we applied paired t-test which is considered robust against normality criterion for larger samples [28], as in our case ($N > 30$). Non-parametric test (Wilcoxon signed-rank test) when applied provided similar outcomes.

5 Discussion

This study explored the impact on students' learning of an assignment that guided them to validate ChatGPT responses by critically contrasting them to human-developed course content. Students formed two groups through free self-sampling process: those who worked and submitted the assignment before course examinations ("*Submitters*") and those who decided to do it afterwords ("*Non-Submitters*"). Results need to be interpreted cautiously as obviously there exists a kind of selective bias in the formation of the two student groups. Admittedly, submitters were a group of students being better prepared overall for the course examination as their decision to submit the assignment beforehand is evidence of their overall effort to prepare well and succeed. Therefore, we explore the "within subjects" results to check for differences within the same group independently of selective bias. We see that submitters perform statistically better (d ~ 0.5) in the "open-rel" items as opposed to the "open-irr" items (Table 3, row 1) included in the assessment sheet. Since the motivation for students in this group is at the same level, we argue that the only reason for this difference is the additional cognitive activity related to the "open-rel" items, induced by the respective assignment tasks. The assignment items increased the "time on task" for the study of "open-rel" material and this resulted in improved learning as demonstrated by the statistical analysis. Non-submitters, as reasonably expected, do not demonstrate such a difference in their respective performance (Table 3, row 2), as they were not engaged in any additional cognitive activity, having skipped the assignment for a later time.

Clearly, any type of learning activity inducing additional cognitive processing of specific material would have led to similar outcomes. However, the key contribution of ChatGPT is that it provided a variety of personalized responses with unknown beforehand possible deficiencies (such as mistakes, typos, conceptual errors, etc.) for each and every student to use as starting material for their subsequent validation activity. Providing this type of personalized material to so many students would have been a challenging task for the human teacher and hard to manage, maintain, adapt for future use, etc. The alternative of providing non-personalized (i.e. the same for all students) starting material would be an easier to manage option, however, it would run the risk of plagiarism, since once the deficiencies of the starting material were identified it would have been easy for late-submitters to copy-paste the known answer in their assignment sheet without any real benefits from additional cognitive activity. Contrastingly, it was simply the prompting of ChatGPT that generated material nicely fitting to the requirements of the assignment being conceptually similar yet with different possible deficiencies for each student. Overall, we believe that these results demonstrate how ChatGPT (and similar AI tools) can be easily used in the role of a "less competent partner" whose generated contribution needs to be further validated by referring to reliable human-produced material.

However, this beneficial pattern is not replicated for the closed-type assessment items (Table 4 r. 1 & 2). There is no statistical difference identified either for the submitters or for the non-submitters group when their performance in the closed-type questions is examined. To explain this, we refer to the type of knowledge required for answering the different types of assessment. To provide improved answers to open-ended questions the students in the submitters group simply required improved domain declarative knowledge relevant to each question, something well supported by the assignment, as students were exposed to valid content resources enriching their understanding and retention. On the contrary, closed-type questions required better understanding of the relations (e.g. similarities and differences) of conceptual knowledge presented in various sections of the course material (and not only relevant to ChatGPT replies), but this was not well supported by the assignment tasks. Perhaps another type of ChatGPT-based task could result in learning benefits also detectable by the closed-type assessment items.

There are two key limitations of the study that should be considered in further research. First, we only tested for differences within subjects of the same group because of selective bias in the formation of the two student cohorts. Although the self-selection design adds to the ecological validity of the study, future studies need to apply also controlled experimentation design to further validate the current outcomes. Additionally, while the authors made considerable efforts to ensure an unbiased assessment of the open-ended questions, a study replication employing more objective measures to validate students' knowledge and performance would certainly enhance the credibility of the reported conclusions.

6 Conclusions and Future Research

In this work we answered the two posed research questions as follows:

- The "AI as a black box" model can be operationalized in the form of a learning scenario where students are asked to reflect on ChatGPT-generated text and validate its responses by contrasting them to valid human-generated content.
- By implementing the above design, we provided evidence that students who validate ChatGPT responses are better prepared to answer open-ended assessment questions relevant to the ChatGPT-based assignment tasks. We consider this to be a result of the additional cognitive processing induced by the ChatGPT-based assignment. However, this result is not replicated for closed-type questions, demonstrating the interaction between the type of assignment task and the format of assessment items.

Based on the outcomes of our study we strongly encourage further exploration on this or similar lines to produce evidence on how ChatGPT-like tools can provide opportunities for improved student learning both at cognitive and metacognitive level. The design of these studies should seek to bypass the "AI agent validity" issue of GC-AI and transform the Human-AI interaction to a unique learning experience independent of the quality of AI responses. This can be achieved by following the "AI as black box" approach (as we demonstrated in this work) or any other theoretical model considered appropriate. Some of the future research questions that we believe are of interest include:

- How to guide students to elaborate in domain knowledge by engaging them in more interesting and sophisticated tasks within the "AI as a black box" perspective.
- How to guide students to develop their critical thinking skills by leveraging the capability of AI to generate material of varied perspective, detail, and argumentation level.
- How to guide students to develop their collaborative skills by "recruiting" appropriately trained AI agents as group member partners.

References

1. UNESCO: ChatGPT and Artificial Intelligence in Education (2023). https://unesdoc.unesco.org/ark:/48223/pf0000385146
2. Atlas, S.: ChatGPT for Higher Education and Professional Development: A Guide to Conversational AI. DigitalCommons@URI, University of Rhode Island (2023). https://digitalcommons.uri.edu/cba_facpubs/548
3. Brown, T.B., Mann, B., Nick, R., at al.: Language models are few-shot learners. arXiv:2005.14165v4 [cs.CL] (2020). https://doi.org/10.48550/arXiv.2005.14165

4. Kasneci, E., et al.: ChatGPT for good? On opportunities and challenges of large language models for education. Learn. Individ. Differ. **103**, 102274 (2023). https://doi.org/10.1016/j.lindif.2023.102274
5. Hwang, G.-J., Chen, N.-S.: Editorial position paper: exploring the potential of generative artificial intelligence in education: applications, challenges, and future research directions. Educ. Technol. Soc. **26**(2) (2023). https://doi.org/10.30191/ETS.202304_26(2).0014
6. Lo, C.K.: What is the impact of ChatGPT on education? A rapid review of the literature. Educ. Sci. **13**, 410 (2023). https://doi.org/10.3390/educsci13040410
7. Bond, M., et al.: A meta systematic review of artificial intelligence in higher education: a call for increased ethics, collaboration, and rigour. Int. J. Educ. Technol. High. Educ. **21**, 4 (2024). https://doi.org/10.1186/s41239-023-00436-z
8. Essel, H.B., Vlachopoulos, D., Essuman, A.B., Amankwa, J.O.: ChatGPT effects on cognitive skills of undergraduate students: receiving instant responses from AI-based conversational large language models (LLMs). Comput. Educ. Artif. Intell. **6** (2024). https://doi.org/10.1016/j.caeai.2023.100198
9. Bender, E.M., Gebru, T., McMillan-Major, A., Shmitchell, S.: On the dangers of stochastic parrots: can language models be too big? 🦜. In: Proceedings of the ACM FAccT 2021 Conference, pp. 610–623. ACM, New York, USA (2021). https://doi.org/10.1145/3442188.3445922
10. Cotton, D.R.E., Cotton, P.A., Shipway, J.R.: Chatting and cheating: ensuring academic integrity in the era of ChatGPT. Innov. Educ. Teach. Int. (2023). https://doi.org/10.1080/14703297.2023.2190148
11. Shoufan, A.: Can students without prior knowledge use ChatGPT to answer test questions? An empirical study. ACM Trans. Comput. Educ. **23**(4) (2023). Article 45. https://doi.org/10.1145/3628162
12. Dawson, S., Joksimovic, S., Mills, C., Gašević, D., Siemens, G.: Advancing theory in the age of artificial intelligence. Br. J. Educ. Technol. **54**, 1051–1056 (2023). https://doi.org/10.1111/bjet.13343
13. Bearman, M., Ajjawi, R.: Learning to work with the black box: pedagogy for a world with artificial intelligence. Br. J. Edu. Technol. **54**, 1160–1173 (2023). https://doi.org/10.1111/bjet.13337
14. Copeland, B.: Artificial intelligence. Encyclopedia Britannica (n.d.). https://www.britannica.com/technology/artificial-intelligence
15. Siemens, G., et al.: Human and artificial cognition. Comput. Educ. Artif. Intell. **3** (2022). https://doi.org/10.1016/j.caeai.2022.100107
16. McTear, M.: Conversational AI: Dialogue Systems, Conversational Agents, and Chatbots. University of Toronto, Graeme Hirst (2020)
17. Song, Y., Li, C.-T., Nie, J.-Y., Zhang, M., Zhao, D., Yan, R.: An ensemble of retrieval-based and generation-based human-computer conversation systems. In: Proceedings of the Twenty-Seventh International Joint Conference on Artificial Intelligence (IJCAI-18), Stockholm, Sweden, pp. 4382–4388 (2018). https://doi.org/10.24963/ijcai.2018/609
18. Vaswani, A., et al.: Attention is all you need. In: Proceedings of NIPS 2017 Conference Red Hook, USA, pp. 6000–6010 (2017). https://doi.org/10.48550/arXiv.1706.03762
19. Ouyang, L., et al.: Training language models to follow instructions with human feedback. arXiv:2203.02155 [cs.CL] (2022). https://doi.org/10.48550/arXiv.2203.02155
20. OpenAI Documentation Models. https://platform.openai.com/docs/models/overview
21. Ramponi, M.: How ChatGPT actually works. AssemblyAI blog post (2022). https://www.assemblyai.com/blog/how-chatgpt-actually-works/
22. Memarian, B., Doleck, T.: ChatGPT in education: methods, potentials, and limitations. Comput. Hum. Behav. Artif. Hum. **1**(2) (2023). https://doi.org/10.1016/j.chbah.2023.100022

23. Zhang, P., Tur, G.: A systematic review of ChatGPT use in K-12 education. Eur. J. Educ. **00**, 1–22 (2023). https://doi.org/10.1111/ejed.12599
24. Hosseini, H., et al.: An exploratory survey about using ChatGPT in education, healthcare, and research. medRxiv 2023.03.31.23287979 (2023). https://doi.org/10.1101/2023.03.31.23287979
25. Tlili, A., Shehata, B., Adarkwah, M.A., et al.: What if the devil is my guardian angel: ChatGPT as a case study of using chatbots in education. Smart Learn. Environ. **10**, 15 (2023). https://doi.org/10.1186/s40561-023-00237-x
26. Dai, W., et al.: Can large language models provide feedback to students? A case study on ChatGPT. EdArXiv Preprints (2023). https://doi.org/10.35542/osf.io/hcgzj
27. Malinka, K., Perešíni, M., Firc, A., Hujňák, O., Januš, F.: On the educational impact of ChatGPT: is artificial intelligence ready to obtain a university degree? In: Proceedings of the 2023 Conference on Innovation and Technology in Computer Science Education V, (ITiCSE 2023), vol. 1, 8–12 July 2023, Turku, Finland. ACM, New York, NY, USA (2023). https://doi.org/10.1145/3587102.3588827
28. Jennings, M., Zumbo, B.D., Joula, J.F.: The robustness of validity and efficiency of the related samples t-test in the presence of outliers. Psicologica **23**, 415–450 (2002)

Integrating Generative Intelligence into Educational Assessment: A Multi-disciplinary Approach for Enhancing Value-Added Measures in Mass Communication and Management Studies

Rafif Faisal[1], Adnan Jawabri[2], and Rouhi Faisal[2](✉)

[1] Digital Media Department, Faculty of Media and Public Relations, Liwa College, Al Ain, United Arab Emirates
rafif.faisal@lc.ac.ae

[2] Management Department, Faculty of Business, Liwa College, Al Ain, United Arab Emirates
{adnan.jawabri,rouhi.faisal}@lc.ac.ae

Abstract. In the evolving landscape of education, the integration of generative intelligence (GI) promises significant enhancements in the pedagogical processes within mass communication and management studies. This paper examines the transformative impact of advanced artificial intelligence technologies, including Generative Adversarial Networks (GANs) and Generative Pre-trained Transformers (GPTs), on educational assessments. By facilitating dynamic and interactive learning environments, GI tools such as large language models extend educational boundaries and foster a continuous, adaptive interaction among students, educators, and AI systems. These technologies not only personalize learning experiences but also support the development of critical thinking skills through tailored content and feedback mechanisms. However, the deployment of such AI-driven innovations necessitates a cautious approach, addressing ethical concerns related to data privacy, algorithmic bias, and the integrity of AI outputs. This study explores both the potential and challenges of GI, providing a balanced perspective on its role in enhancing educational outcomes and shaping future educational practices.

Keywords: Generative Intelligence · Educational Assessment · Artificial Intelligence · Learning Technologies · Ethical Considerations in AI

1 Introduction

The convergence of generative intelligence (GI) and educational assessment heralds a transformative era in the pedagogical landscape, especially within the domains of mass communication and management studies. This paper seeks to elucidate the multifaceted role of generative artificial intelligence (AI), particularly generative adversarial networks (GANs) and generative pre-trained transformers (GPTs), in revolutionizing educational

A. Basiouni and C. Frasson (Eds.): BBGI 2024, CCIS 2162, pp. 53–63, 2024.
https://doi.org/10.1007/978-3-031-65996-6_5

methodologies. By integrating GI, we move beyond traditional learning paradigms to foster a dynamic, interactive educational process that not only enhances student engagement but also deepens learning through continuous and adaptive interactions. Such advancements promise a redefined educational framework where AI is not merely an adjunct but a core component of the educational dialogue, adapting in real-time to the evolving educational needs and contexts. (Andriessen & Sandberg, 1999; Cao & Dede, 2023; Sharples, 2023).

This integration poses significant ethical, technical, and pedagogical challenges, necessitating a nuanced understanding of the implications of AI-driven assessments. As GI technologies streamline and enhance educational assessments, they also raise critical concerns regarding data privacy, algorithmic bias, and the potential depersonalization of learning. Addressing these challenges is imperative to harness the full potential of AI in education, ensuring it acts as an enhancer rather than a disruptor. This paper aims to offer a comprehensive exploration of the integration of GI in educational assessments, presenting empirical evidence, theoretical insights, and forward-looking perspectives on the effective and ethical use of AI in educational settings. (Anderson, 2002).

2 Theoretical Foundations of Generative Intelligence in Education

2.1 Basics of Generative Intelligence – Definitions and Key Principles

Generative Intelligence (GI), particularly in the form of Generative Artificial Intelligence (AI), represents a transformative approach in educational systems, emphasizing interaction between humans and AI within learning environments. This shift views educational interactions not merely as sequences of prompts and responses, but as a dynamic social process. The integration of GI, such as large language models (LLMs) including ChatGPT, extends learning beyond traditional boundaries, creating a pervasive computational medium that facilitates a continuous conversation among students, educators, and AI (Sharples, 2023; Cheung & Xu, 1999).

GI leverages advanced machine learning algorithms, primarily Generative Adversarial Networks (GANs) and Generative Pre-trained Transformers (GPTs), to produce diverse outputs ranging from textual content to multimedia elements. These technologies are grounded in unsupervised or partially supervised learning frameworks, utilizing vast amounts of data to generate content that can mimic human-like outputs in a variety of contexts (Baidoo-Anu & Owusu Ansah, 2023). GPT models, in particular, utilize natural language processing to read and produce text that is indistinguishable from that written by humans, thereby supporting educational applications such as tutoring systems, personalized learning experiences, and the generation of educational content (Hu, 2022; Anderson, 2002).

The pedagogical implications of GI are profound. By incorporating GI systems, educational practices can transition from static knowledge delivery to a more engaging, interactive process that promotes deep learning. These systems can adapt in real-time to the needs of learners, providing personalized feedback and assisting in the development of critical thinking skills. Furthermore, GI fosters collaborative learning environments where AI acts not only as a facilitator but also as an active participant in the educational dialogue (Cao & Dede, 2023; Ge & Hu, 2020; Marquez & Fominykh, 2021).

However, the deployment of GI in education raises ethical considerations, particularly regarding data privacy, the potential reinforcement of existing biases through AI learning processes, and the need for transparency in AI decision-making processes. Educators and technologists must navigate these challenges carefully to harness the benefits of GI while safeguarding against its potential pitfalls (Baidoo-Anu & Owusu Ansah, 2023; Igbokwe, 2023; Lombard, Snyder-Duch, & Bracken, 2002; Marquez & Fominykh, 2021; Richardson & Clesham, 2021; Tyagi, Jain, & Singh, 2020; Zhang & Aslan, 2021; Zhao et al., 2023).

Generative Intelligence redefines educational paradigms by enhancing interactive and personalized learning through advanced AI technologies. Its integration into educational systems promises to enrich learning experiences and outcomes, provided that ethical considerations are rigorously addressed (Landau & Moore, 2010; Ballou, Sanders, & Wright, 2004; Goldhaber & Hansen, 2008; Golding & Van Deventer, 2018; McCaffrey et al., 2004; Ray, McCormack, & Evans, 2009; Rubin, 2003; Sanders, 2000).

2.2 Historical Development and Applications of GI in Educational Settings

Generative Intelligence (GI) in educational settings has evolved through a series of innovations in artificial intelligence (AI) and machine learning, shaping the landscape of education over several decades. This evolution began with early computational models and has matured with the advent of sophisticated algorithms that support dynamic and interactive learning environments. (Ballou, Sanders, & Wright, 2004; Cao & Dede, 2023; Goldhaber & Hansen, 2008; McCaffrey et al., 2004; Ray, McCormack, & Evans, 2009; Rubin, 2003; Sanders, 2000).

The development of GI for educational purposes traces back to the early forms of AI in the 1960s and 1970s, where primitive learning models were employed to simulate basic human cognitive processes (Sharples, 2023). Initial efforts focused on programmed instruction and adaptive learning systems, which laid the groundwork for subsequent developments in intelligent tutoring systems. These systems were designed to adapt the presentation of material based on student responses, essentially customizing the learning experience to meet individual educational needs (Cao & Dede, 2023; Ali & Abdel-Haq, 2021; Heravi, 2017; Houston, 2015; Howard, 2014).

As technology advanced, the 1980s and 1990s saw the introduction of more complex models, including rule-based expert systems, which were capable of simulating the decision-making process of human experts. These systems further enhanced personalized learning by offering tailored feedback and support to students, marking a significant step forward in the application of GI in education (Baidoo-Anu & Owusu Ansah, 2023; Markel et al., 2023; Richardson & Clesham, 2021; Zhang & Aslan, 2021; Zhao et al., 2023).

With the turn of the century, the emergence of deep learning technologies and neural networks introduced a new era for GI in education. These technologies enabled the development of Generative Adversarial Networks (GANs) and Generative Pre-trained Transformers (GPTs), which revolutionized the way educational content could be created and interacted with. Applications of these technologies in education have been broad and impactful (Hu, 2022; Ballou, Sanders, & Wright, 2004; McCaffrey et al., 2004; Sanders, 2000).

1. **Content Generation**: GPT models, like GPT-3, have been used to generate educational content ranging from customized reading materials to interactive dialogue for language learning. These applications not only provide rich, adaptive content but also stimulate student engagement through conversational learning scenarios.
2. **Personalized Learning**: AI-driven platforms utilize GI to adapt learning paths and content to the individual needs of students, thereby supporting differentiated instruction and scaffolding at scale. This personalization extends to assessing student performances and providing feedback that is immediate and formative, enhancing the learning process significantly (Sharples, 2023).
3. **Simulation and Virtual Environments**: GI has been instrumental in creating realistic simulations and virtual environments that offer students hands-on experiences in a risk-free setting. These applications are particularly valuable in fields such as medicine, engineering, and science where practical experience is crucial (Cao & Dede, 2023).
4. **Assessment and Feedback Systems**: Intelligent assessment systems that use GI analyze student responses and adaptively adjust the difficulty of tasks, provide hints, and give tailored feedback to learners, thereby supporting a deeper understanding of the material and improving educational outcomes (Baidoo-Anu & Owusu Ansah, 2023).

3 Value-Added Assessment in Education

3.1 Explanation of Value-Added Assessment – Definitions and Importance

Value-Added Assessment (VAA) is a method used in educational settings to measure the contribution of schools, districts, and teachers to student learning, controlling for the initial conditions and characteristics of students. This method evaluates educational outcomes not only based on student performance at a single point in time but more importantly on the progress students make over time.

VAA is fundamentally about measuring "value added" to students by their educational experiences beyond what is expected based on prior achievement. This assessment framework calculates the growth in student achievement that is attributed to schools or teachers, beyond what is statistically expected given the student's starting point. Value-added models (VAMs) typically use statistical techniques to isolate the school or teacher effect from other influences such as prior achievement and student demographics, which might affect comparisons of educational outcomes (Sanders, 2000; Ballou et al., 2004).

The importance of VAA lies in its potential to provide a fairer and more accurate picture of the impact of teaching and school management on student outcomes. Traditional assessment methods often fail to account for external factors that significantly impact student performance, such as socioeconomic status and initial academic ability. By controlling for these factors, VAA offers several advantages:

1. **Enhanced Accountability**: VAA provides a basis for more effective accountability systems in education by focusing on the progress students make. It shifts the focus from merely achieving a standard score to demonstrating improvement over time, thereby encouraging schools and teachers to prioritize student development (Rubin, Stuart, & Zanutto, 2003).

2. **Informed Decision-Making**: Educators and policymakers can use VAA data to make informed decisions about resource allocation, professional development, and instructional strategies. Understanding which schools or teachers add the most value can help replicate successful practices across educational systems.
3. **Customized Interventions**: With insights from VAA, interventions can be better targeted to meet the needs of students at different achievement levels, potentially leading to more equitable educational outcomes.
4. **Research and Evaluation**: For researchers, VAA provides a robust methodological approach for evaluating educational interventions and policies by measuring their effect on student growth rather than just absolute achievement levels.

Despite its benefits, implementing VAA involves several challenges. The accuracy of VAA is highly dependent on the quality of the data and the statistical models used. Issues such as data missingness, the complexity of model assumptions, and the potential for misinterpretation of the results can impact the reliability and validity of value-added measures. Moreover, there is an ongoing debate regarding the use of VAA results for high-stakes decisions, such as teacher evaluation or school funding, due to concerns about fairness and the potential for incentivizing undesirable teaching practices (Rubin, Stuart, & Zanutto, 2003).

3.2 Current Methodologies and Models Used in Value-Added Assessment

Value-Added Assessment (VAA) methodologies are essential tools in educational research and policy-making, offering insights into the effectiveness of schools and teachers by accounting for baseline student characteristics. Over the years, several methodologies have been developed, each addressing specific aspects of educational assessment and aiming to provide a clearer picture of educational impact beyond initial student conditions.

Value-added models (VAMs) estimate the contribution of schools or teachers to student learning progress, adjusting for students' initial achievement levels and other background variables that might affect their learning trajectory. These models are used extensively in educational research and policy-making to assess teaching effectiveness and school performance.

1. **Fixed Effects Models**: These models control for individual student characteristics that do not vary over time. By focusing on changes in student performance, fixed effects models attribute differences in learning outcomes to external factors like teaching methods or school environment (Tekwe et al., 2004).
2. **Random Effects Models**: Also known as multilevel or hierarchical linear models, these incorporate variability at multiple levels, such as the student, classroom, and school. These models are useful in handling the nested structure of educational data, allowing for the assessment of teacher and school effects while accounting for student-level variability (McCaffrey et al., 2004; Ballou, Sanders, & Wright, 2004; McCaffrey et al., 2004; Sanders, 2000; Rubin, 2003).
3. **Value-Added Mixed Models**: These models are an advancement over traditional fixed and random effects models, accommodating complex and longitudinal data structures. They provide robust estimates by incorporating random components

that capture the unexplained variability at different levels—student, classroom, and school. This approach is particularly effective in assessing the impacts that persist over time, even as students move across schools or classes (Sanders, 2000; McCaffrey et al., 2004).

4. **Propensity Score Matching in VAA**: While not a typical value-added model, propensity score matching is used to simulate randomized control trials by matching students based on observable characteristics. This method ensures that the comparison groups (e.g., students taught by different teachers) are statistically similar on observed characteristics, thus isolating the effect of the teacher or school from other factors (Rubin, Stuart, & Zanutto, 2003).

The methodologies used in VAA play a crucial role in educational assessment by providing policymakers and educators with evidence-based insights into what contributes to effective teaching and successful schools. These models help in identifying high-performing schools and teachers, guiding resource allocation, and informing professional development programs. Moreover, they aid in policy formulation by evaluating the impact of educational reforms and interventions aimed at improving student achievement.

Despite their advantages, value-added models face criticism and challenges regarding their application in high-stakes educational decisions. Issues such as model sensitivity, the robustness of conclusions under different model specifications, and potential biases due to unobserved confounders need careful consideration. Furthermore, ethical concerns about the use of VAA results for evaluating individual teacher performance highlight the need for a balanced approach that considers both statistical evidence and professional judgment.

4 Enhancing Educational Assessments in Mass Communication Studies Through Generative Intelligence

The advent of Generative Intelligence (GI) in educational landscapes, particularly in mass communication studies, heralds a transformative era where the integration of AI-driven technologies promises to refine assessment methods and pedagogical strategies. This paper explores the implementation of GI-enhanced assessment tools, delineates practical guidelines for educators and administrators, and proposes future directions for research in this nascent yet rapidly evolving field.

Mass communication education faces unique challenges and opportunities as it adapts to technological advancements. The integration of GI into educational assessments can potentially elevate the learning outcomes by providing personalized learning experiences and real-time feedback mechanisms. Studies highlight the proliferation of AI applications in higher education, emphasizing adaptive learning technologies that cater to individual student needs through profiling, prediction, and personalization (Ali & Abdel-Haq, 2021; Lombard, Snyder-Duch, & Bracken, 2002; Andriessen & Sandberg, 1999).

For successful implementation, educators and administrators need to consider several practical guidelines:

1. **Curriculum Integration**: Embedding GI tools within the curriculum requires a thoughtful approach to align these tools with educational goals and learning outcomes.
2. **Training and Development**: Both educators and administrators must receive ongoing training to effectively utilize GI technologies. This involves understanding the operational and ethical dimensions of these tools.
3. **Ethical Considerations:** As AI becomes more ingrained in educational processes, ethical concerns related to data privacy, consent, and the potential replacement of human roles must be addressed (Lombard, Snyder-Duch, & Bracken, 2002; Andriessen & Sandberg, 1999).

To deepen the effectiveness and ethical oversight of GI-based educational assessments, research must be meticulously directed toward a range of pivotal areas. This includes a thorough evaluation of how GI tools tangibly enhance student outcomes and engagement in mass communication studies. Equally critical is the exploration of ethical implications that accompany the use of artificial intelligence in educational settings, with a particular focus on issues such as data privacy, algorithmic bias, and the potential for these systems to replace traditional roles. Additionally, there is a need to investigate the long-term impacts of such technologies on students' academic paths and career prospects, ensuring that these tools support rather than undermine educational equity and effectiveness. This comprehensive approach to research will pave the way for informed integration of GI technologies that are both effective and ethically sound in enhancing educational practices. As a conclusion, the research in GI-based educational assessments should focus on several key areas:

1. **Effectiveness of GI Tools**: Investigating how GI tools enhance learning outcomes in mass communication studies.
2. **Ethical Implications:** Exploring the ethical landscape of using AI in education, focusing on privacy, bias, and fairness.
3. **Long-term Impact**: Studying the long-term impact of GI on the educational trajectories and career prospects of students.

The integration of Generative Intelligence into mass communication studies represents a promising frontier for enhancing educational assessments. However, this integration must be approached with careful consideration of ethical standards and a robust framework for implementation. Future research will be crucial in guiding the evolution of this technology and ensuring its beneficial impact on educational practices.

5 Enhancing Educational Assessments in Management Studies Through Generative Intelligence

The integration of artificial intelligence (AI) into educational management is transforming how institutions handle teaching, learning, and administrative tasks. This transformation is particularly significant in management studies, where the need for adaptive and personalized learning environments is critical. AI's capabilities in processing and analyzing vast amounts of data can lead to more nuanced understanding and improvements in educational outcomes (Ge & Hu, 2020; Marquez & Fominykh, 2021; Zhang & Aslan, 2021; Zhao et al., 2023).

AI technologies are utilized in educational management to automate and enhance assessments, providing benefits such as personalized learning paths, real-time feedback, and predictive analytics. These technologies not only streamline assessment processes but also offer detailed insights into student performances, thereby enabling tailored interventions for at-risk students (Ge & Hu, 2020; Marquez & Fominykh, 2021; Zhang & Aslan, 2021; Zhao et al., 2023).

Effective implementation of AI in educational assessments requires careful planning and consideration of ethical, technical, and pedagogical aspects. Institutions must address potential biases and ensure transparency in AI algorithms to maintain fairness and accuracy in assessments. Moreover, educators and administrators need to be equipped with the necessary skills to utilize these advanced technologies effectively (Ge & Hu, 2020; Marquez & Fominykh, 2021; Zhang & Aslan, 2021; Zhao et al., 2023).

To optimize the benefits of artificial intelligence in educational assessments within management studies, institutions need to undertake a series of strategic actions. They should establish clear guidelines that align the use of AI technologies with educational objectives and ethical standards, ensuring that the deployment of these tools supports fairness and transparency. Additionally, robust data privacy measures are essential to protect sensitive student information and maintain trust in the assessment process. Institutions also need to invest in ongoing professional development for educators, enabling them to effectively adapt and leverage AI tools. These steps will help maximize the potential of AI to enhance educational assessments while safeguarding against potential risks associated with technology implementation. As a result, the benefits of AI in educational assessments within management studies, institutions should:

- Develop clear guidelines on AI use that align with educational goals and ethical standards (Ge & Hu, 2020; Marquez & Fominykh, 2021; Zhang & Aslan, 2021; Zhao et al., 2023).
- Ensure robust data privacy measures to protect student information (Ge & Hu, 2020; Marquez & Fominykh, 2021; Zhang & Aslan, 2021; Zhao et al., 2023).
- Provide ongoing professional development for educators to adapt to AI tools effectively (Ge & Hu, 2020; Marquez & Fominykh, 2021; Zhang & Aslan, 2021; Zhao et al., 2023).

Future research should focus on longitudinal studies to assess the impact of AI on learning outcomes over time, explore the scalability of AI applications in larger educational settings, and develop more sophisticated AI tools that can adapt to diverse learning environments and needs. Additionally, there is a need for more empirical studies to validate the effectiveness of AI applications in real-world educational settings (Ge & Hu, 2020; Marquez & Fominykh, 2021; Zhang & Aslan, 2021; Zhao et al., 2023).

AI holds significant promise for enhancing educational assessments in management studies through its ability to personalize learning and streamline administrative tasks. However, its implementation must be handled with care to address ethical concerns and ensure that the technology enhances educational outcomes without compromising the quality of education or privacy of the data (Ge & Hu, 2020; Marquez & Fominykh, 2021; Zhang & Aslan, 2021; Zhao et al., 2023).

6 Conclusion

The exploration of generative intelligence (GI) in educational assessment within mass communication and management studies reveals a compelling trajectory towards more personalized, interactive, and outcome-oriented learning environments. Our investigation underscores the substantial benefits that GI technologies offer, such as enhanced personalization, automated and continuous assessment, and the development of higher-order cognitive skills. However, the deployment of these technologies is not without its challenges. The ethical considerations, particularly concerning data privacy, the reinforcement of biases, and the integrity of AI-driven outputs, are paramount concerns that educators and policymakers must address (Ge & Hu, 2020; Marquez & Fominykh, 2021; Zhang & Aslan, 2021; Zhao et al., 2023).

To navigate these complexities, a robust framework for the ethical implementation of GI technologies is essential. This involves establishing clear guidelines that balance innovation with accountability, enhancing the transparency of AI algorithms, and ensuring that these technologies are used to complement rather than replace traditional educational methods. Moreover, ongoing research is crucial to continuously assess the impact of GI on learning outcomes and to refine AI applications to better suit educational needs (Ge & Hu, 2020; Marquez & Fominykh, 2021; Zhang & Aslan, 2021; Zhao et al., 2023).

In conclusion, while GI presents a promising frontier for enhancing educational assessments, its integration into educational frameworks must be approached with careful consideration and a commitment to ethical standards. Future research should focus on longitudinal and empirical studies to better understand the long-term impacts of GI and to ensure its alignment with educational equity and effectiveness. By addressing these challenges, the potential of GI to revolutionize educational assessment can be fully realized, ultimately contributing to more effective and engaging learning experiences for students across diverse educational settings (Ge & Hu, 2020; Marquez & Fominykh, 2021; Zhang & Aslan, 2021; Zhao et al., 2023).

References

Ali, M., Abdel-Haq, M.K.: Bibliographical analysis of artificial intelligence learning in higher education: is the role of the human educator and educated a thing of the past? In: Advances in Educational Technologies and Instructional Design, pp. 36–53. IGI Global (2021). https://doi.org/10.4018/978-1-7998-4846-2.ch003

Anderson, R.E.: Reforming science teaching: what research says about inquiry. J. Sci. Teacher Educ. **13**(1), 1–12 (2002). https://doi.org/10.1023/A:1015171124982

Andriessen, J., Sandberg, J.: Where is education heading and how about AI. Int. J. Artif. Intell. Educ. **10**(2), 130–150 (1999)

Baidoo-Anu, D., Owusu Ansah, L.: Education in the era of generative artificial intelligence (AI): understanding the potential benefits of ChatGPT in promoting teaching and learning. J. AI **7**(1), 52–62 (2023)

Ballou, D., Sanders, W., Wright, P.: Controlling for student background in value-added assessment of teachers. J. Educ. Behav. Stat. **29**(1), 37–65 (2004). https://doi.org/10.3102/10769986029001037

Cao, L., Dede, C.: Navigating a world of generative AI: suggestions for educators. The Next Level Lab, Harvard Graduate School of Education, Cambridge, MA. Retrieved from Next Level Lab (2023)

Cheung, A.K.L., Xu, W.: Cultural identity and language: a proposed framework for cultural globalization and glocalization. J. Multicult. Discourses **4**(1), 29–47 (1999). https://doi.org/10.1080/17447140802703933

Ge, Z., Hu, Y.: Innovative application of artificial intelligence (AI) in the management of higher education and teaching. J. Phys. Conf. Ser. **1533**(3), 032089 (2020). https://doi.org/10.1088/1742-6596/1533/3/032089

Goldhaber, D., Hansen, M.: Assessing the potential of using value-added estimates of teacher job performance for making tenure decisions. National Center for Analysis of Longitudinal Data in Education Research (2008). http://www.urban.org/sites/default/files/alfresco/publication-pdfs/1001265-Assessing-the-Potential-of-Using-Value-Added-Estimates-of-Teacher-Job-Performance-for-Making-Tenure-Decisions.PDF

Golding, P., Van Deventer, M.O.: The impact of institutional pressures on employee performance and satisfaction: the role of perceived organizational support. J. Manag. **44**(6), 2306–2329 (2018). https://doi.org/10.1177/0149206316655873

Heravi, B.: State of data journalism globally: first insights into the global data journalism survey (2017). https://medium.com/@Bahareh/state-of-data-journalism-globally-cb2f4696ad3d

Houston, B.: Computer-Assisted Reporting: A Practical Guide, 4th edn. Routledge, New York, NY (2015)

Howard, A.B.: The art & science of data-driven journalism (2014). https://towcenter.columbia.edu/news/art-and-science-data-driven-journalism

Hu, X.: Understanding the impact of GPT on education. J. Educ. Technol. **15**(3), 123–134 (2022)

Igbokwe, I.C.: Application of artificial intelligence (AI) in educational management. Int. J. Sci. Res. Publ. **13**(3) (2023). https://doi.org/10.29322/IJSRP.13.03.2023.p13536

Landau, E., Moore, D.: Competence, overconfidence, and excessive risk-taking in banking. J. Bank. Finance **34**(3), 574–585 (2010). https://doi.org/10.1016/j.jbankfin.2009.08.007

Lombard, M., Snyder-Duch, J., Bracken, C.C.: Content analysis in mass communication: assessment and reporting of intercoder reliability. Hum. Commun. Res. **28**(4), 587–604 (2002). https://doi.org/10.1111/j.1468-2958.2002.tb00826.x

Markel, J.M., Opferman, S.G., Landay, J.A., Piech, C.: GPTeach: interactive TA training with GPT-based students. In: Proceedings of the Tenth ACM Conference on Learning @ Scale, pp. 226–236. ACM, Copenhagen Denmark, July 2023. https://doi.org/10.1145/3573051.3593393

Marquez, J., Fominykh, M.: Virtual reality and natural interfaces for learning complex procedural tasks. Comput. Educ. **161**, 104052 (2021). https://doi.org/10.1016/j.compedu.2020.104052

McCaffrey, D.F., Lockwood, J.R., Koretz, D., Louis, T.A., Hamilton, L.: Models for value-added modeling of teacher effects. J. Educ. Behav. Stat. **29**(1), 67–101 (2004). https://doi.org/10.3102/10769986029001067

Ray, A., McCormack, T., Evans, H.: Value added in English schools. Educ. Finan. Policy **4**, 415–438 (2009). https://doi.org/10.1162/edfp.2009.4.4.415

Richardson, M., Clesham, R.: Rise of the machines? The evolving role of AI technologies in high-stakes assessment. Lond. Rev. Educ. **19**(1), 1–13 (2021). https://doi.org/10.14324/LRE.19.1.09

Rubin, D.B.: A potential outcomes view of value-added assessment in education. J. Educ. Behav. Stat. (2003)

Sanders, W.L.: Value-added assessment from student achievement data: opportunities and hurdles. J. Pers. Eval. Educ. **14**(4), 329–339 (2000). https://doi.org/10.1023/A:1012821300683

Sharples, M.: Towards social generative AI for education: theory, practices and ethics. Learn. Res. Pract. **9**(2), 159–167 (2023). https://doi.org/10.1080/23735082.2023.2261131

Tekwe, C.D., et al.: An empirical comparison of statistical models for value-added assessment of school performance. J. Educ. Behav. Stat. **29**(1), 11–36 (2004)

Tyagi, S., Jain, P.K., Singh, A.: Deep learning algorithms in track and trace systems for the pharmaceutical supply chain: a systematic review. Int. J. Inf. Manage. **53**, 102073 (2020). https://doi.org/10.1016/j.ijinfomgt.2020.102073

Zhang, K., Aslan, A.B.: AI technologies for education: recent research & future directions. Comput. Educ. Artif. Intell. **2**, 100025 (2021). https://doi.org/10.1016/j.caeai.2021.100025

Zhao, W.X., et al.: The role of large language models in education. AI Educ. J. **8**(2), 45–67 (2023)

The Reality of Using Artificial Intelligence to Enhance University Education an Applied Study on a Sample of Media Professors in Arab Universities

Ghada Salih and Faisal Kamil Mohammed(✉)

College of Media and Public Relation, Liwa College, Al Ain, UAE
gada.salih@lc.ac.ae, faisalkamil79@gmail.com

Abstract. The overall objective of this study is to explore the role of AI in higher education, focusing on its impact on faculty, students, and the educational system. In addition, the study aims to identify common AI applications, challenges faced in AI adoption, and possible solutions to overcome these challenges. A sample survey method was conducted among lecturers in different media departments in Arab universities to gather information on the use of AI, perceptions of its impact and challenges faced the study the questionnaire included Likert scale items and open-ended questions to elicit detailed responses. Statistical analysis including t-tests and descriptive statistics were used to analyze the data and draw meaningful conclusions.

The study shows the widespread adoption of AI in higher education, using AI tools by faculty and students to improve learning efficiency, support multimedia generation, and create student learning experience types for individuals but challenges to its successful implementation such as AI errors, biases and lack of AI experts lead to significant limitations. Proposed solutions include courses and AI teams, creating AI-integrated courses, and providing training programs for the teachers. AI has tremendous potential to transform higher education by optimizing learning practices, improving student outcomes, and streamlining business processes. However, addressing the demanding situations associated with AI's shortcomings, biases and understanding gaps is vital to make the most of its full blessings. By embracing AI responsibly and proactively, universities can create modern studying environments that empower students and universities.

Keywords: Artificial intelligence · Higher education · Challenges · Solutions · Transformation

1 Introduction

The 21st century has witnessed an exceptional go-sectoral technological improvement, reworking conventional practices and methods of working. In this development, artificial intelligence (AI) stands proud as a device to enhance every field of life consisting of university education. Fostering an inclusive educational environment is an essential

A. Basiouni and C. Frasson (Eds.): BBGI 2024, CCIS 2162, pp. 64–80, 2024.
https://doi.org/10.1007/978-3-031-65996-6_6

step forward. AI technology consist of a wide range of gear and programs from device learning algorithms and herbal language processing to statistics analytics and robotics [1]. Together these technologies make contributions to a greater dynamic and interactive instructional environment. The role of AI in college education is multi-faceted, supplying innovative answers to age-old demanding situations and opening new avenues for educational and expert excellence. The capacity of AI in better education lies in its potential to analyze big amounts of records, predict trends, customize gaining knowledge of studies and automate administrative responsibilities Free up precious time [2]. One of the primary advantages of AI in college education is its ability to streamline getting to know. Traditional one-length-suits-all academic models regularly fail to fulfill college students' person desires and mastering patterns. AI-powered adaptive gaining knowledge of structures can analyze pupil overall performance and getting to know procedures to provide custom designed learning strategies, sources, and comments.

This personalization now not best increases pupil engagement and pleasure however additionally improves learning development via talking to each student. Moreover, AI can dramatically boom the performance and effectiveness of university management [3]. Through automation of ordinary obligations such as grading, scheduling, pupil assist offerings, and so forth. AI can awareness administrative body of workers on more strategic and impactful activities. For example, AI-enabled Chabot can handle a wide variety of pupil questions, offer instantaneous answers and support, for this reason improving the general student level in and decreasing administrative workload. AI additionally performs a vital role in enhancing research competencies in universities. AI algorithms can procedure and examine big quantities of facts with unparalleled velocity and accuracy, permitting researchers to discover insights and patterns that might be not possible to discover manually [4]. This functionality is particularly useful in fields such as genomics, weather, and social sciences. Additionally, the mixing of AI into college education promotes enclosure and accessibility. AI-powered equipment can offer support for college students with disabilities, consisting of speech-to-text apps for college students with hearing loss or textual content-to-speech for those with gaining knowledge of disabilities and predictive information technology. By streamlining training, AI helps universities create an extra comprehensive gaining knowledge of environment in which all college students can be successful [5]. However, the adoption of AI in college schooling isn't always without its demanding situations. Ethical considerations, information privacy worries, and the possibility of dismissal are essential problems for groups to cope with. A.I. Additionally, universities must proactively deal with the trade via reimagining roles and upgrading team of workers capabilities by way of incorporating AI technology to update human professors.

Hence, the reason of this examine is to perform an exploratory survey for analyzing the role of (AI) in improving college schooling, consistent with the perceptions of Arab college professors on this regard and how this influences the studying consequences of college students and researchers. It also discusses the problems involved within the adoption of (AI) in teaching and studying perspectives of professors and the solutions that have been recommend some solutions to conquer these challenges and develop the advancement of (AI) technologies.

2 Research Problem

Arab universities are more and more interested by integrating synthetic intelligence (AI) technology into their teaching and studying applications [6]. However, understanding the reality of the use of these technologies and their impact on the quality of university education still requires further study. Specifically, a thorough understanding of professors' experiences using AI is essential to identify potential opportunities and challenges and contribute to the development of effective strategies to enhance university education.

3 Research Questions

The main research question is "What is the reality of using AI technologies to promote university education in Arab universities?" This broad question is broken down into specific research problems, as given below:
RQ1: How does (AI) contribute to the effectiveness of teachers and their impact on student learning experience?
RQ2: Which (AI) applications are commonly used to promote university learning?
RQ3: What are the challenges in implementing (AI) technology in Arab universities?
RQ4: What are the proposed solutions to overcome challenges and promote the use of (AI) technology in university education?

4 Study Objectives

This research study aims to investigate the realities, impacts, challenges and opportunities of using AI technologies to enhance university education in Arab universities from the perspective of faculty. To understand the use of (AI) in university education from the perspective of faculty in Arab universities. To highlight the challenges faced in the implementation of AI in teaching and learning processes from the point of view of faculty. Solutions proposed by educators to become aware of demanding situations in university schooling and sell the usage of (AI) technologies.

5 Literature Review

Several research have tested in element the professionals and cons of integrating AI into instructional settings [7]. AI generation presents several advantages, inclusive of customized learning studies, automatic collaboration, and actual-time remarks for college students. Individualized lesson plans can be adapted to fulfill college students' character wishes, increasing engagement and educational performance. In addition, AI can extensively reduce instructors' administrative burden with the aid of automating grading and workflow approaches [8]. These advantages, however, are balanced by using several disadvantages, consisting of records privation concerns, capacity for algorithmic bias, and the excessive costs associated with the use of AI technology.

AI applications in training are varies from support equipment to academic functions diagnosed three primary regions in which AI is implemented: company, coaching, and individualized education [9]. Thus, AI is able to be coping with administrative responsibilities, turning in powerful personalized commands within the form of a clever tutoring device, and generating adaptive gaining knowledge of structures that adapt depending on students' modern-day performance. These packages are aimed at enhancing success and accomplishment in studying strategies through making these as green and bendy as viable to fit the particular desires of freshmen. It is important to recognize that the primary area where AI may be effectively applied in HE is in the effectiveness of the learning process using new technologies [10]. These platforms learn how students' study and how they grasp concepts so that it can design customized learning techniques for the students and pace their learning accordingly. AI is also applied in other capacities in higher education such as learning analytics where big data and machine learning help to find patterns and anticipate learners' performance hence making recommendations for improvement of education quality.

Advanced technology such as digital platforms supported by Artificial intelligence has been portrayed to have the potential to enlighten or augment the quality of learning outcomes [11]. These platforms can create individual student learning path, monitor performance, and also offer individual suggestions and resources that are going to be helpful for learning. These platforms allow for student interaction to be consistent and adapted to each of the student's needs that they encounter through their learning process, which is why there is enhanced engagement among the students and high retention rates. Research conducted amongst faculty members in Cairo University highlighted their views on what they deemed necessary in order to successfully incorporate AI in university education [12]. It stressed numerous logistical requirements, extensive professional development of teachers, and solid organizational support to bring in AI technologies. Teaching faculty stressed the need to attend to these requirements to enable the achievement of the intended use of AI in improving the teaching and learning processes.

The current study differs from other similar studies, in that it is an exploratory study conducted on professors from media colleges in the Arab region by having a sample representation of the entire study population. This paper is grounded on literature review of four scholarly articles that examine the opportunities and concerns in using AI in education, but our research is based on pragmatics of a group of teachers in a regional university and a particular discipline. This approach enables the gathering of detailed views and discovery of specific risks and possibilities that can be easily overlooked in other, larger studies.

5.1 Research Gap

The first specializes in studies on the adaptive capacity of synthetic intelligence (AI) to improve university teaching. By growing how AI can enhance teachers' skills and enhance their abilities in using advanced teaching and gaining knowledge of strategies, this examines pursuits to reveal how this generation can improve teachers' performance and gain students' fantastic impact on learning studies. Personalized and tailor-made mastering to meet the specific desires of each scholar is an important results of AI integration, which guarantees to improve academic standards. Second, as technological trends are changing the academic panorama, Arab universities want to hold tempo with those trends [13]. The adoption of AI era not most effective will increase competitiveness globally however also substantially improves the fine of education brought. This observe highlights the want for Arab universities to embody and integrate AI a good way to continue to be relevant and ahead thinking in an increasing number of technologically advanced international. Furthermore, the study addresses the want to identify and understand the challenges associated with enforcing AI in higher education. By resolving these obstacles, studies can pick out efforts to locate effective answers and capitalize on possibilities. This proactive approach guarantees that the integration of AI into university schooling is effective and sustainable, decreasing potential shortcomings.

6 Methodology

6.1 Study Design

This has a look at applies the descriptive research layout the use of a sample survey method. The descriptive studies technique is restricted to describing a particular set of phenomena by way of compiling facts from sample population and then modeling current institutions, tendencies, and patterns. A sample survey allows researchers to collect statistics from a small and achievable sub-phase of the populace to attain an extensive expertise of the phenomenon underneath research, without always seeking to set up the motive and effect relationships of the concerned variables.

6.2 Sample Collection

The population under study was media professors in Arab universities and this was chosen based on the objectives of the study. Faculty members were selected based on their professional experience and qualifies them to offer insight to the problems and potentialities facing the university in the integration of AI. The sample selection was done by selecting professors teaching in different universities in the Arab World to increase variety in terms of cultural, social, geographical differences. Among the variables researched, 60 professors were selected to participate in the study.

6.3 Research Tools

A survey was adopted as the chief data collection instrument employed for this study, which sought to capture the perceptions and trends of respondents toward the application of artificial intelligence in strengthening university learning. The questionnaire structure included demographic data and four axes:

AI, technologies or simply computing intelligence or smartness are innovative tools that have received interest within modern society in the recent past (Table 1).

The survey questions focus on the effects of artificial intelligence on university professors using a Likert scale, the following questions aimed at assessing the challenges of using artificial intelligence in university education with likelihood measured using Likert scale. Possible strategies that can help resolve the problems of artificial intelligence.

The credibility of the questionnaire was tested through pilot testing conducted on nine arbitrators to get their input and make the necessary amendments and improvements accordingly.

Table 1. Different AI tools that evaluate for HE in the current study.

Category	Tools
Search Tools	TutorAI, Perplexity, ChatGPT, Consensus, Elicit, Scholarly, Typeset, Article. Audio, ELIF
Professional Design Tools	Visual Sitemaps, ArtBoard, Uizard, Prototyper
Tools for Creating Educational Content	Narakeet, Munch, Mindsmith, Nolej, Papercup, Video, Pictory, Content Fries, Invideo, Runway, Dubverse, Unscreen
Tools for Writing Articles and Research	Copy AI, Co-writer, Hemingwayapp, Jasper, WriteSonic, Quillbot, Wordtune, Rytr
Tools for Writing and Telling Stories for Students	Subtext, Compose, MarkCopy, Novel AI, Bedtime Story, Tome
Tools for Creating Tests	Yippity, Quiz Gecko, Kwizie
Tools for Making Presentations	Presentation Slides, Designs, Beautiful AI, Pitch, Poised, Presentations AI

6.4 Processing and Statistical Analysis

Respondents were asked to complete a self-administered questionnaire, which was sent to media professors in Arab universities through WhatsApp groups. The questionnaires were administered by the researchers between January and April of the year the study was conducted. The data was then aggregated and analyzed mathematically based on statistical criteria once the data collection was done. For the demographic variables, descriptive statistics were used to provide summary of the result and for the Likert scale items, descriptive statistics was used to analyses the response [14]. To gain insight into the demographic variables that impact students' academic performance, interviews' open-ended response were themes analyzed.

6.5 Spatial and Temporal Framework

Professors who teach media in Arab universities in the context of emirates, Saudi Arabia, Bahrain, Sudan, Egypt, Jordan, Lebanon, Algeria, and Libya were targeted. The data collection and analysis were conducted during the period from January to April to gain an understanding of the phenomenon under study during a particular period.

6.6 Theoretical Aspect

The theoretical foundations are discussed in the literature on artificial intelligence in education. Some of the concepts include individual learning, administrative tasks, and the use of AI in enhancing learners' performance comprise the conceptual framework where the research questions and objectives are established. The literature from accomplished research and reports from universities like Stanford University and consulting organizations such as McKinsey confirm theoretical perspectives to the concept of this study with reference to the effects of AI on university education.

7 Results

The survey results showed a close gender distribution among the sample participants, with 51.7% females and 48.3% males. In terms of academic degrees, assistant professor made up 41.7% of the sample, while Lecturers made up 21.7%. Associate professor and professor each represented 18.3% of the sample (Fig. 1). The use of AI in education showed high adoption, with 56.7% of respondents indicating that they sometimes use AI, highlighting the increasing integration of AI into teaching practices wood adds that 18.3% use AI all the time [15].

This explains the growing importance and adoption of AI in higher education. When asked why they use AI in education, 38.3% cited time savings as a major benefit. Continued technological development was mentioned by 23.3% of respondents, followed by 11.7% who noted that AI helps students achieve the educational outcomes they need [16]. Additionally, 10% emphasized providing exceptional educational experiences for students, and 6.7% used AI for quick feedback during the curriculum. Another 5% refer to curriculum development as a reason for using AI.

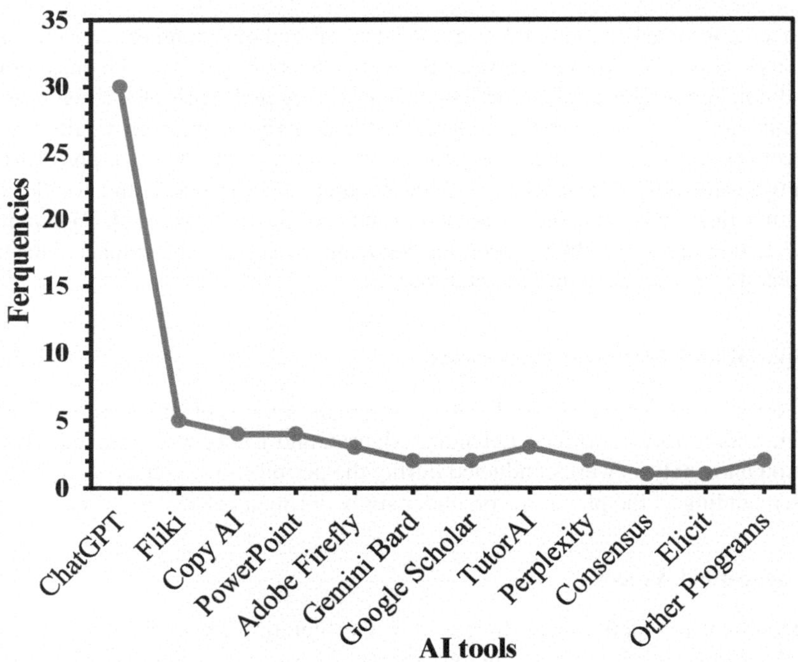

Fig. 1. The frequency of different important AI programs used in higher education.

Regarding the most popular AI applications used, 50% of respondents mentioned Chat GPT. Other AI applications, such as Flicky, Copy AI, PowerPoint, Adobe Firefly, Gemini Bard, and Google Scholar, make up the remaining percentage, reflecting the use of various AI tools in educational settings.

7.1 The Role of Artificial Intelligence on Faculty Progress

According to the data analysis about the impact of artificial intelligence on educators, all of the alternatives' arithmetic averages fell between 4.05 and 3.05. The most often mentioned comment, "AI helps me prepare for science," had a high degree of agreement—4.05, on average. This implies that AI is especially useful for helping teachers prepare for science classes, including making instructional materials and preparing presentations. The statement, "Use AI applications to prepare and evaluate exams and assessments," has the lowest average 3.05 (Table 2). This lower score suggests that although AI has its uses, there are concerns about using it to duties that are essential to upholding academic ethics and integrity, which are generally considered to be the domain of the teacher.

Table 2. The mean and standard deviation of the respondents about the role of AI.

Statement		Standard Deviation	Mean
1	AI helps me achieve learning outcomes with high efficiency	0.823	4.00
2	AI contributes to developing school curricula	0.637	4.03
3	AI helps me prepare for science	0.811	4.05
4	Use AI applications to prepare and evaluate exams and assessments	1.032	3.05
5	I support students in dealing with AI applications in multimedia generation	0.638	4.00
6	Benefit from AI in academic advising	1.030	3.42
7	AI identifies the knowledge and skill gaps of each student, which helps in addressing them	0.946	3.45

According to the data, there is still uncertainty about using AI for test preparation and assessment, even though it is realized as a useful tool in many other areas of education. AI is perceived as improving education rather than taking the place of university professors, emphasizing how technology complements conventional teaching techniques rather than undermines them [17]. This harmony makes sure that although AI can expedite and enhance several educational functions, the human component will always be essential to the learning process (Fig. 2).

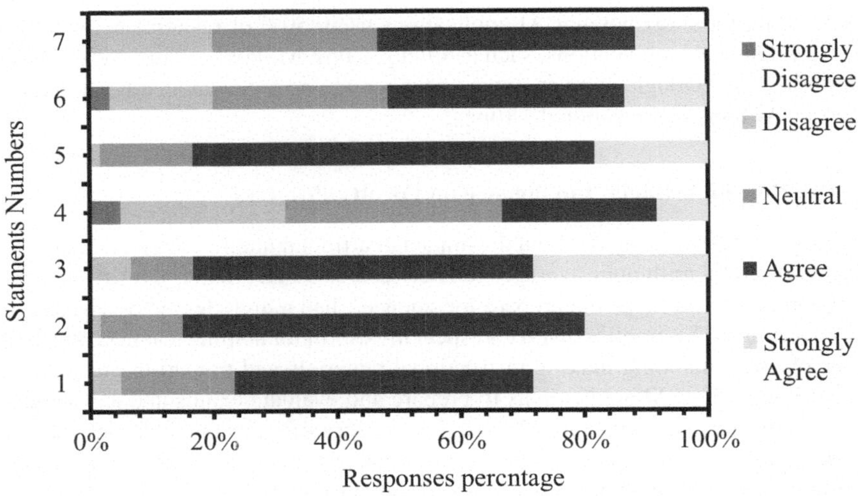

Fig. 2. Likert scale analysis of the statements given in table no 3, for the impact of AI on teachers.

Challenges of Using Artificial Intelligence to Enhance Higher Education.

According to the data in Table 3, there were a range of arithmetic mean values between 4.27 and 3.03 for all difficulties related to the application of artificial intelligence in higher education. The biggest obstacle, with an average score of 4.27, is the support for thinking about moral issues related to keeping an eye on students and making sure they finish assignments and tasks on their own. This high grade indicates a serious commitment for upholding students' independence in their work and upholding academic integrity.

The idea that AI is endangering jobs and removing the need for human resources in education has the lowest average (3.03) [18]. Although there is considerable agreement on this issue, it is not as strong as the ethical concerns, suggesting that although job displacement is a concern, the respondents' main concern is not it (Fig. 3).

The shortage of experts in AI and its applications (average 4.13), as well as some students' difficulties utilizing AI applications (also averaging 4.13), are other noteworthy concerns. These issues show how much more support and training are required to help teachers and students use AI tools effectively. With an average score of 3.87, the worry that students' privacy would be compromised and that their data would be misused also scored well, suggesting a serious concern about data security and privacy while using AI in the classroom. The findings highlight the need to incorporate AI into the educational system even if there are serious concerns regarding privacy, job security, ethics, and availability of knowledge, even though AI is considered as a helpful tool in higher education.

Q 1. To what extent do university professors know about AI technology?

An average test was used to assess the level of artificial intelligence (AI) technology expertise among university teachers (Table 4). The responses had an arithmetic mean of 3.71 and a standard deviation of 0.566. Given that suggest is lots better than the

Table 3. The assessment of challenges while using AI in Higher Education.

Statement		Standard Deviation	Average
1	From my point of view, AI is threatening jobs and eliminating the need for human resources in education	1.207	3.03
2	AI makes mistakes while I deal with it	0.819	3.80
3	AI is characterized by bias and lack of neutrality, reducing chances of justice in education	0.993	3.38
4	Support consideration of ethical aspects around monitoring students and ensuring they complete tasks themselves	0.634	4.27
5	Lack of availability of specialists in AI and its applications	0.700	4.13
6	The difficulty of some students dealing with AI applications	0.713	4.13

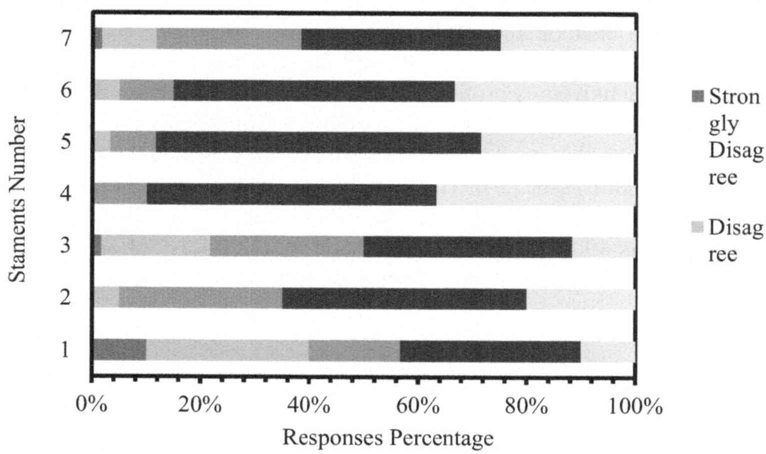

Fig. 3. The response analysis of about multiple challenges of AI in applying at higher education.

size's midpoint, this shows that the professors who participated in the survey had a comparatively full-size level of know-how. Although most professors have a solid hold close of AI era, there are a few versions in their degrees of knowledge, as indicated by using the same old deviation, which factors to a mild degree of variability within the responses.

Table 4. Hypothesis testing of question 1.

Decision	Level of Significance	Standard Deviation	Arithmetic Mean	Degrees of Freedom	Test Value
Accept the Hypothesis	0.000	0.566	3.71	59	43.945

The question of whether university instructors are significantly knowledgeable about AI technology was put to the test. At a significant level of 0.000, the test result of 43.945 is extremely significant. The strength of the results is further supported by the significance level, which is much below the widely accepted cutoff of 0.05 [19]. Consequently, it is acknowledged that university professors have a significant understanding of AI technology. A p-value of 0.000 indicates the statistical significance of the test, indicating that the observed link in the data is not the result of chance. The decision that university professors are knowledgeable about AI technology is strongly supported by this substantial evidence. The analysis reveals that university professors possess a high and statistically significant degree of knowledge regarding AI technology, indicating that they are well-equipped to incorporate AI into their professional and academic endeavors.

Q 2. How does Ai contribute to improving the performance of teachers and their impact on the learning experience of students?

The mean numerical response was 3.40, and the standard deviation was 0.451. This instrument shows that university professors generally agree that AI contributes positively to their work and affects students' learning experiences (Table 5). The relatively low standard deviation indicates that most responses were clustered around the mean, indicating teacher consensus on this issue [20]. The hypothesis tested was whether AI significantly contributes to teachers' performance and improves students' learning experience. The obtained test value is 49.877, which is significant at 0.000 level of significance. This level of significance is well below the criterion of 0.05, indicating the robustness of the results.

Table 5. AI contribution to enhance the performance of professor regarding student learning.

Decision	Level of Significance	Standard Deviation	Arithmetic Mean	Degrees of Freedom	Test Value (t)
Accept the Hypothesis	0.000	0.451	3.40	59	49.877

Thus, the hypothesis that AI positively impacts teacher performance and student learning experience is supported. Statistical significance indicated by a p-value of 0.000

indicates that the observed relationship is not due to chance. This strong evidence supports the claims that AI contributes positively to the effectiveness of the curriculum and improves the academic achievement of the students [21]. The research provides compelling evidence that AI plays an important role in improving teacher performance and positively impacting students' learning experiences. University professors recognize the benefits of AI, demonstrating the value and effectiveness of its incorporation into educational practices.

Q 3. What are the most widely used applications of AI in enhancing higher education?

T-tests were conducted to determine the extent of universities' knowledge of artificial intelligence (AI) technologies (Table 6). The results are detailed in the table above. The mean numerical response was 3.58, and the standard deviation was 0.629. This median value indicates that the university respondents have a moderate to high level of knowledge about AI technologies. The standard deviation shows some variation in the responses, but the overall agreement is clear.

Table 6. The evaluation of AI in enhancing higher education.

Decision	Level of Significance	Standard Deviation	Arithmetic Mean	Degrees of Freedom	Test Value (t)
Accept the Hypothesis	0.000	0.629	3.58	59	37.909

The hypothesis tested was whether universities have greater knowledge of AI technologies. The obtained t-test value is 37.909, which is significant at 0.000 level. This level of significance is much lower than the traditional threshold of 0.05, confirming that the results were statistically significant. Thus, the notion that universities have enough AI technology has been accepted. The significance level reached 0.000, well below the threshold of 0.05 (Table 6). This suggests that the observed relationship is highly unlikely to emerge spontaneously, thus confirming that universities are aware of commonly used AI initiatives to enhance higher education.

Q 4. What are the challenges facing the adoption of Ai technologies in Arab universities?

The hypothesis tested was to identify the challenges faced by the implementation of AI technologies in Arab universities (Table 7). The obtained t-test value was 49.377, which is significant at 0.000 level. This level of significance is well below the traditional limit of 0.05, confirming the statistical significance of the results. Thus, the view that university professors are aware of the challenges of adopting AI in Arab universities is supported.

The calculated mean of 3.78 with a standard deviation of 0.515 indicates that university lecturers have a relatively high level of knowledge about AI technologies [22]. An exponential stage of 0.000 suggests a distinctly significant relationship, indicating that the located consequences are not distinctly possibly to occur by danger. This confirms that university, college's expertise of AI technology and demanding situations related to its adoption is sufficient and statistically vast. The statistical evaluation affords sturdy

Table 7. The analysis of specific challenges of AI facing by Arab Universities.

Decision	Level of Significance	Standard Deviation	Arithmetic Mean	Degrees of Freedom	Test Value (t)
Accept the Hypothesis	0.000	0.515	3.78	59	49.377

evidence that college professors have enough knowledge approximately AI technology. Respondents' perceptions in their know-how of AI and the demanding situations related to its adoption in Arab universities are sturdy and statistically extensive [23]. This indicates that university academics are nicely aware about the capability and demanding situations of integrating AI technology into the gaining knowledge of surroundings.

8 Discussion

Intelligence (AI) is rapidly becoming an integral part of the curriculum in universities worldwide, as it is now embedded in university management systems. This requires AI education and career plans to motivate faculty at all universities. AI technology has changed educational tools, such as educational games and competitions that increase interaction, student engagement, and data storage (Luan et al., 2020). The results of the study reveal insightful demographic data as well as important findings on university faculty knowledge and use of artificial intelligence (AI) in higher education. Demographic breakdown shows a nearly even split between female (51.7%) and male (48.3%) participants, indicating a balance between male and female participants. Most respondents hold the position of Assistant Professor (41.7%), followed by Lecturer (21.7%), Assistant Professor (18.3%) and Professor (18.3%). These positions ensure a broad understanding in different levels of AI technologies adopted in various fields of study.

The integration of AI into teaching practices is surprisingly high, with 56.7% indicating that they sometimes use AI, and 18.3% always using it [23]. This widespread adoption is consistent with global trends, where AI is becoming a tool of great educational importance. The main reasons for using AI are to save time (38.3%), to keep up with technological developments (23.3%), and to help students achieve academic achievement (11.7%) [24]. These statements include the benefits of AI characteristics that have been highlighted in other studies, such as the increased productivity gains reported by [25]. Among the AI applications used, Chat GPT is the most popular, with 50% of respondents using it. This aspiration highlights the increasing reliance on conversational AI for a variety of educational tasks ranging from curriculum support to rapid feedback. A variety of AI tools including PowerPoint, translators, and other systems feature AI the ability to meet a variety of educational needs has been demonstrated [26].

The role of AI in improving teachers' performance and its impact on students' learning experience was tested using a series of case studies with different perspectives. The numerical means for these statements ranged from 4.05 to 3.05, indicating a generally positive view of the role of AI in education. The highest opinion (mean of 4.05) was the statement that AI helps teachers prepare for science lessons, indicating that AI tools are particularly effective in facilitating subject-specific learning activities in facilitating subject-specific teaching tasks (Huang & Qiao, 2024). In contrast, there was little intention (median 3.05) to use AI applications to prepare for and test exams and tests. This finding highlight concerns about the reliability of AI and the ethical implications of its use in high-stakes trials, a sentiment documented by [27]. Although with this background, all positive comments indicate that AI is viewed as a complementary tool that enhances rather than replaces traditional teaching methods.

It was also determined that the challenges associated with the adoption of AI in higher education highlight a number of concerns. The highest mean (4.27) was ethical considerations in supervising students and ensuring that tasks were completed independently. This highlights important concerns about academic integrity and the ethical use of AI, which has been an important topic of discussion in educational technology literature. Other notable challenges include the scarcity of AI experts (mean 4.13) and difficulties some students have in handling AI applications (mean 4.13) [28]. These issues highlight the importance of support and in-depth training difficult for teachers and students to use AI tools effectively. The average test was used to determine the extent of university faculty's knowledge of AI technology, which is calculated as 3.71 which is 0.566. Higher scores indicate adequate AI knowledge among faculty, with a t-test value of significance level of 43.945 at 0.000 level of significance. This indicates that the determined stage of understanding is not coincidental and shows that university professors are gifted with AI technology.

An arithmetic implies of three.40 and a fashionable deviation of 0.451 imply that AI has a useful impact on both teaching performance and scholar learning. A t-check price of 49.877 is statistically good sized, lending credence to the concept that AI has a beneficial effect on both instructor effectiveness and student fulfillment. Previous look at has proven that AI can enhance the excellent of guidance and boom pupil engagement [29], that's in line with this locating. The widespread use of AI services, with an arithmetic suggest of 3.Fifty eight and preferred deviation of zero.629, indicating a excessive level of know-how approximately AI tools with a giant T-test value of 37.909 amongst university respondents regarding the most frequent use of AI programs to enhance higher schooling This indicating that the sturdy motives are steady with the growing use of AI equipment in academic settings around the world. The difficulties related to implementing AI at Arab establishments have been investigated; the imply score turned into 3. Seventy-eight and the usual deviation become zero.515. A t-check rating of 49.377 shows that human beings are quite aware of these difficulties. There is a want for specialized AI education and support because the consequences convey attention to troubles which includes college students' struggles with AI programs, the moral utilization of AI, and the demand for AI experts. The findings spotlight each the advantages and demanding situations of adopting AI, and underscore the importance of ethical considerations, support, and education to maximize the ability of AI in instructional settings. Several solutions were proposed to address these demanding situations:

- Establishing an AI team to monitor AI developments in universities and provide training. Design courses that integrate AI, making it more interactive and responsive to student needs.

- Provide new AI-enabled instructional equipment, including educational robots and self-mastering applications.
- A clever assessment gadget the use of AI to analyze pupil performance and offer development steerage.
- Promoting research and development in educational technology and AI.
- Using AI for administrative tasks, such as attendance, assessment, testing, and storing student documents.
- Teaching AI as a curriculum in all majors and ensuring that students use AI ethically and correctly.
- Establishing clean rules and oversight for the use of AI in education to reduce errors and make certain information privateness.
- Tailored AI applications for private establishments and ongoing training for students to use AI responsibly in research.

These answers are in step with Al-Hindi's have a look, which emphasizes the need for sturdy infrastructure, ok technical help, ongoing training for school members, and a tradition of AI adoption in education to buy modern-day machinery, maintain gadget, college the use of AI successfully Useful and suitable economic aid is likewise needed.

9 Conclusion

This look at sheds light on how and why college teachers are the use of synthetic intelligence (AI) within the classroom. There is a considerable variety of educational tiers and a balanced distribution of genders, consistent with the demographic information. Artificial intelligence (AI) is turning into more and more critical in academia because of its excessive adoption fee and widespread utilization in educational approaches [30]. Chat GPT is the most widely used utility of AI, that is primarily used to store time and enhance instructional outcomes. According to the results, AI has a profoundly useful impact on both the pleasant of practice and the gaining knowledge of stories of students [31]. The public has a positive effect of AI, regardless of positive concerns which include ethical dilemmas and the opportunity of task loss. Academic advising, filling in college students' information gaps, and curriculum constructing are all areas where professors see its cost [32]. Increased investment, schooling, and interest to moral worries are important considering the difficulties encountered even as the use of AI, especially at Arab schools. According to the report, college instructors are well informed about the AI era and can effectively incorporate AI into their teaching strategies, so one can enhance students' academic enjoy.

10 Future Work

The studies envision a transformative future for university schooling, where AI technology and its gear dramatically beautify the training and mastering procedure. it explain study the current role of AI in journalism faculties in Arab universities, and opens the way for further research on its impact on students, course guides and business processes Let's do it This future-focused approach will help to assess whether AI is such a slow development or potential threat to the university teaching profession, thus providing researchers with more opportunities to explore multiple influences of AI in higher education. Overall, future research should seek to maximize the benefits of generative AI in medical education while resolving current limitations and constraints.

References

1. Akgun, S., Greenhow, C.: Artificial intelligence in education: addressing ethical challenges in K-12 settings. AI Ethics **2**(3), 431–440 (2022). https://doi.org/10.1007/s43681-021-00096-7
2. Alam, A.: Should robots replace teachers? Mobilisation of AI and learning analytics in education. In: 2021 International Conference on Advances in Computing, Communication, and Control (ICAC3) (2021)
3. Alharbi, W.: AI in the foreign language classroom: a pedagogical overview of automated writing assistance tools. Educ. Res. Int., 1–15 (2023). https://www.hindawi.com/journals/edri/2023/4253331/
4. Alhumaid, K., Naqbi, S., Elsori, D., Mansoori, M.: The adoption of artificial intelligence applications in education. Int. J. Data Netw. Sci. **7**(1), 457–466 (2023). https://doi.org/10.5267/j.ijdns.2022.8.013
5. Awang, Z., Afthanorhan, A., Mamat, M.: The Likert scale analysis using parametric based Structural Equation Modeling (SEM). Comput. Methods Soc. Sci. **4**(1), 13 (2016). https://www.ceeol.com/search/article-detail?id=418522
6. Bates, T., Cobo, C., Mariño, O., Wheeler, S.: Can artificial intelligence transform higher education? **17**, 1–12 (2020)
7. Berg, S.: The Acceptance of Assessment AIs in Formal Higher Education: an Exploratory Study University of Twente (2023). https://purl.utwente.nl/essays/94567
8. Borger, J.G., et al.: Artificial intelligence takes center stage: exploring the capabilities and implications of ChatGPT and other AI-assisted technologies in scientific research and education. Immunol. Cell Biol. **101**(10), 923–935 (2023). https://doi.org/10.1111/imcb.12689
9. Brynjolfsson, E., Rock, D., Syverson, C.: Artificial intelligence and the modern productivity paradox. Econ. Artif. Intell. Agenda **23**, 23–57 (2019). https://doi.org/10.3386/w24001
10. Castro, D., New, J.: The promise of artificial intelligence. Center Data Innov. **115**(10), 32–35 (2016). https://datainnovation.org/2016/10/the-promise-of-artificial-intelligence/
11. Chen, L., Chen, P., Lin, Z.: Artificial intelligence in education: a review. IEEE Access **8**, 75264–75278 (2020). https://doi.org/10.1109/ACCESS.2020.2988510
12. Chivose, E.M.: The Adoption and Usage Patterns of ChatGPT Among Students and Faculty Members in Higher Education: a Study of the University of Nairobi, Faculty of Education University of Nairobi (2023). http://erepository.uonbi.ac.ke/handle/11295/164663
13. Dahabreh, F.: The continued usage of artificial intelligence in the United Arab Emirates public sector organisations: An extended information system success model Northumbria University (2023). https://nrl.northumbria.ac.uk/id/eprint/51629/
14. Di Leo, G., Sardanelli, F.: Statistical significance: p value, 0.05 threshold, and applications to radiomics—reasons for a conservative approach. Eur. Radiol. Exp. **4**, 1–8 (2020). https://doi.org/10.1186/s41747-020-0145-y
15. Elsayed, A.M.: The use of academic social networks among Arab researchers: a survey. Soc. Sci. Comput. Rev. **34**(3), 378–391 (2016). https://doi.org/10.1177/0894439315589146
16. González-Carrillo, C.D., Restrepo-Calle, F., Ramírez-Echeverry, J.J., González, F.A.: Automatic grading tool for Jupyter notebooks in artificial intelligence courses. Sustainability **13**(21), 12050 (2021). https://doi.org/10.3390/su132112050

17. Hitka, M., Schmidtová, J., Lorincová, S., Štarchoň, P., Weberová, D., Kampf, R.: Sustainability of human resource management processes through employee motivation and job satisfaction. Acta Polytechnica Hungarica **18**(2), 7–26 (2021). https://real-j.mtak.hu/21037/2/APH_2021_18_02_.pdf
18. Hooda, M., Rana, C., Dahiya, O., Rizwan, A., Hossain, M.S.: Artificial intelligence for assessment and feedback to enhance student success in higher education. Math. Prob. Eng. **2022**, 1–19 (2022). https://doi.org/10.1155/2022/5215722
19. Huang, X., Qiao, C.: Enhancing computational thinking skills through artificial intelligence education at a STEAM high school. Sci. Educ. **33**(2), 383–403 (2024)
20. Igbokwe, I.C.: Application of artificial intelligence (AI) in educational management. Int. J. Sci. Res. Publ. **13**(3), 300–307 (2023). https://www.ijsrp.org/research-paper-0323.php?rp=P13512782
21. Inayah, N., Yusuf, Q., Fibula, N.: Exploring undergraduate students' perception toward the use of Duolingo in learning English. Hum. Soc. Sci. Rev. **8**(3), 76–85 (2020). https://core.ac.uk/download/pdf/327122519.pdf
22. Khodeir, L.M., Nessim, A.A.: Changing skills for architecture students employability: analysis of job market versus architecture education in Egypt. Ain Shams Eng. J. **11**(3), 811–821 (2020). https://doi.org/10.1016/j.asej.2019.11.006
23. Kong, S.-C., Cheung, M.-Y.W., Tsang, O.: Developing an artificial intelligence literacy framework: evaluation of a literacy course for senior secondary students using a project-based learning approach. Comput. Educ. Artif. Intell. **6**, 100214 (2024). https://doi.org/10.1016/j.caeai.2024.100214
24. Luan, H., et al.: Challenges and future directions of big data and artificial intelligence in education. Front. Psychol. **11**, 580820 (2020). https://doi.org/10.3389/fpsyg.2020.580820
25. Osakwe, J., Dlodlo, N., Jere, N.: Where learners' and teachers' perceptions on mobile learning meet: a case of Namibian secondary schools in the Khomas region. Technol. Soc. **49**, 16–30 (2017). https://doi.org/10.1016/j.techsoc.2016.12.004
26. Pedro, F., Subosa, M., Rivas, A., Valverde, P.: Artificial intelligence in education: challenges and opportunities for sustainable development (2019). https://hdl.handle.net/20.500.12799/6533
27. Ryosuke, M., Ogino, H.: Linking entrepreneurial education and interactive learning with post-graduate success for biotechnology programs: identifying the moderating role of the usefulness of co-teaching R&D. J. Commercial Biotechnol. **28**(1), 212–224 (2023). https://doi.org/10.1504/IJLC.2021.111670
28. Sanusi, I.T., Ayanwale, M.A., Chiu, T.K.: Investigating the moderating effects of social good and confidence on teachers' intention to prepare school students for artificial intelligence education. Educ. Inf. Technol. **29**(1), 273–295 (2024). https://doi.org/10.1007/s10639-023-12250-1
29. Sarker, I.H.: AI-based modeling: techniques, applications and research issues towards automation, intelligent and smart systems. SN Comput. Sci. **3**(2), 158 (2022). https://doi.org/10.1007/s42979-022-01043-x
30. Wentzel, K.R., Muenks, K., McNeish, D., Russell, S.: Peer and teacher supports in relation to motivation and effort: a multi-level study. Contemp. Educ. Psychol. **49**, 32–45 (2017). https://doi.org/10.1016/j.cedpsych.2016.11.002
31. Zhang, X., Gossett, C., Simpson, J., Davis, R.: Advising students for success in higher education: an all-out effort. J. Coll. Student Retention Res. Theory Pract. **21**(1), 53–77 (2019). https://doi.org/10.1177/1521025116689097
32. Zing, K.: Harnessing the power of artificial intelligence in personalized learning. Educia J. **2**(1), 7–14 (2024). https://www.eurchembull.com/uploads/paper/835e4f9a9da2bd3a8178f9a8b882d15c.pdf

Comparative Performance of GPT-4, RAG-Augmented GPT-4, and Students in MOOCs

Fatma Miladi(✉), Valéry Psyché, and Daniel Lemire

TELUQ University, 5800 rue Saint-Denis, Montreal, QC H2S 3L5, Canada
{fatma.miladi,valery.psyche,daniel.lemire}@teluq.ca

Abstract. Generative Pretrained Transformers (GPT) have significantly improved natural language processing, showcasing enormous versatility across diverse applications. Although GPT models have enormous potential, they frequently encounter issues such as mistakes and hallucinations, which may limit their practical use. Addressing these shortcomings, Retrieval-Augmented Generation (RAG) represents an innovative approach that potentially enhances the accuracy and reliability of these models by leveraging external databases to correct and enrich their outputs. In our study, a RAG-augmented GPT-4 model was tested within an AI-focused Massive Open Online Course (MOOC) and outperformed a standard GPT-4 model, achieving an 85% success rate compared to 81%. Notably, it also surpassed the average student performance, underscoring its ability to deliver precise and contextually relevant responses. These findings suggest the potential of RAG in enhancing AI models for educational use and indicate that instructors can leverage this technology to refine assessment methods and that students can achieve more personalized and engaging learning experiences.

Keywords: Large Language Models · GPT · Text Embeddings · MOOC · Online Education · Evaluation · Retrieval-Augmented Generation

1 Introduction

The introduction of Large Language Models (LLMs), such as the generative pre-trained transformer (GPT), has significantly transformed the field of artificial intelligence, specifically in the domain of natural language processing [1–4]. These models have shown impressive performance in diverse fields such as finance, technology, and healthcare [5–7]. Nevertheless, although large language models possess remarkable capabilities, they are not without limitations. They tend to 'hallucinate', whereby they produce content that may be factually inaccurate [8,9]. This phenomenon has the potential to give rise to information that may contradict established facts.

To overcome this issue, researchers developed the Retrieval Augmented Generation (RAG) technique, which was first proposed by Lewis et al. in 2020 [10].

A. Basiouni and C. Frasson (Eds.): BBGI 2024, CCIS 2162, pp. 81–92, 2024.
https://doi.org/10.1007/978-3-031-65996-6_7

RAG enhances LLMs by dynamically incorporating external knowledge during the generation process, which enhances the model's capacity to produce precise and pertinent responses. This marks a significant advancement in LLMs, especially for generative tasks [11,12]. Although RAG has demonstrated potential in different fields, its application in educational settings, particularly within Massive Open Online Courses (MOOCs), remains underexplored. This research gap motivated us to investigate how large language models enhanced with RAG could improve content accuracy in educational settings.

In our previous research, we explored how RAG enhances the performance of GPT models across four MOOC modules, finding significant improvements in response accuracy [13]. We continue the work initiated in [13] by conducting a more in-depth analysis, not only of accuracy but also of the relevance of the responses. Additionally, we are introducing a new personalized prompt designed to align the language model more precisely with the pedagogical requirements of learners. This innovation aims to foster richer and more engaging interactions between students and the GPT model, which is used as a learning companion in the online course. Such enhancements are expected to improve the effectiveness of autonomous learning.

Our study is guided by two main research questions. (RQ1): Does integrating RAG into the GPT-4 model improve the pedagogical quality (accuracy and relevance) of answers in MOOCs? Hypothesis 1 (H1): We hypothesize that GPT-4 enriched with RAG will exhibit improved performance over standard GPT-4 with respect to the pedagogical quality of generated responses. The second question (RQ2) is: How does the performance of RAG-augmented GPT-4 compare with that of students in MOOC exercises? We propose two hypotheses: (H2) the RAG-augmented GPT-4 will exceed the average scores of students, and (H3) the RAG-augmented GPT-4 will exceed the highest scores obtained by students.

2 Model

Our architecture enhances user interaction by augmenting GPT model with the Retrieval-Augmented Generation technique, as depicted in Fig. 1. The workflow starts with the submission of a query by a user, which is subsequently converted into a vector representation using OpenAI's text-embedding-ada-002 model [14] for retrieval-augmented generation. This embedding model was selected based on its capacity to accurately capture the semantic details of text within contexts that are specific to a particular domain. After vectorizing the query, the system navigates through a database of domain-specific text embeddings to detect segments, referred to as "chunks", that have the highest cosine similarity scores. These selected segments were then combined with the initial user query to enhance the prompt by providing additional context. The prompts are based on White et al. [15]'s description of the Persona Pattern Prompt (see Fig. 2). The goal of this strategy is to increase student engagement and facilitate learning in educational contexts. The enriched prompt is then fed into a Large Language Model such as GPT-4 to generate responses that are precise, contextually appropriate, and reflective of domain-specific knowledge. Our model aims to achieve superior response quality by utilizing both retrieval-based methods and the generative capabilities of the GPT-4.

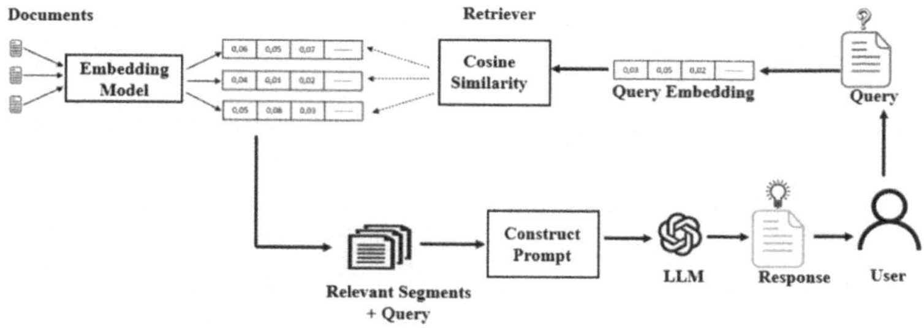

Fig. 1. Overview of the model architecture: From user query processing to response generation, taken from [13].

"""Act as a learning companion in an artificial intelligence course.
Provide outputs that a learning companion would create for each question.

Question:""" + question + """

Context: {text}

Answer:

"""

Fig. 2. Prompt configuration for RAG-augmented GPT-4.

3 Methods

In this section, we first describe the dataset used in our study. Following this, we outline two experiments designed to evaluate the performance enhancements that Retrieval-Augmented Generation technology provides to GPT-4 model, particularly within MOOC environments.

3.1 Dataset

Our research employs the AI MOOC focused on artificial intelligence developed by University TELUQ [16]. This course is segmented into four modules, each focusing on different AI aspects: general AI concepts, symbolic AI, connectionist AI, and AI applications in education. Our analysis focuses on the first module, which includes 33 assessment exercises for the purposes of this study. There are eight true/false questions, seven multiple-choice questions, four matching exercises, and fourteen fill-in-the-blank exercises in this set of exercises. Table 1 presents examples of these questions to provide a better understanding of the assessment types used in evaluating GPT models.

Table 1. Examples of exercises used for GPT models evaluation.

Question Type	Example
True/false	Indicate whether the following statement is true or false: An intelligent agent cannot adapt its actions to its environment nor act upon it. 1. True 2. False
Multiple Choice Question	Select the correct answer: According to Yann LeCun, making a machine intelligent allows it to: A. dream. B. memorize. C. learn. D. perceive.
Matching exercise	Match each definition with its corresponding term from the following: Definitions: 1. Various digital technology, mathematical, and other components that enable the design of an autonomous car. 2. The ability of a neural network to adjust itself, changing its behavior based on an environment, this ability can be used during the learning phase. 3. A robotic arm that has learned through trial-and-error manipulation to handle a Rubik's Cube. Terms: A. Artificial Intelligence B. Adaptability C. Intelligent Agent
Fill-in-the-blank	Fill in the blank: To pass the test of ..., the computer must be equipped with an artificial vision device to perceive objects and a robotic capability to manipulate objects and move.

3.2 Experiment Design

Our experimental approach consists of two distinct components, each designed to provide comprehensive insights into the effectiveness of the RAG-augmented GPT-4 model. The first experiment evaluates the efficacy of the RAG-augmented GPT-4 comparing it to the standard GPT-4 model. The second experiment aims to conduct a comparative analysis between the responses of students and those of the RAG-augmented GPT-4, focusing specifically on the same MOOC exercises.

Experiment 1: GPT-4 Models Performance Evaluation (RQ1)

Objective. In Experiment 1, the objective is to evaluate the impact of incorporating the retrieval technique on GPT-4 model outputs, which involves integrating external information to enhance response quality. Specifically, we aim to compare the accuracy and the relevance of responses produced by the RAG-enhanced GPT-4 model with those generated by the conventional GPT-4 model.

Procedure

- Data: We utilized the 33 assessment exercises from the first module of the MOOC as queries for both models, as detailed in Table 1.
- Prompt Configuration for RAG-augmented GPT-4: The prompt depicted in Fig. 2 is structured as follows:
  - Persona Prompt: "Act as a learning companion in an artificial intelligence course. Provide outputs that a learning companion would create for each question."
  - Query and Contextual Integration: Each exercise's text replaces the 'question' placeholder, and the 'context' placeholder is filled with segments that are contextually appropriate. These segments are selected based on high cosine similarity scores from a domain-specific text-embedding database, as detailed in Sect. 2.
- Standard GPT-4 Model Configuration: The standard model uses a similar persona prompt but without additional contextual data integration.

Evaluation Process. The answers from both models were processed sequentially as they appeared in the MOOC, without feedback on incorrect responses. An independent reviewer, a Ph.D. candidate in cognitive computing, scored the answers using a binary scale (0–1) based on two criteria: accuracy and relevance.

For accuracy, a score of "1" was assigned to answers that were factually correct, while a score of "0" was given to those that were factually incorrect or contained fabrications, referred to as hallucinations.

Relevance was assessed based on how well an answer addressed the specific question posed; accurate answers received a score of "0" if they did not directly relate to the question.

This binary scoring system simplified the assessment process, enabling a direct comparison of the two models' performance on the same set of exercises, consistent with the MOOC's established grading standards.

Experiment 2: Comparison of RAG-Augmented GPT-4 and Student Performance (RQ2)

Objective. This experiment aims to assess the effectiveness of the GPT-4 model augmented with Retrieval-Augmented Generation by comparing it to the performance of students on the same set of 33 MOOC exercises.

Participants. The sample for this study consisted of twenty students, with a gender distribution of seven males and thirteen females. The participants' ages ranged from 22 to 35 years. The study included participants with diverse educational backgrounds, with 60% pursuing computer science, 25% pursuing education, and 15% pursuing engineering. All participants voluntarily participated in this study.

Procedure. The procedure involved conducting 33 exercises under controlled, exam-like conditions without any external assistance for both the students and the GPT-4 model augmented with RAG. This approach guarantees that the evaluation closely matches real testing situations, allowing for an equitable comparison of performance between human learners and the AI model.

Evaluation Process. The exercises were part of the course evaluations for the students, who completed them in a conventional academic environment. In parallel, the RAG-augmented GPT-4 produced responses under identical conditions to ensure consistency. We then conducted a direct comparison between the students' responses and those generated by the augmented model, assessing both for accuracy. This comparative approach facilitated a fair evaluation and provided valuable insights into the practical efficacy of the RAG-enhanced GPT-4 model in an educational setting.

4 Results

In this section, we present the results of using Retrieval-Augmented Generation with the GPT-4 model in MOOC environments. We organize the results around the main research questions.

4.1 Research Question 1 (RQ1): Does Integrating RAG into the GPT-4 Model Improve the Pedagogical Quality (accuracy And relevance) of Answers in MOOCs?

In addressing RQ1, we evaluated the performance of the standard GPT-4 model and its enhancement with Retrieval-Augmented Generation technology using a dataset of 33 exercises from an AI MOOC. The results indicate a slight improvement in both accuracy and relevance when the GPT-4 model is augmented with RAG. The standard model achieved a success rate of 81% in both accuracy and relevance, while the augmented model showed an improvement to 85% in accuracy and 84% in relevance. Table 2 summarizes the comparative results of the exercise assessments in module 1 of the MOOC.

Table 2. Exercise assessment results on module 1.

Exercise Type	GPT-4		RAG-augmented GPT-4	
	Accuracy	Relevance	Accuracy	Relevance
True False	8/8 (100%)	8/8 (100%)	8/8 (100%)	8/8 (100%)
Multiple-Choice	5/7 (71%)	5/7 (71%)	5/7 (71%)	5/7 (71%)
Matching	3/4 (75%)	3/4 (75%)	4/4 (100%)	4/4 (100%)
Fill in the blank	11/14 (79%)	11/14 (79%)	10/14 (71%)	9/14 (64%)
Total	81%	81%	85%	84%

4.2 Research Question 2 (RQ2): How Does the Performance of RAG-Augmented GPT-4 Compare to that of Students in MOOC Exercises?

Concerning RQ2, we evaluated the performance of the RAG-augmented GPT-4 across 33 different types of exercises within an MOOC and compared its results with those of an average student. The model demonstrated superior performance, surpassing the average for all exercise types. It achieved an overall success rate of 85% compared with a student average of 60%, as indicated in Fig. 3. Notably, the model scored 100% in the True/False and matching exercises, whereas its performance in the Fill in the blank tasks was 71%, which is still well above the student average of 35%.

As detailed in Table 3, the performance analysis of students reveals diverse outcomes across various exercise types. Both the median and mode in True False exercises achieve a perfect score of 100%. In multiple-choice question (MCQ) exercises, the median success rate decreases to 57%, while the most frequent score (mode) is even lower at 43%. The matching exercises demonstrate a median success rate of 75% and a mode of 100%. Fill in the blank exercises are particularly challenging, as indicated by a median and mode score of 43%.

Table 3. Median and mode for each exercise type.

Exercise Type	Median Success Rate (%)	Mode Success Rate (%)
True False	100	100
MCQ	57	43
Matching	75	100
Fill in the blank	43	43

Further analysis of the RAG-augmented GPT-4's performance indicates its superior capabilities compared to students. For instance, the model's 52th percentile ranking in the True/False and Multiple Choice exercises suggests competitive performance, with the model either exceeding or matching the scores of more than half of the students. Regrading the matching exercises, the RAG-augmented GPT-4's percentile ranking of approximately 67th demonstrates its superior performance, surpassing the scores of the majority of students. Moreover, the model's 95th percentile ranking in the Fill in the Blank exercises highlights its exceptional performance, placing it within the top 5% of student scores. This indicates that the RAG-augmented GPT-4 outperformed 95% of students in Fill in the Blank exercises.

5 Discussion

The findings obtained from experiment 1 demonstrate that the GPT-4 model when enhanced with Retrieval-Augmented Generation, attains an average accuracy rate of 85% and an average relevance rate of 84%. In contrast, the standard

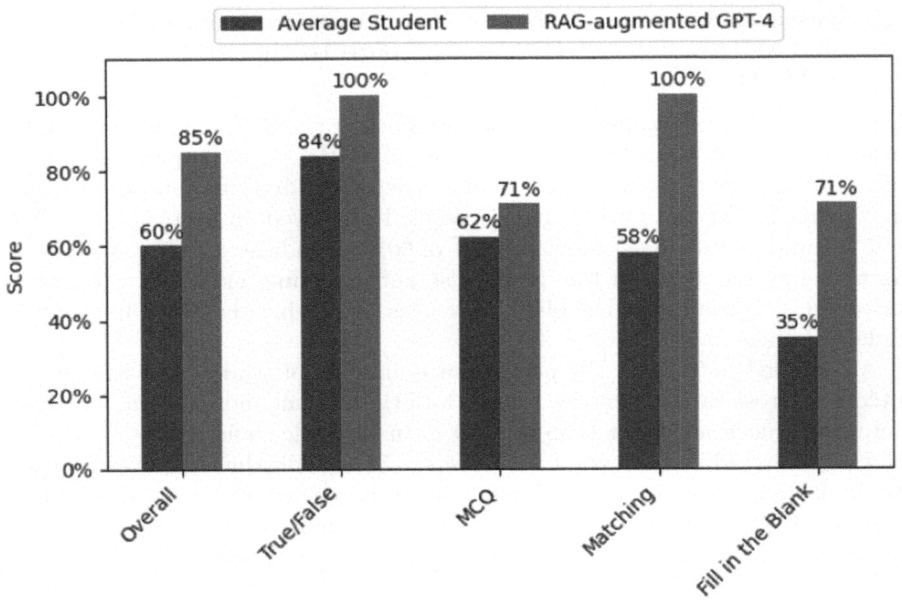

Fig. 3. Average student (blue) and RAG-augmented GPT-4 (green) percentage scores across different types of exercises. (Color figure online)

GPT-4 model recorded a success rate of 81% for both accuracy and relevance. The findings of this study provide evidence in support of Hypothesis 1 (H1), which claimed that incorporating retrieval capabilities would enhance the performance of the GPT-4 model in generating responses within MOOC settings.

The results of experiment 2 not only confirm that the RAG-augmented GPT-4 performed better than the average student, thus validating Hypothesis 2 (H2), but they provide partial support for Hypothesis 3 (H3). This evidence indicates that the model performs exceptionally well in different types of exercises, especially in fill in the blank exercises, where it consistently achieved scores within the top 5% of student performance. These tasks, which are characterized by the need to both remember factual information and apply it in a specific context, often pose a challenge for students, as indicated by their relatively low median and mode scores. Nevertheless, the RAG-augmented GPT-4 shows exceptional proficiency in these exercises. Its advanced understanding and data processing abilities are specifically designed to perform effectively in tasks that frequently present significant challenges for human learners.

In our study, we focused specifically on the capabilities of GPT models enhanced with Retrieval-Augmented Generation. This technique enables the GPT models to access external databases or documents, retrieving information that is then incorporated into their responses. This process enhances the accuracy and relevance of the content generated. The results of our study demonstrate the potential of GPT-4 augmented with RAG to improve educational experiences, providing advantages for students as well as instructors.

For students, the Persona Prompt, designed to act as a 'learning companion', could significantly enhance student engagement and improve learning outcomes. This role enables the technology to guide learners effectively by providing constructive feedback, posing thought-provoking questions, and encouraging the exploration of new perspectives. Consequently, the integration of RAG-augmented GPT-4, which utilizes the Persona Prompt, has the potential to further enrich educational experiences through the creation of immersive and dynamic dialogues. It serves as a sophisticated 'learning companion', as envisioned by Chan and Baskin [17], offering students instant clarifications and in-depth explanations that are customized to their levels of understanding.

However, it is crucial to recognize that the RAG-augmented GPT-4 is not a substitute for human instructors. It lacks the deep understanding that human instructors have of their learners' backgrounds, cultures, and individual learning needs. While this technology can deliver accurate answers and facilitate learning, it cannot replace the nuanced understanding and adaptability of an instructor.

Instructors should adopt a more sustainable assessment approach that prioritizes the cultivation of higher-order cognitive abilities, including critical thinking [18], problem-solving, and creativity [19]. These skills are less susceptible to replication by GPT models. It is recommended that instructors prioritize the improvement of learning and skill acquisition over solely preparing students for traditional evaluations [19]. This can be achieved by integrating more complex assessments such as problem-solving activities and collaborative learning that necessitate active demonstration of comprehension. These methods enhance students' understanding and utilization of knowledge, cultivating a more comprehensive educational approach.

In Retrieval-Augmented Generation systems, the effectiveness of the retrieval component is crucial, as it sources relevant information for content generation. Enhancing this component, particularly through the Hybrid Retrieve approach, has significantly improved RAG systems [20]. Hybrid Retrieve combines dense and sparse retrieval methods, capitalizing on dense retrieval's ability to capture semantic similarities and sparse retrieval's efficiency in keyword matching. This combination results in a more effective retrieval process, enhancing the quality and relevance of the information provided to the generator [21,22]. Consequently, RAG systems based on Hybrid Retrieve could become more capable of producing accurate and contextually relevant outputs, paving the way for advancements in educational technologies and beyond.

Although our study yielded encouraging results, it is crucial that we recognize and address its limitations in order to attain a thorough comprehension. The relatively small sample size (N=20) may affect the statistical robustness and generalizability of our findings. Additionally, our research was conducted on a single MOOC platform and exclusively assessed French language exercises, including multiple choice, true/false, matching, and fill-in-the-blank questions.

This specialization may limit the generalizability of our findings to other educational contexts that utilize a diverse array of assessment types and languages.

To overcome these limitations, future research should incorporate a larger sample size and a broader selection of MOOCs featuring varied exercise formats and languages. Addressing these limitations will enhance our understanding of the effectiveness of GPT-4 augmented with RAG across different educational settings.

6 Conclusion and Future Work

Our study has demonstrated the enhanced capabilities of the GPT-4-augmented model in handling diverse assessment exercises within a MOOC setting. By integrating Retrieval-Augmented Generation with GPT-4, we have not only enhanced the accuracy and relevance of responses but also demonstrated clear superiority over the average performance of students across various types of exercises.

Looking ahead, we plan to extend our research by conducting two detailed case studies involving students from diverse geographical backgrounds. These studies aim to analyze the broader impact of our RAG-augmented GPT-4 model on the online learning experience. We will evaluate not only academic performance but also factors such as students' motivation, engagement, and feelings of isolation. The ability of the RAG-augmented GPT-4 to serve as a learning companion through the Persona Prompt and provide contextually relevant information can enhance the learning experience, making it more engaging and motivating. Furthermore, by delivering timely and relevant responses, the augmented model can help reduce feelings of isolation, particularly in online learning environments. This comprehensive analysis will offer deeper insights into how such advanced AI tools can be effectively integrated into various educational settings, ultimately improving learning experiences.

The integration of RAG-augmented GPT-4 into educational environments promises transformative changes. This innovative technology can revolutionize traditional teaching methods by equipping instructors with advanced tools to enhance student engagement and enrich the learning experience. The RAG-augmented GPT-4 enables customized learning experiences by adjusting educational content to meet the specific needs of individual students. This ensures that learning is not standardized but personalized, addressing each individual's needs. Additionally, the model promotes a more engaging and interactive learning environment through its natural language processing capabilities. As a sophisticated learning companion, the RAG-augmented GPT-4 can significantly enhance student engagement, motivation, and learning outcomes.

References

1. Vaswani, A., et al.: Attention is all you need. Adv. Neural Inf. Process. Syst. 30 (2017)
2. Radford, A., Wu, J., Child, R., Luan, D., Amodei, D., Sutskever, I.: Language models are unsupervised multitask learners. OpenAI blog **1**(8), 9 (2019)
3. Devlin, J., Chang, M. W., Lee, K., Toutanova, K.: Bert: Pre-training of deep bidirectional transformers for language understanding. arXiv preprint arXiv:1810.04805 (2018)
4. Brown, T., et al.: Language models are few-shot learners. Adv. Neural. Inf. Process. Syst. **33**, 1877–1901 (2020)
5. Wu, S., Irsoy, O., Lu, S., Dabravolski, V., Dredze, M., Gehrmann, S., Mann, G.: Bloomberggpt: A large language model for finance. arXiv preprint arXiv:2303.17564 (2023)
6. Chen, M., Tworek, J., Jun, H., Yuan, Q., Pinto, H. P. D. O., Kaplan, J.,Zaremba, W.: Evaluating large language models trained on code. arXiv preprint arXiv:2107.03374 (2021)
7. Yang, X., et al.: A large language model for electronic health records. NPJ Digital Med. **5**(1), 194 (2022)
8. Zhang, Y., Li, Y., Cui, L., Cai, D., Liu, L., Fu, T., Shi, S.: Siren's song in the AI ocean: a survey on hallucination in large language models. arXiv preprint arXiv:2309.01219 (2023)
9. Zhou, C., Neubig, G., Gu, J., Diab, M., Guzman, P., Zettlemoyer, L.,Ghazvininejad, M.: Detecting hallucinated content in conditional neural sequence generation. arXiv preprint arXiv:2011.02593 (2020)
10. Lewis, P., et al.: Retrieval-augmented generation for knowledge-intensive nlp tasks. Adv. Neural. Inf. Process. Syst. **33**, 9459–9474 (2020)
11. Shi, W., et al.: REPLUG: Retrieval-Augmented Black-Box Language Models. ArXiv, abs/2301.12652. https://doi.org/10.48550/arXiv.2301.12652 (2023)
12. Liu, J., Jin, J., Wang, Z., Cheng, J., Dou, Z., Wen, J.: RETA-LLM: A Retrieval-Augmented Large Language Model Toolkit. ArXiv, abs/2306.05212. https://doi.org/10.48550/arXiv.2306.05212 (2023)
13. Miladi, F., Psyché, V., Lemire, D.: Evaluating Generative Pre-trained Transformers in MOOC Assessments: A Comparative Study of GPT Models. In International Conference on Artificial Intelligence in Education (2024)
14. Neelakantan, A., et al.: Text and code embeddings by contrastive pre-training. arXiv preprint arXiv:2201.10005 (2022)
15. White, J., et al.: A prompt pattern catalog to enhance prompt engineering with chatGPT. arXiv preprint arXiv:2302.11382 (2023)
16. Clom-motsia, https://clom-motsia.teluq.ca/,Accessed 17/MAR/2024
17. CHAN, Tak-Wai et BASKIN, Arthur B.: Studying with the prince: The computer as a learning companion. In Proceedings of the International Conference on Intelligent Tutoring Systems (1988)
18. Smolansky, A., Cram, A., Raduescu, C., Zeivots, S., Huber, E., Kizilcec, R. F.: Educator and student perspectives on the impact of generative AI on assessments in higher education. In Proceedings of the tenth ACM conference on Learning@ Scale, pp. 378-382 (2023)
19. Savelka, J., Agarwal, A., An, M., Bogart, C., Sakr, M.: Thrilled by your progress! Large language models (GPT-4) no longer struggle to pass assessments in higher education programming courses. In: Proceedings of the 2023 ACM Conference on International Computing Education Research-Vol 1, pp. 78-92 (2023)

20. Zhao, P., Zhang, H., Yu, Q., Wang, Z., Geng, Y., Fu, F., Cui, B.: Retrieval-Augmented Generation for AI-Generated Content: A Survey. arXiv preprint arXiv:2402.19473 (2024)
21. Wang, W., Wang, Y., Joty, S., Hoi, S. C.: Rap-gen: Retrieval-augmented patch generation with codet5 for automatic program repair. In: Proceedings of the 31st ACM Joint European Software Engineering Conference and Symposium on the Foundations of Software Engineering, pp. 146-158(2023)
22. Lu, S., Duan, N., Han, H., Guo, D., Hwang, S. W., Svyatkovskiy, A.: Reacc: A retrieval-augmented code completion framework. arXiv preprint arXiv:2203.07722 (2022)

The Optimisation of Genetic Assessment Test Generation Based on Fuzzy Scoring

Doru Anastasiu Popescu[1(✉)], Nicolae Bold[2], and Ovidiu Domșa[3]

[1] Department of Mathematics and Computer Science, Pitești University Center, National University of Science and Technology POLITEHNICA Bucharest, Buchares, Romania
dopopan@gmail.com

[2] Faculty of Management and Rural Development, University of Agronomic Sciences and Veterinary Medicine Bucharest, Slatina Branch, Romania

[3] 1 Decembrie 1918 University of Alba Iulia, Alba Iulia , Romania

Abstract. The most important aspect of an educational assessment is related to the closeness of the results to the actual knowledge level of the assessee. In this way, the fidelity of the assessment is ensured. In this matter, this paper presents the description and potential results of a model that determines a recognition of a detailed knowledge report related to the assessment topic, including the situation of partial knowledge. Thus, a model that details the usage of genetic algorithms (GAs) for establishing a method of partial scoring using fuzzy logic and weights given to specific parts of the assessment items is presented in this paper. Shortly, assessment items such as MCQ (multiple-choice) or cloze questions are given as examples of situations where this method of partial scoring can be applied. The genetic algorithm is used to generate the optimal scoring weights to the option of the assessment items related to a given value of entropy or scoring equilibrium between the scores chosen for the items. The purpose of this analysis is to obtain an optimal score configuration for an item which can offer chosen score equilibrium between the options score and which could give the opportunity of partial scoring, which has multiple benefits for the assessment process.

Keywords: genetic algorithm · fuzzy logic · entropy · scoring

1 Introduction

Genetic Algorithms (GAs) are inspired from the natural processes. They can be used in test generation to search for optimal or sub-optimal solutions according to several evaluation criteria and proved efficient for solving complex issues with strategies inspired by nature, as shown in [1], including the use of fuzzy logic to evaluate responses. This paper presents the development of a previous model for educational assessment related to the generation of assessment tests, an issue that was studied in a large volume of literature research papers, with main focus on the context of assessment, as detailed in [6]. In addition, the current paper

A. Basiouni and C. Frasson (Eds.): BBGI 2024, CCIS 2162, pp. 93–101, 2024.
https://doi.org/10.1007/978-3-031-65996-6_8

deals with the particularity of allowing partial or graded points to be awarded for each answer, thus reflecting the degree of correctness of the answers given by the student. The genetic algorithm can be adapted accordingly to search for optimal or sub-optimal solutions in this formulation, aiming to maximize or optimize the total test score, taking this fuzzy logic into account. The first part presents a short review of the most important concepts from the literature related to the topic, while the next section presents the description of the theoretical model of the described issue related to assessment. The latter sections present a short area related to several practical results and the conclusions related to these results.

2 Literature Review

The usage of fuzzy logic combined with evolutionary algorithms has proven a good solution and was studied thoroughly, as shown in [14]. Introducing fuzzy logic into test generation using genetic algorithms, whose applicability has been studied for a prolonged period of time, as detailed in [3], can bring several benefits within the assessment process, including for the assessment authenticity, especially related to partial knowledge, a concept detailed in [15]. Also, it can influence the assessment results and the optimization process in several ways:

- **flexibility in answering**: using a fuzzy scoring system, students can receive partial recognition for correct answers, rewarding even partial knowledge, even if they are not completely correct. This can lead to a fairer assessment of students' skills and encourage deeper and more complex approaches to the subject;
- **item complexity**: by allowing items to be fuzzy scored, you can create more complex and engaging items that require critical thinking and sophisticated reasoning from students;
- **adaptability to student diversity**: adaptability is a powerful characteristic of the assessment, as detailed in [8], which relates to the fact that students may have different approaches to problem solving and may have different skill levels depending on the domain, raising the necessity of the accurate depiction of the knowledge, in many cases partial, a topic subjected in [4];
- **optimizing the test generation process**: genetic algorithms can use this fuzzy logic to search for optimal or sub-optimal solutions for test generation, taking into account multiple evaluation criteria and tools, including question types and structures. A particular case related to polytomous and dichotomous scoring related to question types and structure is shown in [5]. Also, the assessor must take into account the aspect of allowing items to have different degrees of difficulty and importance.

Amongst the benefits of the usage of the fuzzy scoring we can include the diversification of the item generation [2], fair assessment, adaptability and automatic generation. Because the model generates items that are variate related to correctness, we can reduce predictability and stimulate the critical thinking ability of the students. The weighted distribution of points allows for a more correct assessment of the knowledge and skills of the students, regardless of their response strategy.

Thus, the introduction of fuzzy logic in the generation of tests with the help of genetic algorithms can improve the assessment process [7]. This aspect provides a more balanced and informative assessment of the skills obtained and acquired by the students and allow the adaptation of tests to their diversity and to the specific requirements of the subject.

3 Model Description

For a better understanding of the entire model, we will describe shortly in the first part of this section the model of generating educational assessment tests using genetic algorithm.

3.1 Assessment Test Generation

The purpose of this model is to create balanced and relevant tests that measure students' knowledge and skills in an objective way. Genetic algorithms are used to optimize the test generation process, taking into account constraints such as solving time and item difficulty. The model can be analyzed in details in previous authors work, comprised in papers such as ([9–11]).

The structures that are used in the model are:

- *population*: the set of initial and evolved tests. Each individual in the population represents a test;
- *item*: each question or problem that a student needs to solve. Each item can be characterized by requirements, e.g., its difficulty, average time to solve;
- *chromosomes*: the result of coding a test. Chromosomes are usually represented as strings of genes, each gene corresponding to an item;
- *fitness function*: evaluation of the quality of a test, taking into account the mathematical representation of the requirements. In the latter representations of the model for the same subject developed by the authors, the fitness function was established as an average value of a series of sigmoid functions applied for each requirements.
- *requirements*: the given restrictions or constraints for the test generation. They may consist in solving time, the degree of the difficulty or the topic of the items within the test.

As for the encoding process, within the chromosomes each gene represents the index of an item in the database.

3.2 Weighted Item Assessment

Purpose. The purpose of the described model is to automatically generate items with weighted scores to assess students' knowledge and skills. The model uses genetic algorithms to optimize the distribution of points per option within the items, ensuring a variety of correct answers and a fair assessment of student performance. The entire model is visually presented in Fig. 1.

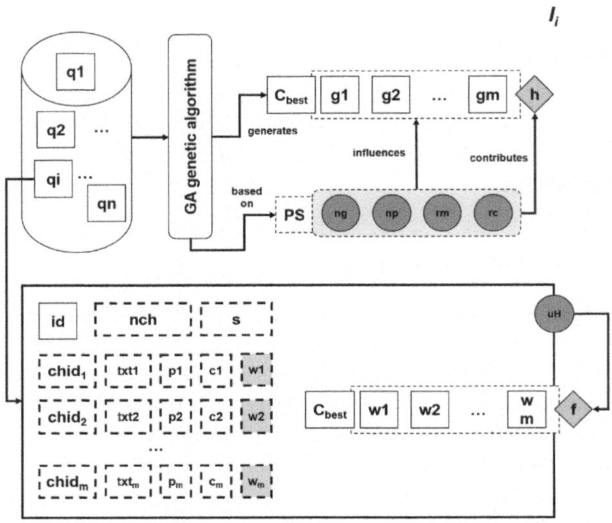

Fig. 1. The visual depiction of the assessment model and fuzzy scoring mechanism

Figure 1 presents the integrated visual depiction of the entire model, including the assessment test generation phase. In the upper part of the figure, the test generation process is described, while the lower part presents the mechanism of generating optimal weights for the options related to a specific item.

Shortly, the upper part starts from a pool or a dataset of items of various types which are used for the selection of the items for a specific test. From this dataset, chromosomes in form of assessment test formed of items are formed. Basically, a chromosome is the genetic representation of an assessment test. The chromosomes are formed and a fitness value is calculated for each chromosome, based on the fitness function h, which comprises the restrictions (requirements) given by the user. The best chromosome (C_{best}) is then obtained after the appliance of genetic operators and genetic parameters (PSI). It represents the assessment test that complies best with the user requirements. This mechanism is sketched in Sect. 3.1 and was detailed in several previous research papers published by the current authors.

The lower part of the Fig. 1 depicts visually the model presented in the current section. As shown, for the generated items which have a specific structure

(MCQ, cloze etc.), a partial scoring can be made and even adjusted related to entropy (balance between the scoring weights). It can allow the assessor to score the same item differently from assessment to assessment, based on the assessee learning profile. Thus, each item is formed, amongst other characteristics, by a set of options that have a specific score and a weight that can be adjusted and customized. The genetic algorithm presented in the lower part depicts the genetic process of finding the optimal configuration of options weights based on the entropy, calculated as a fitness value using the function f and related to assessor desired, expressed using uH value.

Item Examples. We will give two examples of items and the mechanism of establishing the score calculation.

The two examples are related to an MCQ and a cloze question:

- MCQ item:
  - the statement: "Which of the following are open-source operating systems? Select the two variants that are correct:"
  - the choices, their corectness, their score and weight:
    - ("Windows", False, 0, 0.0);
    - ("macOS", False, 0, 0.0);
    - ("Linux", True, 5, 0.3);
    - ("Android", True, 5, 0.7).
- cloze item:
  - the statement: "Fill in the blanks in the next paragraph: A computer's operating system is the ... that manages the ... and ... resources of a computer. It provides a platform for the applications to run and allows users to interact with the computer through a ... (GUI) or a command-line interface (CLI)."
  - the correct answers (choices), their corectness, their score and weight:
    - ("software", True, 3, 0.3);
    - ("hardware", True, 3, 0.3);
    - ("software", True, 2, 0.3);
    - ("graphical user interface", True, 2, 0.1).

The final score of the item is calculated as the sum of weighted scores (the product between the score and the weight) of each option, if answered correctly. For a specific item, if the user desires that an item has a fixed score, than all the choices have a fixed and unique score. Then, the total score of the assessment test can be determined as the weighted sum of all items, even if the score of a specific item changes, changing the importance of an item within the test according to a specific context.

Elements. The most important element of the model are the item and the choice. We will take into account the representation of an item as a multiple-choice item. In this matter, the two elements are:

- the choice ch, a tuple $(chid, txt, w, p, correct)$, where the components of the tuple are:
  - $chid$, $chid \in \mathbb{N}$: the unique identification particle of the choice, formed of the identification particle of the item id and the identification particle of the choice;
  - txt: the textual component of the choice;
  - w, $w \in [0, 1]$: the scoring weight of the choice;
  - p, $p \in \mathbb{Q}$: the scoring value of the choice;
  - $correct$, $correct \in \{0, 1\}$: determines whether the choice is correct; obviously, when $correct = 0$, $w = 0$.
- the item q, a tuple (id, nch, ch, s), generated and stored in a database, where the elements of the tuple are:
  - id, $id \in \mathbb{N}$: the unique identification particle of the item;
  - nch, $nch \in \mathbb{N}$: the number of choices of the items;
  - ch, $ch = \{ch_i | i \in \{1, nch\}\}$: the set of identification particle of the choices of the item;
  - s, $s \in \mathbb{Q}$: the total score of the item, calculated as a fuzzy number, with specific advantages for the scoring strategy of the entire test, as follows:

$$s = \sum_{i=1}^{nch} w(ch_i) \times p(ch_i) \tag{1}$$

Also, particular forms of items can be used besides multiple-choice items, such as cloze items, pair items etc.

The genetic structures are presented as follows:

- $g \in \mathbb{N}$: the gene, which encodes the choices $ch_i, i \in \{1, nch\}$, within an item;
- $C = \{g_i \mid i \leq nch\}$ the chromosome which encodes an item choices weights set ch;
- pch: a quadruple of variables which defines the set of the genetic algorithm parameters, $pch = (NP, NG, rm, rc)$, where NP is the initial population size, NG the number of generations, rm the mutation rate and rc the crossover rate, $np, ng \in \mathbb{N}; rm, rc \in [0, 1]$;
- $f : C \rightarrow [0, 1]$ is the fitness function, defined as an entropy function, as follows:

$$f(q) = - \sum_{ch_i \in ch} p(ch_i) \log_2 p(ch_i), \tag{2}$$

where

$$p(ch_i) = \frac{w(ch_i) * p(ch_i)}{s} \tag{3}$$

In the context of weighted-scored items, $w(ch_i)$ represents the weight (score) assigned to option ch. For each correct option (ch_i), the f function calculates the probability $p(ch_i)$ as the product of the weight $w(ch_i)$ and the score $p(ch_i)$, divided by the final score s. A higher entropy value indicates a more even distribution of probabilities over correct options, promoting response diversity. In this matter, the chromosomes which converge to a desired value uH will be selected by establishing a penalty margin.

Genetic operators are mutation, crossover and selection, described as follows:

- *mutation operator* ***Mut***, defined as the replacement of a randomly-selected gene within a randomly-selected chromosome with a randomly-selected gene;
- *crossover operator* ***Csv***, where two parent chromosomes combine related to a randomly-selected position in a manner that two new child chromosomes are obtained;
- *selection operator* ***Sel***, which selects the chromosomes with the best fitness function values.

Algorithm. For the usual GA methodology, the next steps are applied:

Step 1: The input data (*ch* set, q and uH) is read.
Step 2: The genetic algorithm is applied, as follows:
(a) the generation of the initial population of items is made;
(b) the mutation operation is applied;
(c) the crossover operation is applied;
(d) the resulted chromosomes are selected;
(e) after NG generations, the best chromosome is selected.
Step 3: The best chromosome is input.

4 Results and Discussions

The results presented are resulted based on a Python implementation. The initial *pch* set is determined as follows:

- the population size NP is 100;
- the chromosome length nch is 5;
- the crossover rate rc is 0.8;
- the mutation rate rm is 0.1;
- the maximum number of generations NG is 200.

For the implementation, the wrong answers of the items are omitted from the calculation. The results are shown in Table 1.

Table 1. The research implementation results

No.	Choice score	Desired entropy	Obtained weights
1	[7, 10, 7, 5, 9]	0.1	[0.14 0.14 0.14 0.29 0.29]
2	[8, 2, 3, 6, 5]	0.2	[0.125 0.125 0.125 0.5 0.125]
3	[8, 1, 7, 2, 7]	0.3	[0.67 0.083 0.083 0.083 0.083]
4	[4, 1, 5, 9, 10]	0.4	[0.71 0.07 0.07 0.07 0.07]
5	[1, 3, 8, 1, 9]	0.5	[0.076 0.69 0.076 0.076 0.076]
6	[6, 9, 5, 2, 8]	0.7	[0.11 0.11 0.11 0.11 0.53]
7	[9, 3, 4, 3, 9]	1.0	[0.11 0.33 0.11 0.33 0.11]

We can observe that the results are converging to a more balanced entropy. Thus, the described model provides an innovative solution for the automatic generation of weighted-scored items, contributing to a more efficient and fair assessment of student learning.

5 Conclusions

By modifying the objective function and extending the genetic algorithm to handle the point related to items, the relative importance of each correct answer within the generated items can be taken into account. This approach allows the creation of items that assess even partial knowledge and skills of the assessee in different ways based on the complexity and correctness of the answers.

Using entropy in the objective function of the genetic algorithm can be an effective way to generate weighted-scored items that promote a variety of correct answers and a fairer assessment of student knowledge and skills. This approach is particularly relevant for items that assess critical thinking, problem solving, and creativity, where there is no single correct answer.

In the previous research, specific implementations of the model were made and can be studied in [12,13]. Future work would consist in the development of current implementations that would comprise the functionality described in this paper in real-time environments.

References

1. Akopov, A.S., Beklaryan, L.A.: Traffic improvement in manhattan road networks with the use of parallel hybrid biobjective genetic algorithm. IEEE Access (2024)
2. Betts, J., Muntean, W., Kim, D., Kao, S.c.: Evaluating different scoring methods for multiple response items providing partial credit. Educ. Psychol. Meas. **82**(1), 151–176 (2022)
3. Chahar, V., Katoch, S., Chauhan, S.: A review on genetic algorithm: Past, present, and future. Multimedia Tools Appl. **80** (2021)
4. Coombs, C.H., Milholland, J.E., Womer, F.B.: The assessment of partial knowledge. Educ. Psychol. Measur. **16**(1), 13–37 (1956)
5. Grunert, M.L., Raker, J.R., Murphy, K.L., Holme, T.A.: Polytomous versus dichotomous scoring on multiple-choice examinations: development of a rubric for rating partial credit. J. Chem. Educ. **90**(10), 1310–1315 (2013)
6. Hook, D.W., Porter, S.J., Herzog, C.: Dimensions: building context for search and evaluation. Frontiers Res. Metrics Analytics **3**, 23 (2018)
7. Kansup, W., Hakstian, A.R.: A comparison of several methods of assessing partial knowledge in multiple-choice tests: I. scoring procedures. J. Edu. Measur, pp. 219–230 (1975)
8. Levin, H.M.: The importance of educational adaptability. Teachers College, Columbia University, Columbia (2012)
9. Popescu, D.A., Bold, N., Domşa, O.: Generating assessment tests with restrictions using genetic algorithms. In: 2016 12th IEEE International Conference on Control and Automation, pp. 696–700. IEEE (ICCA) (2016)

10. Balas, V.E., Jain, L.C., Balas, M.M. (eds.): SOFA 2016. AISC, vol. 634. Springer, Cham (2018). https://doi.org/10.1007/978-3-319-62524-9
11. Popescu, D.A., et al.: The determination of the learning performance based on assessment item analysis. In: CSW@ WSDM, pp. 59–76 (2023)
12. Cheung, S.K.S., Lam, J., Li, K.C., Au, O., Ma, W.W.K., Ho, W.S. (eds.): ICTE 2018. CCIS, vol. 843. Springer, Singapore (2018). https://doi.org/10.1007/978-981-13-0008-0
13. Popescu, D.A., Victor, T., Bold, N.: C. pp. 153–158. Springer (2020)
14. Richter, J.N., Peak, D.: Fuzzy evolutionary cellular automata. In: Proceedings of International Conference on Artificial Neural Networks In Engineering. vol. 24, p. 185 (2002)
15. Wilkinson, A.C.: Theoretical and methodological analysis of partial knowledge. Dev. Rev. **2**(3), 274–304 (1982)

Analyzing the Performance of Distributed Web Systems Within an Educational Assessment Framework

Doru Anastasiu Popescu[1(✉)], Marian Ileana[1], and Nicolae Bold[2]

[1] Department of Mathematics and Computer Science, Pitesti University Center, National University of Science and Technology Politehnica Bucharest, Bucharest, Romania
dopopan@gmail.com

[2] University of Agronomic Sciences and Veterinary Medicine Bucharest, Slatina Branch, Romania

Abstract. This paper examines the usage of genetic algorithms for performance analysis and optimization in distributed web systems. The selected system for distributed systems performance analysis pertains to educational assessment domains. Genetic algorithms (GA) offer a promising approach for automating the optimization process. In this study, the GA is used to generate educational assessment tests within an educational framework. The assessment tests are formed of items stored in data structures and used in the generation process. This process is delimited by several requirements of the assessment objectives, such as the degree of difficulty or solving time. A typical GA approach leads to optimised sequences of items or tests, whereas the usage of distribution within the process can surpass usual GA issues, such as local optimisation. The distribution consists in the generation of the assessment tests on several nodes within a network, where each node has generative tasks. Moreover, they have been successfully applied and solved a wide range of problems, including scheduling, routing, and load balancing in distributed systems. This article also presents a comparative analysis of GA performance: centralized GA and distributed GA. Centralized GAs run on a single computer, while distributed GAs run on multiple computers. This work represents an important step in the understanding and application of genetic algorithms in the context of distributed web systems, providing a solid foundation for future research in this area. The conclusions of this paper demonstrate the effectiveness of genetic algorithms in developing the performance of distributed systems.

Keywords: Distributed web system · Genetic algorithms · Educational Assessment · Optimization

1 Introduction

The paper presented in this research presents an innovative use of Genetic Algorithms (GA) within educational assessment contexts, highlighting the potential

A. Basiouni and C. Frasson (Eds.): BBGI 2024, CCIS 2162, pp. 102–115, 2024.
https://doi.org/10.1007/978-3-031-65996-6_9

benefits of distributed approaches in optimizing test generation processes and overcoming inherent GA limitations.

In this matter, this paper illustrates a new scheduling method in distributed web systems. The scheduling problem in distributed web systems is challenging because it has to consider a multitude of factors, such as the time required to transfer data between servers, the load on each server, and the need to balance the load between all servers [1]. In this paper, the analysis is focused on the network balance issues.

In distributed web systems, the correct distribution of tasks is an essential component of the overall efficiency of the system. A distributed computing system consists of a group of computers (each computer having its own set of resources) interconnected through communication networks [2]. By properly managing the tasks to the available nodes, the total execution time is reduced and the proper use of the available resources within the network is made.

Also, this paper illustrates an instance of generative systems (D-GA-CO model), where GAs are used in three directions:

- GA component, consisting in the initial generation of the assessment test, using random genetic parameters (i.e., size of initial population, number of generations etc.);
- D-CO component for the parameters set, consisting in the determination of the optimal values of the GA parameters; in this matter, four essential parameters were chosen;
- D-CO component for the distributed system, used for the optimal balance of the network node computing loads, where each node in a network computes an individual genetic algorithm.

In the end, a comparative analysis of the centralized and distributed GA instances is made, in order to assess the efficiency of the distributed approach.

2 Literature Review

The section aims to provide a summary of existing research and investigations on increasing the energy efficiency of distributed web systems using genetic algorithms [3]. It brings to the discussion an understanding of the historical evolution of the subject and sets the stage for current research on performance optimization using genetic algorithms.

An article written by E. Alba and J. M. Troya [4] examines recent changes and future trends in the field of Parallel Genetic Algorithms (PGAs), which are grouped into coarse-grained and fine-grained models. PGAs are not just a parallel variant of sequential algorithms; they are a new category of meta-heuristics that is highlighted by parallel execution and structured populations. This differentiates them from sequential adaptations to achieve higher speeds. Applications in fields such as artificial intelligence, numerical and combinatorial optimization, business, and engineering have grown as a result of its remarkable robustness in complex problems. The work of the two authors addresses both traditional and recent technical aspects, formalizing these algorithms and providing useful summaries of key applications and references to online resources. This will facilitate access for researchers in this ever-expanding field.

Research by S. Sadeghiram, H. Ma, and G. Chen [5] they studied the automatic construction of web services and concluded that their focus should shift to data-intensive concepts. Metaheuristics, especially evolutionary computation (EC) techniques, have been used to solve complex problems. However, much of the current research has ignored the distributed nature of data-intensive web services. The article by the three authors explored the distributed structure of these services and proposed a model that integrates the characteristics of web and network services. The main idea is to create a communication time and cost model for a composite web service, taking communication delay and costs into account. Starting with an innovative approach based on the Genetic Algorithm (GA) that includes a variant of K-means clustering for implementation.

Through the dynamic analysis of a distributed web system topic, especially that of genetic algorithms, the literature offers a multitude of publications from a multitude of authors. In carrying out this empirical investigation, Dimensions.ai was used as the database, and the search engine was used for the search. The returned results were processed with the help of Vos Application Viewer [6] to be able to easily analyze the authors who publish on this topic on a chart. Author-obtained clusters are clusters from an author network, as illustrated in Fig. 1. The data was found to include 12356 authors. In order for an author to be relevant, the condition that he appear as an author in at least five papers has been added. The total number of authors who met these conditions was 268, as it can be seen in Fig. 1a.

(a) A graphic map of authors for the search term "distributed web systems and genetic algorithms"

(b) A country map of authors for the search term "distributed web systems and genetic algorithms"

Fig. 1. The term occurrence map

Using the same data set, it was sorted by the countries where more were published on the topic. A total of 106 were obtained. For a country to be considered relevant, a condition was added that there should be at least 5 documents from that country, and the minimum number of citations should be at least 3, as seen in Fig. 1.

3 Theoretical Foundation of the D-GA-CO Generative Model

The D-GA-CO (**D**istributed **G**enetic **A**lgorithm **C**onfiguration **O**ptimizer) generative model has as purpose the improvement of a genetic algorithm used for generating educational assessment tests [10]. The improvement consists in the transformation of the generative component of the genetic algorithm into a distributed system in order to obtain the optimal parameters of the genetic algorithm (e.g., size of initial population, number of generations, mutation and crossover rate). In this matter, each component of the distributed system can run one or multiple instances of the genetic algorithm run for a distinct random set of parameters [11]. The distributed system can consist in nodes in a network or cores in a computing system that run the algorithm instances. The network distribution of D-GA-CO runs will be obtained using a genetic algorithm as well.

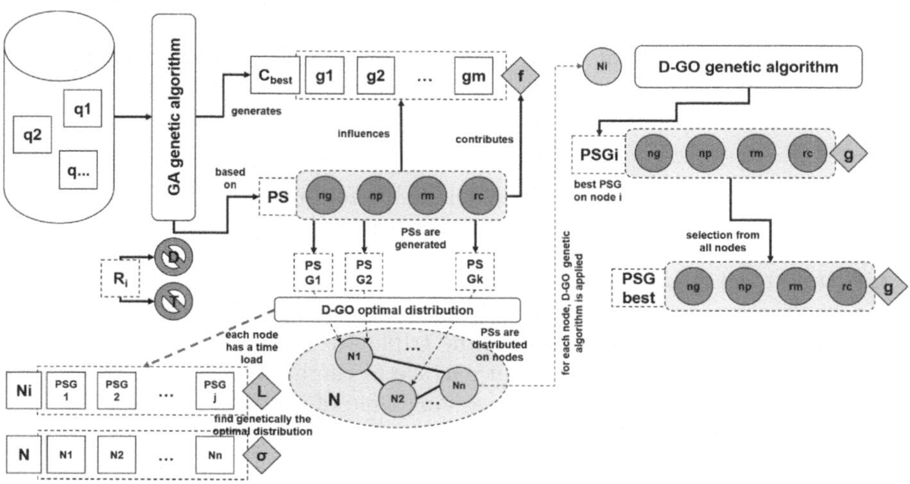

Fig. 2. The general form of the D-GA-CO generative model

As we can observe in Fig. 2, the model has three important areas, related to the usage of the GA, marked with yellow rhombuses (fitness functions). The items (q) are stored in a database. From the database, an educational assessment test (sequence of items) is generated based on specific restrictions. The chromosomes with the highest values of the f fitness function are selected (C_{best}). In order to optimise the generation, a second GA is applied for the determination of the best set of parameters for the generation PSG_{best}, where the parameters are the mutation and crossover rates, the number of generations and the size of initial population. For this second GA, the fitness function is the f value and several results of GA parameter sets are obtained. In order to create a more efficient determination, several instances of the second GA are run in parallel on network nodes. The distribution of the generated sets of parameters is made using a third GA, which determines the optimal distribution of the generated sets on the network nodes in order to create a balanced load based on total runtime of the algorithm. The two main components of the model (GA component and D-CO component) are described in the next two sections.

3.1 The GA Component

The GA component of the model is related to the main framework of the model, which consist in the generation of educational assessment test using previously-generated items stored in a database using genetic algorithms [13]. We will describe the main characteristics of this component further.

GA Purpose. The purpose of the GA component is the obtaining of optimized sequences of items, referred as assessment tests. The optimization characteristic of the GA is connected to the existence of several requirements given by the user to generate assessment tests. Thus, the optimal test which complies with the given requirements must be found. The requirements taken into account in this paper are the total solving time and the test degree of difficulty.

GA Elements. The main elements of the GA component are the GA structures (test and genetic) and operators, presented as follows:

- GA test structures:
  - q: the item, a triple (id, t, d) which codifies an item generated and stored in a database. The elements of the triple are:
    - $id \in \mathbb{N}$ is the identification particle of the item;
    - $t > 0, t \in \mathbb{Q}$ is the average solving time of the item in seconds;
    - $d \in [0, 1]$ is the degree of difficulty of the item.

    The triple is a particular case for a generalized tuple with several additional characteristics of an item (e.g., the usual characteristics of a question within the test). The simplified construction of an item was chosen for this paper in order to focus on the generative aspects of the model. A more detailed description of a tuple may be found in [16].
  - SI: the assessment test, a quintuple (id, m, Q, T, D) which codifies an educational assessment test generated based on requirements using genetic algorithms. The elements of the quintuple are:
    - $id \in \mathbb{N}$ is the identification particle of the test;
    - $m \in \mathbb{N}$ is the test size (number of questions);
    - $Q = \{q_i | i \leq m\}$ is the set of items that form the test;

  * $T > 0, T \in \mathbb{Q}$ is the total solving time of the test, calculated as the sum of the solving times of all items that form the test:

$$T = \sum_{i=1}^{m} q_i(t) \tag{1}$$

  * $D \in [0, 1]$ is the degree of difficulty of the item, calculated as an average of the degrees of difficulty of all the items that form a test, as follows:

$$D = \frac{1}{m} \sum_{i=1}^{m} q_i(d) \tag{2}$$

- R: the set of requirements $\{R_1, R_2 \ldots R_k\}$, where $R_i, i \leq k$ is a requirement for the test generation. The current paper uses two requirements: the solving time T and the degree of difficulty D.

– GA genetic structures (genotype):
- $g \in \mathbb{N}$: the gene, which codifies the items q within a test;
- $C = \{g_i | i \leq m\}$ the chromosome which codifies an assessment test SI;
- $f : C \to [0, 1]$ is the fitness function, defined as a sigmoid function, as follows:

$$f(C_i) = \sum_{i=1}^{2} f_i(R_i) \tag{3}$$

where $f_i(R_i) = \frac{1}{1+e^{-R_i}}$ and R_i is the value of the absolute difference between the C_i chromosome calculated values for the R_i requirement and the value given by the user for the requirement;
- PS quadruple, which defines the set of the genetic algorithm parameters, $PS = (np, ng, rm, rc)$, where np is the initial population size, ng the number of generations, rm the mutation rate and rc the crossover rate, $np, ng \in \mathbb{N}; rm, rc \in [0, 1]$.

– GA operators:
- *mutation operator* ***Mut***, defined as the replacement of a randomly-selected gene within a randomly-selected chromosome with a randomly-selected gene;
- *crossover operator* ***Csv***, where two parent chromosomes combine related to a randomly-selected position in a manner that two new child chromosomes are obtained;
- *selection operator* ***Sel***, which selects the chromosomes with the best fitness function values.

GA Methodology. The GA methodology comprises several steps:

Step 1: The input data (Q set, PS, uT and uD) is read.
Step 2: The genetic algorithm is applied, as follows:
(a) the generation of the initial population of items is made;
(b) the mutation operation is applied;

(c) the crossover operation is applied;
(d) the resulted chromosomes are selected;
(e) after ng generations, the best chromosome is selected.

Step 3: The best chromosome is input.

Algorithm 1: GA algorithm

Data: Q, PS, uT, uD
Result: sol
The initial population is generated $pop \leftarrow initialpopulation$ The genetic algorithm starts $k \leftarrow 0$;
while $k \leq ng$ **do**
  The mutation operation is applied
  The crossover operation is applied
  The selection operation is applied
  $k \leftarrow k + 1$
The first chromosome is selected
$sol \leftarrow C_1$;

3.2 D-CO Component

The D-CO component is the part of the model that optimize the instances of the GA component [12]. As we have seen, the GA uses a PS set in order to run the instance of the algorithm. In this matter, the D-CO component establishes the PS optimal configuration in order to obtain the best results. The distributed characteristic of the model resides from the search mechanism of the optimal configuration, which implies the existence of a network of several nodes (either nodes within a web or cores within a computing system) which computes the GA instances in parallel. These will be made using genetic approaches.

D-CO Purpose. The main purpose of the D-CO component of the model is to obtain the optimal PS configuration of GA parameters. The optimum is reached when the number of generations of each node, common for every node, is reached. Also, the component also has as secondary objective the reduction of the time used to generate the optimal configuration.

D-CO Elements. The main elements of the D-CO components are the genetic structures used in the generative processes and the genetic operators, which are the same as the ones described before, as well as the network characteristics. Shortly, the D-CO component runs a genetic algorithm on GA sets of parameters PS in order to obtain optimal PSs [15]. In the same time, the generative process is run on a network of nodes, the initial population of PSs being distributed on the nodes, where the D-CO genetic algorithm is run for each node. The distribution process also uses a genetic algorithm to create a balanced load of nodes related to the runtime of each PS parameters set.

Thus, we will limit to the short description of the structures:

- the genetic structures used for finding the optimal configuration:
  - psg: the gene, which is a specific parameter of the GA component (i.e., the size of the initial population $np \in \mathbb{N}$, the number of generations $ng \in \mathbb{N}$, the mutation rate $rm \in [0, 1]$ and crossover rate $rc \in [0, 1]$);
  - PSG: the chromosome, which is a quadruple which has the form (np, ng, rm, rc);
  - the parameters of the D-GO genetic algorithm dnp, dng, drm, drc;
  - g: the fitness function of each chromosome, which has as values the best f GA fitness function value for the given configuration, as follows:

$$g(PSG_j) = max(f(C_i)), i \in \{1, np\}, j \in \{1, dnp\} \tag{4}$$

- the network parameters
  - NN: the size of the network, i.e., the number of nodes in a network;
  - $N_i, i \in \{1, NN\}$: a node in the network. The node can be a terminal in a network of computing devices or a core in a processor. The main performance metric taken into consideration for the node is the maximum load time L_{max_i};
  - $N = \{N_i | i = 1, NN\}$: the network of nodes, which gives the general structure of the network;
- the genetic structures used for the optimal distribution of parameters sets on the network nodes:
  - $g_{N_i}, i \in \{1, NN\}$: a gene which codifies a node in the network.
  - a chromosome CN, which is defined as a set of tuples, each element of the set being a tuple of PSGs
  - the parameters of the distribution algorithm: nnp, nng, nrm, nrc;
  - the fitness function σ, which calculates the distribution of the PSG parameters sets on all the nodes. Each node can compute one or multiple sets of nodes, depending on its L_{max}. In this matter, the form of the fitness function is as follows:

$$\sigma(CN) = \frac{1}{L + P} \tag{5}$$

    where:
    * L is the total time load, computed as the sum of the time loads $(L_1, L_2, \ldots, L_{NN})$ of all the nodes within the network:

$$L = \sum_{i=1}^{NN} L_i \tag{6}$$

      For a parameter set $PSG(np, ng, rm, rc)$, the time load is calculated as follows:

$$L_{PSG} = ng \times (T_{Mut} + T_{Csv} + T_{Sel}) \times np \times rm \times rc \tag{7}$$

where T is the time needed to compute the operations of mutation, crossover and selection and which can be estimated based on tests or calculated theoretically. Thus, for a given node N_i who computes the fitness values for k parameter sets, the total load time L_i is the sum of all load times of each parameter set computed on the node N_i:

$$L_i = \sum_{j=1}^{k} L_{PSG_j} \tag{8}$$

* P is the total penalty value of the network, computed as the sum of all penalties from all the nodes. A penalty P_i for a node N_i is calculated as the normalized differences between the total load time of a node L_i and the maximum load time of the respective node L_{max_i}:

$$P = \sum_{i=1}^{NN} max(0, L_i - L_{max_i}) \tag{9}$$

D-CO Methodology. The GA methodology comprises several steps:

Step 1: The input data (NN, N set, L_{max} set, nnp, nng, nrm, nrc, dnp, dng, drm and drc) is read.

Step 2: The optimal distribution algorithm is applied, as follows:
- (a) the generation of the initial population of distributions is made;
- (b) the mutation operation is applied;
- (c) the crossover operation is applied;
- (d) the resulted chromosomes are selected;
- (e) after dng generations, the best chromosome is selected.

Step 3: The D-GO algorithm is applied on each network node N.
- (a) the generation of the initial population of PSG parameters is made;
- (b) the mutation operation is applied;
- (c) the crossover operation is applied;
- (d) after nng generations for the node N, the best chromosome is selected.

Step 4: The fitness values from all the best chromosomes resulted from the N nodes are compared and the one with the highest fitness is selected.

Step 5: The best chromosome is input.

3.3 Characteristics of Distributed Web Systems

A distributed Web system includes locally distributed server nodes that allow client applications to see multiple IP addresses [9]. A diagram of the architecture is available in Fig. 3. Because this part plays an important role in routing requests for distributed web systems, the authoritative DNS is included in the system box. A front-end Web switch is not a component of a distributed Web system architecture.

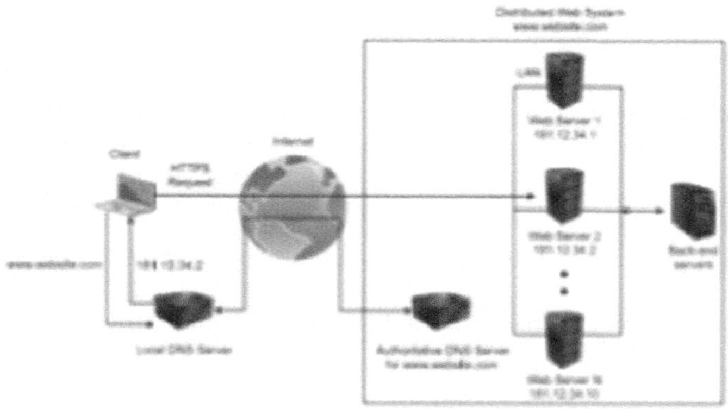

Fig. 3. Distributed Web System architecture diagram

The DNS mechanism typically assigns the client's request to a target Web server during the Web site name address resolution process (the lookup phase) [14]. In some systems, there is also a second level of routing. This is usually accomplished through a redirect mechanism that is activated by a Web server that cannot fulfill a request.

4 Results and Discussions

An implementation built in Python programming language was used for the obtaining of the results. In this matter, the parameters of all the GAs had the next values:

- for the GA algorithm:
  - the items *id* maximum value is 1000;
  - the number of questions in the sequence is 10 ($m = 10$);
  - the target difficulty is 0.5 ($uD = 0.5$);
  - the target time is 3600 s ($uT = 3600$);
  - the initial population size is 100 ($np = 100$);
  - the maximum number of generation is 100 ($ng = 100$);
  - the mutation rate is 0.2 ($rm = 0.2$);
  - the crossover rate is 0.5 ($rc = 0.5$).
- for the D-CO algorithm:
  - the initial population size is 10 ($dnp = 10$);
  - the maximum number of generations is 10 ($dng = 10$);
  - the mutation and crossover rate were equal to 0 ($drm = drc = 0$).
- for the D-CO distributed algorithm:
  - the initial population size is 100 ($nnp = 100$);
  - the maximum number of generations is 100 ($nng = 100$);

- the mutation rate is 0.1 ($nrm = 0.1$);
- the crossover rate is 0.8 ($nrc = 0.8$).

The number of nodes (NN) was set to 5 and their parameters were randomized. The algorithm was run for 3 times. The results are shown in Tables 1, 2 and 3.

Table 1. The research implementation results for the GA algorithm

No.	Run	Best fitness	Running time
1	Run 1	0.779	0.886
2	Run 2	0.785	0.956
3	Run 3	0.780	1.243
	Average	*0.781*	*1.028*

The average value of the fitnesses of the best chromosomes after running the GA algorithm for 3 times is 0.781, with the highest being 0.785. The average running time is 1.028 s.

Table 2. The research implementation results for the D-CO algorithm

No.	Run	Optimal configuration	Fitness value	Running time
1	Run 1	[71, 77, 0.028, 0.763]	0.799	39.607
2	Run 2	[66, 495, 0.059, 0.712]	0.794	304.313
3	Run 3	[76, 441, 0.012, 0.590]	0.795	330.239
	Average		*0.796*	*224.720*

For the D-GO algorithm, the average fitness value for the best chromosomes for all the 3 runs is 0.796, higher than the one shown in Table 1. The best configuration for the highest fitness value (0.799) consisted in an initial population size of 71 chromosomes, 77 generations, a mutation rate of 0.028 and a crossover rate of 0.763. The average running time of the algorithm was 224.720 s.

For the D-GO distributed algorithm, the average value of fitness was 0.8, with the highest one obtained for a configuration of an initial population size of 89 chromosomes, 321 generations, 0.098 rate of mutation and 0.692 rate of crossover. The configuration was obtained for Node 2, where 6 PSG configurations were run on the same node. The average running time for the D-GO distributed algorithm was 929.180 s

Table 3. The research implementation results for the D-CO distributed algorithm

No.	Run	Node 1	Node 2	Node 3	Node 4	Node 5	Best fitness	Running time
1	Run 1	5, [56, 212, 0.011, 0.638], 0.794	6, [89, 321, 0.098, 0.692], 0.808	6, [92, 484, 0.054, 0.583], 0.799	5, [68, 367, 0.029, 0.871], 0.798	5, [31, 107, 0.093, 0.773], 0.805	0.808	863.601
1	Run 2	10, [42, 251, 0.075, 0.525], 0.794	1, [85, 364, 0.018, 0.502], 0.795	6, [71, 499, 0.023, 0.576], 0.792	9, [62, 402, 0.079, 0.640], 0.798	10, [26, 155, 0.018, 0.886], 0.792	0.798	1007.030
1	Run 3	9, [46, 324, 0.059, 0.749], 0.792	5, [80, 463, 0.034, 0.602], 0.794	6, [67, 256, 0.052, 0.514], 0.792	5, [96, 133, 0.070, 0.759], 0.793	6, [22, 390, 0.080, 0.655], 0.795	0.795	916.909
	Average						*0.800*	*929.180*

5 Conclusions

In conclusion, the study brings an innovative perspective on the optimization of distributed web systems. The results obtained using genetic algorithms show a significant improvement in performance, which indicates that the proposed approach could be a useful solution to the problems currently raised in this field.

This study found and highlighted critical elements that influence the performance of distributed web systems. This sets the groundwork for the future development of optimization strategies. In addition, our research will pave the way for other future research, which could include extending the application of genetic algorithms to other aspects of distributed web systems.

Limitations can be referred to the input data, the efficiency of genetic algorithms in generating assessment tests critically depending on the quality and representativeness of the input data. Also, implementing and executing genetic algorithms on multiple nodes in a network can be technically challenging and require considerable computational resources. These limitations will be dealt with in future work.

A deep understanding of how distributed web systems work is an essential component in the ever-changing digital world. Consequently, we want this research to help create more efficient technological solutions and optimize resources within distributed web systems.

References

1. Bittencourt, L.F., Goldman, A., Madeira, E.R.M., Da Fonseca, N.L.S., Sakellariou, R.: Scheduling in distributed systems: a cloud computing perspective. Comput. Sci. Rev. **30**, 31–54 (2018). https://doi.org/10.1016/j.cosrev.2018.08.002
2. Shukur, H.M., et al.: A State of Art Survey for Concurrent Computation and Clustering of Parallel Computing for Distributed Systems. Comput. Sci. Rev. 1, 148-154 (2020). https://doi.org/10.38094/jastt1466
3. Ileana, M.: Optimizing Energy Efficiency in Distributed Web Systems. 2023 7th International Symposium on Innovative Approaches in Smart Technologies (ISAS) (2023). https://doi.org/10.1109/isas60782.2023.10391617
4. Alba, E., Troya, J.M.: A survey of parallel distributed genetic algorithms. Complexity. 4, 31-52 (1999). https://doi.org/10.1002/(sici)1099-0526(199903/04)4:4
5. Sadeghiram, S., Ma, H., Chen, G.: Cluster-Guided Genetic Algorithm for Distributed Data-intensive Web Service Composition. 2018 IEEE Congr. Evol. Comput. (CEC). (2018). https://doi.org/10.1109/cec.2018.8477729
6. Effendi, D.N., et al.: Bibliometric analysis of scientific literacy using VOS viewer: analysis of science education. J. Phys: Conf. Ser. **1796**(1), 01209 (2021). https://doi.org/10.1088/1742-6596/1796/1/012096
7. Lambora, A., Gupta, K., Chopra, K.: Genetic Algorithm- A Literature Review. 2019 International Conference on Machine Learning, Big Data, Cloud and Parallel Computing (COMITCon). (2019). https://doi.org/10.1109/comitcon.2019.8862255
8. Mirjalili, S.: Evolutionary Algorithms and Neural Networks. SCI, vol. 780. Springer, Cham (2019). https://doi.org/10.1007/978-3-319-93025-1
9. Kulesza, R., de Sousa, M.F., de Araújo, M.L.M., de Araújo, C.P., Filho, A.M.: Evolution of web systems architectures: a roadmap. In: Roesler, V., Barrére, E., Willrich, R. (eds.) Special Topics in Multimedia, IoT and Web Technologies, pp. 3–21. Springer, Cham (2020). https://doi.org/10.1007/978-3-030-35102-1_1
10. Jangdoost, A., Keypour, R., Golmohamadi, H.: Optimization of distribution network reconfiguration by a novel RCA integrated with genetic algorithm. Energy Syst. **12**, 801-833 (2020). https://doi.org/10.1007/s12667-020-00398-5
11. Shaheen, A.M., Elsayed, A.M., El-Sehiemy, R.A., Abdelaziz, A.Y.: Equilibrium optimization algorithm for network reconfiguration and distributed generation allocation in power systems. Appl. Soft Comput. 98, 106867 (2021). https://doi.org/10.1016/j.asoc.2020.106867
12. Gong, Y.-J., et al.: Distributed evolutionary algorithms and their models: A survey of the state-of-the-art. Applied Soft Computing. **34**, 286-300 (2015). https://doi.org/10.1016/j.asoc.2015.04.061
13. Pambudi, R.A., Lubis, W., Saputra, F.R., Maulidina, H.P., Wijayaningrum, V.N.: Genetic Algorithm for Teaching Distribution based on Lecturers' Expertise. Kinetik: Game Technology, Information System, Computer Network, Computing, Electronics, and Control. 297-304 (2019). https://doi.org/10.22219/kinetik.v4i4.859
14. Xiong, G., Yan, K., Zhou, X.: A distributed learning based sentiment analysis methods with Web applications. WWW **25**, 1905-1922 (2022). https://doi.org/10.1007/s11280-021-00994-0

15. Stańczak, J.: Optimal control of multistage deterministic, stochastic and fuzzy processes in the fuzzy environment via an evolutionary algorithm. Control. Cybern. **34**, 525–552 (2005)
16. Popescu, D.A., Bold, N., Nijloveanu, D.: A method based on genetic algorithms for generating assessment tests used for learning. Polibits **54**, 53–60 (2016)

New Paradigm Shift to STEM Education in the United Arab Emirates

Ahmed Al-Gindy(✉)

Department of Electrical Engineering, Canadian University Dubai, Dubai, United Arab Emirates
agindy@cud.ac.ae

Abstract. Science, technology, engineering, and mathematics represent powerful STEM education methods and concepts. STEM is the new paradigm shift in the education system that enables students to learn real-life scenarios and the proper thinking process to solve real-life problems requiring using integrated concepts. This type of learning improves students' 21st-century skills to make decisions, solve real-life problems, learn lifelong, innovate, and think creatively and critically in solving problems. STEM education is new in the United Arab Emirates, and there are no or few types of research applied to it. The primary purpose of this paper is to propose a framework for STEM education to be taught in UAE schools that meets the objectives of the strategic action plan (2015–2021) of the Ministry of Education MOE. The introduced framework is structured in four levels. Each education level performs a relative difficulty, complexity, and depth hierarchy. Going higher in the qualification's framework levels hierarchy means excellent challenges will be faced, advanced knowledge and skills are required, and high demand is expected of a student.

Keywords: component · 21st Century Skills · STEM Education · National Qualification Framework

1 Introduction

One of the most significant reforms in the educational sector is integrating interdisciplinary science, technology, engineering, and mathematics (STEM) methods in the k-12 education system. STEM education is called meta-discipline as it is the integration between STEM educational mechanisms and concepts combined to form a new curriculum to be taught as a whole. According to [1], the STEM disciplines are like the parts of the human body: "science is the musculoskeletal system, technology is the hand, engineering is the brain, and mathematics is the heart and blood." So, it is obvious that these disciplines are intertwined with each other in teaching real-life projects, problems and Scenarios. Constructing or designing robots, submarines, automobiles, gliders, and supersonic aircraft without knowledge of STEM concepts is unmanageable.

The four strands of STEM—science, technology, engineering, and mathematics—have consistently influenced students' academic levels.

A. Basiouni and C. Frasson (Eds.): BBGI 2024, CCIS 2162, pp. 116–127, 2024.
https://doi.org/10.1007/978-3-031-65996-6_10

Science is a systematic way of studying the laws of nature and different environmental materials based on recognition, observation, classification, measurements, and experiments [2]. Technology is a STEM field that works with technical topics and projects and their correlations with human life and the surrounding environment, such as education, the health sector, industrial projects, machines, etc. Engineering is more about applying theoretical knowledge in physics, science, mathematics, and chemistry to real-life projects. Mathematics is the science of numbers and equations, including Algebra equations, measurements, and geometries.

The STEM educational approach aims to show a paradigm shift from teaching different subjects to teaching authentic problems in a constructivist environment [3]. Guilford [4] The emphasis was on integrating critical thinking and creativity in teaching strategies to develop students' skills. However, many types of research pointed out a gap between teachers' practices and students' learning [5]. Authors at [6] Pointed out that teachers have deep information about the content knowledge but don't have the pedagogical content knowledge based on Shaulman's idea.

STEM discipline-specific content should not be divided, and it should be taught as one subject to solve real-life scenarios. According to [7], there are many ways that STEM can be taught in schools. The first way is known as S-T-E-M, it is to teach the concepts of STEM with little or no integration. Some curriculums introduced this type as a "cross-curricular link". It is like some problems or questions in the books of separate subjects.

The second method is STEM, which focuses on two subjects. This method is also applied in some schools, with collaboration between science and math teachers.

The third way is known as E→STM; it combines the three disciplines, science, technology, and math, into one main discipline, engineering. It is applied to teaching subjects like robotics. Robotics is an engineering project that requires integration from other subjects. Authors at [7] I recommend the third way, which integrates the three disciplines within the fourth main discipline, as the most comprehensive.

STEM fields were identified as vital to the United States' economic progress and development [8]. According to a study by the U.S Bureau of Labor Statistics (Vilorio 2014), STEM careers will increase to more than nine million by 2022; moreover, by 2020, 90% of all jobs require knowledge about at least one STEM skill, which is happening now by 2020. Thus, integrating STEM literacy in early education will help students prepare well for advanced education levels and future professions.

The literature review illustrates that students must know about technology and its tools to be viable job candidates in the future [2], so integrating STEM concepts in education is a practical endeavor that empowers the abilities and perceptions of k12 students about STEM concepts.

Integrating STEM concepts will transform traditional school organizations to enhance students' capabilities and skills effectively, enrich the school's curriculum, and be prepared to meet a vision for competency-based curriculum reform. According to [9], two analysis methods were used:

1. Literature review and statistics about the importance and needs of reforming schools' requirements.

2. Qualitative surveys were conducted in some schools that initiated curriculum reform to improve the interdisciplinary curriculum in STEM concepts in the U.S. The results from surveys, statistics, and the literature review illustrate that curriculum reform in STEM concepts shifted it to a more integrated curriculum that significantly impacts the students' progress and achievements.

In the United Arab Emirates, the government shows a great interest in STEM concepts, especially in the educational field, where STEM concepts reform the education system to be "innovation-based," according to a survey conducted among students in the UAE (2012). The survey's primary purpose was to ask the students why they were motivated by STEM concepts. The result of analyzing the survey's data is illustrated in Fig. 1.

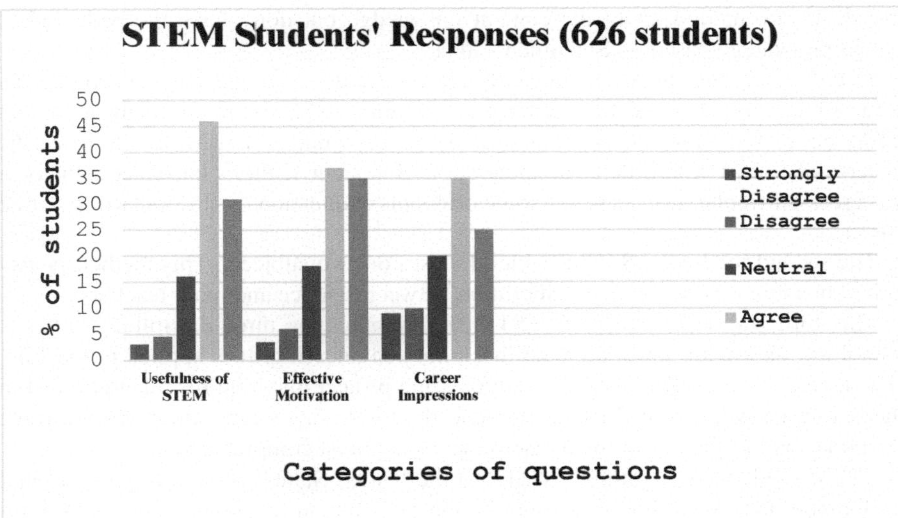

Fig. 1. STEM Student's responses to the different categories of questions

According to the final results of the data of all categories in Fig. 1 (Usefulness of STEM, Effective Motivation and Career Impressions), around 77% of the students agree that STEM education is useful and effective, at the same time, the majority of the students agree on the effective motivation of STEM activities in the education system, Also 60% of the students believe that STEM concepts can provide a variety of opportunities in students' future careers [10]. Reforming the education system in schools is a necessary reaction to match the required developments for preparing k-12 students to follow up with the continuous world progress in the technological era.

2 21St Century Skills

A huge body of literature confirmed that STEM education suits all learning styles where the pedagogy, technology, and content are combined [1]. This is why the different teaching strategies used to teach STEM disciplines, such as Inquiry, Constructivism learning, problem-based learning, and project-based learning. According to [11] Embraces the view that STEM education is not mainly about "convenient integration" of its four concepts; it comprises real-life problems that require STEM-based solutions. Learning STEM methods requires solving well-structured or ill-structured problems, which sets a guide to new strategies for teaching and learning. As a result, there are three types of learning: cognitive, collaborative, and content [12]. Author at [5] Developed a framework based on the Hewlett Foundation (2010), which stated that each type develops a skill students can acquire. Cognitive learning focuses on solving complex problems, which creates the student's critical thinking, creativity, and motivation skills. Collaborative learning focuses on the interaction between the students in solving real-world problems. It develops students' soft skills such as problem-solving, decision-making, communication, and conflict resolution. Authors [13] Focused on the social interaction between learners in the learning process. STEM concentrates on the deep meaning of the concepts by presenting new ideas, connecting STEM methods to real life, utilizing STEM knowledge in solving real-life problems, and reflecting on the strengths and restrictions of the results [1]. This leads the students to higher-order thinking skills, where they acquire experience in collaboration, creativity, critical thinking, communication, connection, and the use of technology as a tool.

3 STEM Education and Innovation in UAE

Although there is a wide interest in STEM concepts in the developed communities that have proliferated recently, it is a new common concept in the United Arab Emirates. STEM education was introduced in the UAE after 2010. Research has been conducted to measure the impact of teaching STEM on students [5]. Different companies in UAE have proposed after school activities and programs in Robotics as one of the famous curricula of STEM that include knowledge from physics, chemistry, technology, electrical and mechanical engineering, and mathematics. However, the resources and the model that can be combined to be compatible with the schools and their respective curriculums should be in place. STEM activities have to be mapped to the curriculum in each grade horizontally and vertically within grade levels and across grade levels. This will enable STEM education to be a part of the school rather than being an after-school activity.

UAE has adopted its vision, mission, and goals for 2020–2021. UAE is concentrating on empowering creativity and innovation through all educational levels in UAE to develop research skills and knowledge of the students in different aspects of STEM, space, and green energy from early ages to produce basic assets for higher education levels in the future. The UAE government encourages students to enrich their knowledge of STEM concepts by conducting and announcing many STEM activities related to innovation in artificial intelligence, robotics, and advanced science, such as an annual national science fair named the National Science, Technology, and Innovation Festival (NSTIF) and the Artificial Intelligence and Robotics competition series (AIR).

The UAE Vision 2021 states that the Ministry of Education plans to replace the current educational strategies with strategies based on creativity, innovation, and STEM concepts [14]. The strategic action plan 2015–2021 of the Ministry of Education in UAE recommended the following:

1. Develop the curriculum to create innovative learners knowledgeable in all relevant subjects.
2. Improve learners' critical thinking, analytical reasoning, and communication skills.
3. In leading their learning path, students can get inspiration and self-direction skills.
4. Using new and creative teaching methods enables teachers to easily convey information in the classrooms and be imaginative throughout the education process.

Learners need to be able to do much more than memorize information. They should be able to apply knowledge creatively in solving real-life problems, have personal values of honesty and integrity, and be committed to engaging in lifelong learning. Such a person should have the ability to communicate efficiently, including reasonable and professional use of information technology, and the ability to take individual and group activities initiatives. The framework defined how integrating STEM concepts will lead to such an improvement in the knowledge and skill levels of the learners.

These characteristics include teaching approaches that take students well beyond learning knowledge and abilities and continue to emphasize their use in practical circumstances.

4 Proposed STEM Education Framework in UAE

This study will suggest appropriate learning outcomes for each level of the STEM education system and compare them with levels 1–4 of QFEmirates to improve the student's skills, knowledge, and experience to meet the expectations and the goals of the Ministry of Education in the UAE. The Qualifications Framework for the Emirates (QFEmirates) [15].

It provides comprehensive details on the qualification architecture in the UAE and also specifies the criteria that will enable the comparison and valuation of UAE qualifications alongside foreign qualifications.

The QFEmirates set out the policies, frameworks, criteria, standards, and procedures for the Emirates Qualification Process. It provides a logical, comprehensible, and robust approach to the design of qualifications for higher education levels, general and technical education, vocational and professional education, and training. It specifies the criteria for both the accreditation of qualifications and for public and private organizations. Also, QFEmirates provides some guidelines and a reference tool for certification and awarding bodies and designers of qualifications.

The structure of the United Arab Emirates' national qualification framework is divided into 10 level descriptors, each comprised of 5 learning outcomes strands. These five strands indicate what students must accomplish and what knowledge and skills to learn for each certificate at each level. A qualification is first identified, benchmarked, and matched to the required standard.

The ten levels involve the broadest possible learning outcomes. Level 10 qualifications demonstrate the ability to discover and develop new knowledge and skills required at the frontiers of research and scholarship. In contrast, Level 1 students can demonstrate the ability to perform practical and elementary tasks [15].

Table 1. Level Descriptors of QFEmirates

		Titles Used in the QFEmirates		
Level Descriptor	Degree	Vocational Education	Higher Education	General Education
10	Doctoral Degree		Doctoral	
9	Master Degree	Applied Master	Master	
8	Graduate Diploma	Applied Graduate Diploma	Postgraduate Diploma	
7	Bachelor Degree	Applied Bachelor	Bachelor	
6	Diploma	Advanced Diploma	Higher Diploma	
5	Diploma/Associate Degree	Diploma	Associate Degree	
4	Certificate	Certificate/4		Secondary School Certificate (G 12)
3	Certificate	Certificate/3		TBA
2	Certificate	Certificate/2		
1	Certificate	Certificate/1		

Table 1 shows the five strands of learning outcomes: knowledge, skill, and aspects of competence in autonomy and responsibility, role in context, and self-development (Table 2).

Table 2. Strands of Learning Outcomes

	Strand 1	Strand 2	Strand 3	Strand 4	Strand 5
Level Descriptor X	Knowledge	Skills	Autonomy & Responsibilities	Role in Context	Self-Development
			Aspect of Competence		

The Proposed STEM education Framework is relevant because it ensures consistency within UAE Schools in the standards of STEM students' learning outcomes regardless of the institution attended. The Framework will help provide sufficient reference points between schools and activity providers and help consider the strengths and abilities of students who should be taught.

Primary and secondary education are available for all UAE citizens. The standing educational system, released in the early 1970s, is a four-tier system covering 14 years of education, starting with kindergarten and ending with secondary school (Table 3).

Table 3. Four-Tier Education System in UAE

Structure	*Length*	*Age*
Kindergarten	2	4 to 5 years
Primary	6	6 to 12 years
Preparatory	3	12 to 15 years
Secondary (Certificate awarded)	3	15 to 18 years

The Introduced Framework has been incorporated into the four levels of the General education title of the NQFemirates, where Level 4 is the high school certificate, Level 3 is the preparatory certificate, Level 2 is the primary certificate, and finally, Level 1 is for Kindergarten. Accordingly, Table 1 can be modified to accommodate the four-tier education system, as shown in Table 4 below.

Table 4. Updated Level Descriptor of QFEmirates

Titles Used in the QFEmirates				
Level Descriptor	Degree	Vocational Education	Higher Education	General Education
4	Certificate	Certificate/4		**Secondary School Certificate (G 12)**
3	Certificate	Certificate/3		**Preparatory**
2	Certificate	Certificate/2		**Primary**
1	Certificate	Certificate/1		**Kindergarten**

Each educational level represents relative difficulty, complexity, and depth. Starting from the lower levels with fundamental knowledge and simple challenges and ending up with higher levels that include more significant challenges and advanced expertise. Added levels numbered and linked to Kindergarten, Primary, preparatory, and secondary structures to illustrate the change in the intellectual demand, complexity of knowledge, and skills expected from students. The Level Descriptors are cumulative, e.g., the descriptor for Level 4 assumes the inclusion of all of the outcomes in the preceding levels.

Table 5. Learning Outcomes of Each Strand at Level 4

	Strand 1	Strand 2	Strand 3	Strand 4	Strand 5
	Knowledge	Skills	Autonomy & Responsibilities	Role in Context	Self-Development
Level Descriptor 4	Broad knowledge of how to apply STEM concepts in real-world contexts effectively Advanced knowledge of the basic theoretical and practical STEM, Awareness of the most significant recent developments in STEM fields Knowledge of available sources of information about new innovative ideas, their development, and their implementation possibilities	Advanced mathematical skills for measurements, calculations, and data analysis Can investigate practical and theoretical problems in the STEM field of study Ability to ask questions and define solutions using STEM techniques in undertaken study Creativity, leadership, organization, and coordination skills to propose potential solutions to solve problems and develop new ideas Technical skills to solve a wide range of STEM-based problems, including diagnosing, testing, and implementing solutions using appropriate information retrieval STEM methods, tools, and techniques independently with autonomy	Can act responsibly and can be relied upon to complete assigned STEM tasks Can seek advice and guidance and act constructively with some initiative in response Can work effectively in group situations and make group decisions Can break down complex STEM topics into smaller portions to be understandable Can demonstrate an ability to represent ideas and explain STEM concepts using digital media and modern technology tools Can collect and analyze data related to a predetermined research/ project topic, identify project goals and objectives, develop a project plan and timeline, draw conclusions from research or experiments' results, and communicate findings effectively with others	Can effectively use routine STEM skills to develop solutions for challenges & real-world issues Can complete assigned tasks independently or under supervision when dealing with complex issues Can obtain relevant new information from some available sources of information and use techniques of inquiry that have been developed in the educational programs with some guidance	Can demonstrate independence and become more focused and aware of post-secondary study and STEM careers Can analyze and critique some topics in the STEM field and contribute to its advancement Evaluate self-learning and identify strengths and weaknesses in learning familiar or unfamiliar topics
			Aspect of Competence		

Table 6. Learning Outcomes of Each Strand at Level 3

	Strand 1	Strand 2	Strand 3	Strand 4	Strand 5
	Knowledge	Skills	Autonomy & Responsibilities	Role in Context	Self-Development
Level Descriptor 3	Broad knowledge of specified tasks and processes related to STEM areas Fundamental knowledge and understanding of science, mathematics, and technology tools based on asking questions and connecting various subjects to the STEM disciplines Fundamental knowledge and understanding of complex ideas, phenomena, and vocabularies used in explaining STEM concepts	Participate in challenges that require STEM-based solutions Demonstrate ability to plan, design, and create a solution for a proposed problem Engage in Argument for Evidence of ideas that were discussed during STEM activities Thinking skills to obtain new knowledge and integrate STEM methods creatively into the surrounding environment	Can represent STEM topics using simple and understandable diagrams, arts, and text Can work and collaborate with others to propose potential solutions and produce results for STEM-based challenges or activities	Can apply knowledge gained through STEM education to a wide range of familiar topics Can pay attention to details, record data accurately, perform calculations if required, and write instructions Can initiate and deploy science and mathematics principles associated with STEM ideas within groups and teams	Can demonstrate the ability to take out-of-the-box approaches to problems and then propose STEM-based solutions Can lead, contribute, and implement STEM ideas outside the school environment Can do STEM activities Individually that include building, measurements, collecting data, and experimentation
			Aspect of Competence		

For example, The STEM education level for Primary School (Grades 1 to 6) includes activities such as basics of mathematics, counting, numbering, programming and assembling simple robotics, Social Responsibility, and Environmental Science, as well as activities to encourage basic life Skills that are connected to STEM concepts such as thinking and problem-solving skills. Preparatory School Level (Grades 7 to 9) includes more advanced STEM activities such as aero modeling, making Balsa gliders, Structures, Robotics with EV3, Sustainable Energy, Animation, and Data-logging; furthermore, students have the ability to propose STEM-based solutions for simple real-world problems. Finally, at the secondary school level (Grades 10 to 12), the activities will be upgraded from simple to more complex three-dimensional activities: Printing, data analysis and prediction, technological design, atmospheric sciences, and artificial intelligence (Tables 5, 6, 7 and 8).

Table 7. Learning Outcomes of Each Strand at Level 2

	Strand 1	Strand 2	Strand 3	Strand 4	Strand 5
	Knowledge	Skills	Autonomy & Responsibilities	Role in Context	Self-Development
Level Descriptor 2	A primary knowledge of Basic Science, mathematics, and the use of technology tools Demonstrate ability to understand and connect between STEM-related fields (Science, technology, engineering, and math)	Measurement and calculation skills with applying the appropriate units Demonstrate the ability to suggest potential STEM solutions to children's real-world problems Can connect understandings from various STEM fields to propose solutions to various challenges	Can receive, understand, respond to instructions, and recall STEM techniques Accept and act upon all reasonable directions given by the instructor Can share and explain their ideas about STEM concepts and activities during classroom discussions and the team's work Can you suggest the engagement of STEM activities and ideas in different life aspects?	Accurate data records can be kept in a notebook during the investigations and results can be communicated, whether orally or through standard written reports Can apply knowledge gained through STEM education to a limited range of structured and mainly sequential tasks	Can do the STEM activities within groups that include building, measurements, collecting data, and experimentation Can observe, estimate, classify, and propose solutions for simple real-world problems
			Aspect of Competence		

Table 8. Learning Outcomes of Each Strand at Level 1

	Strand 1	Strand 2	Strand 3	Strand 4	Strand 5
	Knowledge	Skills	Autonomy & Responsibilities	Role in Context	Self-Development
Level Descriptor 1	Elementary knowledge and understanding of the concepts of science and mathematics Knowledge of essential life skills that are connected to STEM concepts, such as thinking skills, problem-solving, and communication skills	Demonstrate ability to engage in conversations and experiments using primary math concepts, such as measurements and temporal and spatial realization Observe, classify, and recognize the characteristics of human senses, natural objects, and demographic variables such as age, gender, location, etc	Can demonstrate an appropriate understanding of STEM concepts and articulate questions related to these concepts Can participate in a responsive conversation with others about their classroom STEM discussions	Can understand the elementary vocabulary used through verbal communication and written instructions while performing STEM activities Can communicate and collaborate within groups to complete or perform a given task	Can interact and observe closely the surrounding environment Can connect STEM concepts to the outside environment
			Aspect of Competence		

5 Conclusion

This research paper proposes upgrading STEM-based educational systems' learning outcomes to improve the level and quality of education in UAE schools. The adopted research methodology could improve education to an advanced level.

Integrating STEM concepts in schools' curricula provides students with various opportunities in their future careers. It prepares them for continuous technological advancement, a critical part of the UAE's vision.

In general, the impact of reforming the education system in UAE to be "innovation-based" has many significant results in students' achievements, improved analyzing skills, and developed abilities to propose and implement STEM-based solutions to their real-world problems.

References

1. ElSayary, A.: The Effectiveness of Problem-Based Learning Strategy in STEM Education for Enhancing Students' 21st Century-Skills. The British University in Dubai (BUiD) (2014)
2. Barcelona, K.: 21st century curriculum change initiative: a focus on STEM education as an integrated approach to teaching and learning. Am. J. Educ. Res. **2**, 862–875 (2014)
3. Broadbear, J.T.: Essential elements of lessons designed to promote critical thinking. J. Scholarsh. Teach. Learn. **3**, 1–8 (2003)
4. Capraro, R., Capraro, M., Morgan, J.: Stem Project-Based Learning: An Integrated Science, Technology, Engineering, and Mathematics (STEM) Approach. Rotterdam, The Netherlands (2013)
5. Council, National Academy of Engineering and National Research: STEM Integration in K-12 Education: Status, Prospects, and an Agenda for Research. The National Academies Press (2014). https://doi.org/10.17226/18612
6. Du, X.Y., de Graaff, E., Kolmos, A.: PBL-Diversity in Research Questions and Methodologies, Research on PBL Practice in Engineering Education. Sense Publishers, Boston (2009)
7. Dugger, W., Fellow, J.: Evolution of STEM in the United States. International Technology and Engineering Educators Association and Emeritus Professor of Technology Education Virginia Tech (2011)
8. Guilford, J.P.: Creativity. Am. Psychol. **5**(9), 444–454 (1950). https://doi.org/10.1037/h0063487
9. Mayer, R.: Should there be a three-strikes rule against pure discovery learning? The case for guided methods of instruction. Am. Psychol. **59**(1), 14–19 (2004)
10. Report, STEM Task Force: Innovate: a blueprint for science, technology, engineering, and mathematics in California public education. The Californians Dedicated to Education Foundation (2014)
11. Makhmasi, S., Zaki, R., Barada, H., Al-Hammadi, Y.: Students' Interest in STEM Education, A survey from the UAE. Khalifa University of Science, Technology, and Research, Abu Dhabi, United Arab Emirates (2012)
12. Unit, The Economist Intelligence: UAE Economic Vision: Women in Science, Technology and Engineering. A Report from the Economist Intelligence Unit Limited (2014). https://www.eiuperspectives.economist.com
13. Vilorio, D.: Intro to tomorrow's jobs. Occupational Outlook Quarterly (2014). https://www.bls.gov/careeroutlook/2014/spring/art01.pdf
14. Vygotsky, L.S.: Mind in Society: The Development of Higher Psychological Processes. Harvard University Press, Cambridge (1978)
15. Sondergeld, T.A., Johnson, C.C., Walten, J.B.: Assessing the impact of a statewide STEM investment on K–12, higher education, and business/community STEM awareness over time. School Sci. Math. Assoc. **116**, 104–110 (2016)

Exploring the Role of Generative AI in Medical Microbiology Education: Enhancing Bacterial Identification Skills in Laboratory Students

Ray Al-Barazie[1](✉), Azza Mohamed[2], and Fuhua Lin[3]

[1] Faculty of Medical and Health Sciences, Liwa College, Al-Ain, UAE
ray.albarazie@lc.ac.ae

[2] Faculty of Information Technology, Liwa College, Al-Ain, UAE
azza.basiouni@lc.ac.ae

[3] School of Computing and Information Systems, Faculty of Science and Technology, Athabasca University, Athabasca, AB, Canada
oscarl@athabascau.ca

Abstract. The precise identification of pathogens in biological material is critical for appropriate medical diagnosis and therapy. Medical laboratory students must be proficient in laboratory skills since they play a critical part in the diagnostic process. Using appropriate microscope techniques, one must be able to identify a wide range of pathogens, including bacteria, viruses, parasites, and fungi. Traditional methods of skill development include on-campus practical lessons and field training in hospital microbiology departments. However, the emergence of generative artificial intelligence (AI) opens new avenues for educational enhancement. This study investigates the feasibility of using generative AI, specifically Gemini, to train medical laboratory students in bacterial identification using morphological traits seen in micrographs. The study assessed student learning results using Gemini-generated case studies and quizzes. The results showed that Gemini-generated quizzes helped pupils identify different bacteria based on the micrographs supplied. However, limitations were identified, such as the requirement for teachers to manually add photographs. Overall, the study highlights the potential of generative AI tools in educational contexts, arguing that they could supplement traditional teaching techniques and improve the learning experience for medical laboratory students. More research into generative AI's educational applications is needed to fully realize its potential in medical education.

Keywords: Generative Artificial Intelligence · Medical education · Medical Microbiology · Micrographs · Generative AI · AI-assisted learning

1 Introduction

1.1 Generative Artificial Intelligence (AI) Language Models

Generative Artificial Intelligence (AI) language models, also known as large language models (LLMs), are capable of understanding and producing text sequences and categorizations within natural language, computer code, and even protein chain

A. Basiouni and C. Frasson (Eds.): BBGI 2024, CCIS 2162, pp. 128–144, 2024.
https://doi.org/10.1007/978-3-031-65996-6_11

structure [1, 2]. ChatGPT (OpenAI), Bing AI (Microsoft), and Gemini (Google) are examples of natural language specific LLMs. Category of AI systems that specialize on processing and producing text with human-like characteristics. These models are built using advanced machine learning techniques and trained on large volumes of text data, allowing them to understand the patterns, structures, and meanings of human language. As a result, they can understand and produce material that is very similar to human writing, making them great assets in a variety of disciplines, including education and research [3].

One of the primary advantages of AI language models is their ability to obtain and analyze a wide range of information, including specialized expertise in domains such as biomedicine. For example, ChatGPT has shown outstanding knowledge performance in this domain, as proved by recent research showing its capacity to pass the United States Medical Licensing Exam (USMLE) without any specialized training or reinforcement algorithms [4, 5]. The exam is a highly regarded assessment that focuses on foundational science, pharmacology, and pathophysiology. It is usually taken by medical students following two years of lecture-based and problem-solving education, and they often devote roughly 300–400 h of concentrated study time to this exam [6]. Such findings underscore AI models' potential as educational tools, providing students with accurate and relevant information to augment their study. Nonetheless, AI language models have substantial limitations. Even the most advanced models available today may struggle to handle ambiguous, complex, or highly specialized inputs, affecting the quality and accuracy of their outputs [5]. Furthermore, these models may accidentally produce misleading or inaccurate medical information, especially if their training data is poor or biased [7]. AI models may also generate information that appears convincing but is factually inaccurate, a process known as "hallucinations" [5]. These inaccuracies are linked to their incapacity to interpret information and make logical deductions in the nuanced manner that people do, as they are trained to generate text based on learned patterns, rather than genuine knowledge or reasoning [8].

Furthermore, AI models' short memory and attention spans can be a substantial impediment to their ability to keep track of various pieces of information or consider multiple potential solutions to a problem. This is especially challenging when dealing with complicated inputs that necessitate the examination of various variables and information sources. For example, most AI models struggle with multimodal inputs, such as reading and integrating information from images, charts, and text all at once, which is frequently required in medical education.

1.2 AI in Medical Microbiology Education

Medical microbiology is an important discipline in the medical field. The identification of pathogens like bacteria and parasites, is crucial for proper diagnosis and successful treatment. Studies showed the use of machine learning technology for the identification of species and determining antimicrobial susceptibility seems to be promising yet applying it in clinical settings is still challenging [9]. Generative AI potential and capabilities in the medical microbiology consultation has been studied. This paper showed AI potential in the field of clinical microbiology despite having its limitations and concerns [10]. We present realistic ways for recognizing and evaluating student contributions when they work with AI models to create replies, sometimes known as AI-assisted learning. Understanding the possibilities and limitations of AI language models can help teachers. We believe teachers will be able to incorporate these technologies into the educational process, supporting a fruitful learning experience that leverages AI's potential while simultaneously developing students' critical thinking and problem-solving skills.

The major purpose of this article is to explore the potential of generative AI in the medical field, and its potential in education. Hence, the aim of this study is to investigate the potential of generative AI in education, principally preparing medical laboratory students to gain the required skills in medical microbiology, as well as to propose simple principles for adapting present educational methodologies to a scenario in which students rely on these tools to learn. It has been suggested that AI models such as ChatGPT can improve medical students' communication, problem-solving, and critical thinking [11], but there are currently no systematic approaches for evaluating the usage of such technologies in the classroom.

1.3 Study Objectives

a. Selecting a suitable generative artificial intelligence tool: The first goal is to find and evaluate generative AI tools that suit the unique requirements for developing evaluations targeted to the training needs of medical laboratory students.
b. Generation of learning assessments: After selecting an acceptable AI tool, the goal is to use it to create assessments that will instruct medical laboratory students on case studies containing micrographs in the field of medical microbiology.
c. Evaluation of outcomes: This goal entails evaluating the effectiveness of the generated evaluations and determining the amount to which they contribute to student learning. It also seeks to highlight the advantages and disadvantages of using the selected AI technology to create assessments in medical microbiology.

Overall, the study seeks to investigate the viability of employing generative AI tools to create evaluations for educating medical laboratory trainees, specifically in the field of medical microbiology. It also aims to assess the results of this strategy and provide insights into its potential benefits and drawbacks.

2 Literature Review

2.1 Utilization of Technology in Teaching Support

Over the last two decades, the usage of digital tools in educational contexts has skyrocketed due to a variety of variables, including increased tool availability, and changed student expectations [12]. The learning management system (LMS) is the major digital tool in education's technological transition, and it is nearly universally adopted by secondary and tertiary educational institutions [13, 14]. Because of their flexibility, LMSs can serve as one-stop shops for all aspects of a certain course, such as facilitating collaboration and debate through forums [15] or sharing lessons and other relevant materials such as self-assessment quizzes or instructional films [16–18]. Furthermore, LMSs have built-in data collection functionalities that record all user interactions, allowing educators to not only monitor their students' overall engagement but also use that data to identify struggling students [19, 20] and provide timely feedback.

Other potentially interesting forms of bringing technology into the classroom, such as the use of augmented reality [21] or the Georgia Institute's AI-powered teaching assistant Jill Watson [22], have also received positive feedback from students, despite the fact that these implementations are not as widespread as the LMS. The use of information tools in education has been suggested to provide significant benefits from both administrative and academic perspectives, particularly in higher education settings [23, 24].

2.2 The Applications of Generative AI in Education

Generative AI models are algorithms that recognize patterns and rules in training data and produce new observations that follow those rules [24]. These have progressed from simple statistical algorithms like the Naive Bayes classifier [25] to complex deep-learning models with billions of parameters. LLMs, such as the Generative Pre-trained Transformer (GPT) or Meta's Llama-2, are deep learning models trained on large quantities of text and deployed to generate new text from a prompt. While the literature on the use of LLMs in education is still in its early stages, there is mounting evidence that these tools will play a critical role in altering the educational landscape in the years ahead. When exploring the possibilities of LLMs in education, Kasneci et al. [3] stated that these models might benefit teachers in a variety of domains, including student assessment and evaluation, teaching assistance, and individualized learning. In their evaluation of studies on artificial intelligence applications in higher education, Zawacki-Richter et al. [26] proposed a similar typology, adding profiling and prediction to the three previously identified domains.

In terms of assessment and evaluation, the use of LLMs falls into two groups. The first is automatic question generation (AQG), which prompts the LLM to generate relevant problems for students to solve. AQG has become a requirement in large-scale courses, and while the long-term effectiveness of LLM-generated questions is unknown, exploratory studies on English [25], arithmetic, and data science have been well appreciated by educators and human specialists. The second category involves automating the correction of free-form answers. Moore et al. [27] employed a revised Bloom taxonomy to classify a group of chemistry students' short-form answers and discovered that a fine-tuned LLM matched the human-expert rating in 32% of cases. ChatGPT was also proven to provide comments on open-ended programming challenges in the same way as field specialists would [28].

The literature also discusses the use of LLMs in instructional situations. Using the cutting-edge GPT-4, Srihdar et al. [29] developed learning objectives for a university-level artificial intelligence course. The objectives were determined to be appropriate and well-suited to the course's modules. In another work, Jauhiainen and Guerra [30] used the content generating capabilities of generative AI to construct numerous versions of a history lesson, each matched to a distinct student knowledge level.

The AI-enhanced lessons were well accepted, with reviews indicating that they were both enjoyable and educational. In a more technical discipline, such as programming, Sarsa et al. [31] discovered that LLMs are effective not only in creating unique introductory programming problems, but also in delivering full and accurate explanations of most of the lines of code that comprise the answer. MacNeil et al. [32] proved ChatGPT's ability to explain code fluently.

2.3 Applications of Generative AI in the Medical Field

Generative AI is a fascinating tool which has found its applications in the medical field. In a study, pathology generative AI built on establishment model was used to enhance the system in the laboratory and assess in training as it can support in analyzing images, writing reports as well as other tasks [33]. AI has shown immense use during COVID-19 pandemic as it was used for early detection by analyzing symptoms and patterns related to the disease, follow-up the treatment, prediction of hot-spots, development of antiviral drugs and vaccines among others [28]. In a study machine learning (ML) was used in medical microbiology field. ML was used to identify different types of pathogens including viruses, parasites, bacteria, and fungi using different data set. Furthermore, ML has shown potential in the antimicrobial susceptibility tests. Though ML showed great potential in the field of medical microbiology, still the extend of its application in real clinical settings remains unclear [34]. Analyzing microscopic images is an important pillar in the medical microbiology which aids in identifying the causative agent and thus have a proper diagnosis. Neural network was used to analyze and identify bacteria from a micrograph, where the model showed generally a high sensitivity and accuracy in classifying bacteria based on their Gram staining results and morphology [35].

2.4 Using Google Gemini in Educational Settings

The integration of Gemini and other generative AI technologies offers great promise in the educational field, particularly in activities like generating test questions, assessing student performance in evaluations, and assisting with writing assignments. However, there are significant worries about data privacy and potential biases in algorithmic procedures [36]. Ensuring the trustworthiness of these AI technologies is critical and necessitates continuous evaluation. A recent study investigated the usefulness of Gemini in answering biology-related questions and found a disturbing proportion of erroneous responses due to a variety of variables. As a result, the study underlines the need for continuous evaluation until these tools achieve greater consistency [37]. Furthermore, Google has made breakthroughs in Gemini models designed exclusively for medical applications, known as Med-Gemini. Google reported outstanding accuracy rates of up to 91.1% in a recent article [38]. This idea has the potential to significantly improve medical education and practice.

2.5 Ethical Aspects of Generative AI

Since generative AI became widely available, there has been a great deal of controversy about its ethical applications. There have already been lawsuits over AI utilizing someone else's work, particularly when creating photographs and videos [39]. Aside from the legal element, one of the most important ethical considerations when employing generative AI techniques is prejudice. Overcoming obstacles is especially critical when utilizing AI to create learning materials. ChatGPT, like the current study, uses the GPT-3.5 and GPT-4 models and has been connected to a variety of gender, ethnic, cultural, language, ideological, and cognitive biases. Mitigation measures include resampling and pre-processing of data used for training the models [40], employing diverse and representative datasets [41], and feedback loops [42].

Other ethical considerations for the current level of generative AI models include their tendency to provide erroneous or deceptive data. LLMs have been accused of "hallucinations" [39], which occur when these models generate information that is intelligible and grammatically correct but factually erroneous and incoherent. Self-reflection methodology, answer weighting strategies, and double checks are some of the methods for mitigating such behavior.

2.6 Research Gap

One research gap that has emerged is the need for additional investigation into the specific processes by which generative AI tools influence student learning outcomes in medical laboratory science teaching. While the study found that AI-generated quizzes can improve laboratory skills, there is still a dearth of understanding of the underlying processes and elements that lead to this result.

Future research should explore deeper into the cognitive and pedagogical mechanisms that influence student learning via AI-generated quizzes, including engagement, motivation, and information processing. By explaining these mechanisms, researchers can get significant insights into how to design and deploy AI-based educational interventions that are most effective.

Furthermore, comparative studies are required to assess the efficacy of generative AI tools in comparison to traditional teaching approaches or other types of educational technology. Such research would serve to situate this study's findings within the larger landscape of educational innovation, as well as provide a foundation for evidence-based decision-making in curriculum creation and instructional design.

3 Methodology

The methodological approach used in this paper is described in the next part, which provides extensive insights into each procedural stage. Figure 1 gives a visual summary of the methodological phases carried out in this study, providing an organized picture of the research process. Through this complete approach, the report assures clarity and transparency in explaining the methods, methodologies, and processes used to achieve the research objectives and support the conclusions given here. The described approach was used to create an assessment through generative AI tool that can be employed for educational purpose in medical microbiology. The methodology used was to assess and create a quiz that can train the students on medical cases and assess their practical skills in recognizing bacterial micrographs. Nevertheless, implementing AI generated assessments in the educational sector can be challenging as the assessor should be familiar with the available tools and qualified to utilize these tools in generating suitable assessments that aligns with students' level and subject's learning outcomes.

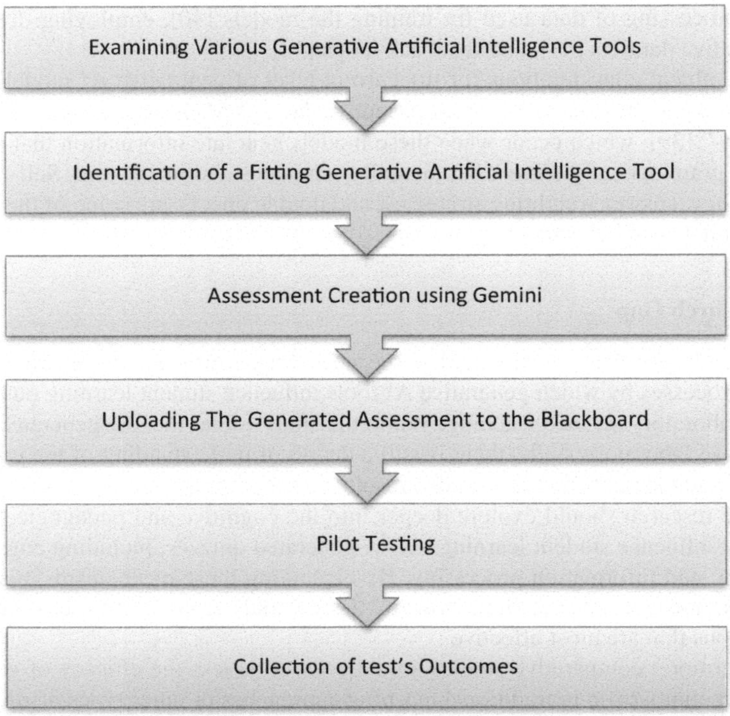

Fig. 1. Summary of the methodological phases used in this study.

3.1 Examining Different Generative Artificial Intelligence Tools

In this section, we conduct a thorough assessment of various generative artificial intelligence (AI) technologies to determine their suitability for meeting the study's aims, see Table 1. The goal is to assess each tool's usefulness and applicability in answering the study objectives and requirements.

Through a comprehensive analysis of these generative AI tools, we aim to determine their adequacy and suitability for fulfilling the aims of the study. By assessing factors such as accuracy, coherence, domain specificity, and task relevance, we seek to identify the most appropriate tools to support our research endeavors and contribute to meaningful insights in the field.

Table 1. Description of Generative AI tools and Evaluation

Generative AI Tool	Description	Evaluation Criteria
ChatGPT	Variant of the GPT architecture designed for natural language conversations and text generation based on input prompts	–Relevance to research focus –Coherence and context retention –Limitations or areas of improvement
GPT-4	Latest iteration of the GPT series, incorporating advancements in language understanding and text generation capabilities	–Performance compared to earlier iterations –Adaptability to diverse tasks and domains –Contributions to study objectives
Google PaLM 2	Advanced language model developed by Google, utilizing probabilistic techniques for text generation and linguistic analysis	–Contextual relevance of generated text –Scalability across various tasks –Alignment with research requirements
Google Gemini	Specialized AI model tailored for tasks such as generating test questions, analyzing student performance, and writing tasks	–Effectiveness in educational contexts –Reliability in generating accurate assessments - Alignment with study objectives

3.2 Identification of a Fitting Generative Artificial Intelligence Tool

Among the different AI tools, Google Gemini was the most suitable tool that attained more than 80% of the necessities needed to create the assessment. The criteria were to have an AI tool that can create case study about medical microbiology along multiple choice questions (MCQs). Gemini had the advantage of including the correct answers, although micrographs could not be uploaded to train the tool. Furthermore, the tool was unable to include images, but it was able to describe them which was an acceptable alternative.

3.3 Assessment Creation using Gemini

Gemini was requested to generate a quiz using clinical case of meningitis which suits advanced levels of students. The request was as follows: Create a quiz using case study about meningitis with multiple-choice questions (MCQs) based on bacterial microscopic images. Gemini responded by creating a case study and 5 MCQs related to the case as shown in Fig. 2. As the tool does not include images, images were added manually and they were obtained from the Public Health Image Library (PHIL) [43].

A strong quiz structure was produced by combining Gemini's textual data with hand-picked photos from PHIL. This technique guaranteed that learners had a comprehensive and immersive learning experience by combining textual analysis with visual assistance to reinforce essential concepts in meningitis diagnosis and therapy.

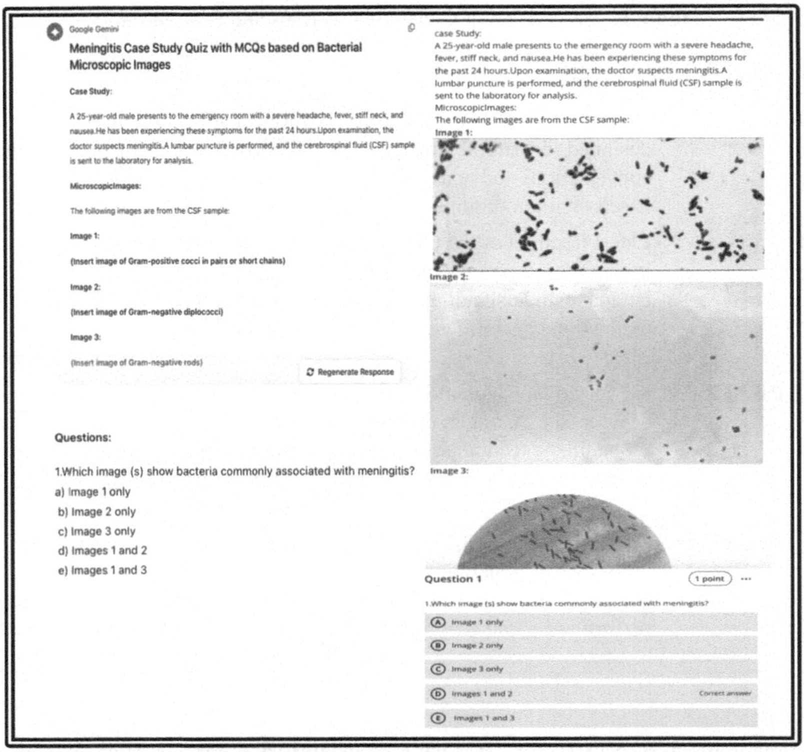

Fig. 2. Example of the generated questions and the question as used in Blackboard.

3.4 Uploading the Generated Assessment to the Blackboard

The generated quiz was uploaded to the Blackboard to assess the students (Fig. 2). The images were uploaded as well to have full assessment of the student's ability to recognize and identify bacteria based on data provided and bacterial micrographs. This can assess and identify weaknesses in a crucial skill each medical laboratory student should have.

By introducing visual aspects into the exam, students were forced to apply their theoretical knowledge to real-world circumstances, which improved their critical thinking and diagnostic abilities. This approach allows the instructors to identify and rectify any shortcomings in students' ability to analyze microbiological data, which is a critical skill for medical laboratory students. The use of Blackboard as an assessment tool not only makes administration and grading easier, but it also provides vital insights into students' comprehension and competency in microbiological identification, which is an important part of their training and future practice in medicine.

3.5 Pilot Testing

During this phase, the quiz underwent a pilot test involving students from different levels, specially targeting second- and third-year majors in medical laboratory science. The goal of this pilot testing was to determine the effectiveness and acceptability of the quiz structure and material for various skill levels. During the pilot test, students were instructed to take the quiz, and each correct answer was worth one point. This scoring system established a clear metric for assessing student performance and comprehension of the quiz material.

The pilot test, which involved students from various levels within the medical laboratory science program, was designed to confirm the quiz's relevance and effectiveness for a broad range of learners. This iterative process of testing and refining contributes to the development of a robust and dependable assessment tool for future use in the curriculum.

3.6 Collection of Test Results

After the students completed their examinations, the outcomes and performance data were collected and examined. This procedure sought to provide significant insights into the efficacy and benefits of using quiz-based tutoring in medical microbiology education. The collected data included a variety of indicators, such as individual student scores, overall class performance trends, and any observable patterns or connections between performance and characteristics like academic level or experience. This phase enabled a full assessment of the tutoring method's efficacy by collecting and evaluating test results in a methodical manner. Data insights guided decisions on optimizing teaching tactics, refining assessment formats, and identifying places for more instructional support.

Finally, collecting and analyzing test results was an important step in determining how the tuition approach affected student learning and performance in medical microbiology.

4 Results and Discussion

The performance of students on the test was analyzed utilizing Blackboard question analysis tools, as shown in Table 2. Additional statistical analysis could not be done due to the low number of students who took the quiz (13 students). The analysis includes determining the percentage of difficulty for each question, which is a critical metric shown in Table 2 and Fig. 3A. This proportion revealed the amount of difficulty posed by each question, with Questions 1 and 2 classed as difficult since they received less than 30% accurate responses, while Questions 4 and 5 were classified as easy because their correct responses exceeded 80%.

Simultaneously, the average score per question was calculated, providing information about students' competency levels in several skill areas. Questions 1 and 2, which focused on bacterial micrograph recognition, had lower average scores than the other theoretical questions, as shown in Table 2 and Fig. 3B. This disparity shows that students may benefit from more laboratory practice, even though their theoretical comprehension appears to be rather solid.

Furthermore, discrimination was measured using the Pearson correlation coefficient, as shown in Table 2. This statistical measure looked at the correlation between individual question scores (X) and overall quiz results (Y) for each student. This type of analysis helps to uncover questions that successfully differentiate between high and low-performing students, improving the assessment process's reliability and validity.

$$\mathbf{r} = \frac{1}{n-1}\sum_{i=1}^{n}\left(\frac{X_i - \overline{X}}{s_X}\right)\left(\frac{Y_i - \overline{Y}}{s_Y}\right)$$

The variables are the standard score, sample mean and sample standard deviation correspondingly:

$$\frac{X_i - \overline{X}}{s_X}, \overline{X}, \text{and } s_X$$

Discrimination is an important sign of a question's usefulness in determining pupils' levels of competency and comprehension in a specific area. Discrimination ratings typically range from −1.0 to +1.0, with values greater than 0.3 considered good, values between 0.1 and 0.3 labeled fair, and values less than 0.1 considered poor.

Our research, shown in Fig. 3C, demonstrated that Questions 1, 3, and 4 had high discrimination, effectively differentiating between students with varying levels of skills and knowledge in the subject. This shows that the questions were carefully prepared to test students and assess their level of comprehension.

Question 2 showed fair discrimination, indicating moderate effectiveness in determining students' competence levels. While not as robust as Questions 1, 3, and 4, Question 2 made an important contribution to the assessment process.

However, Question 5 had poor discrimination, implying that it failed to properly distinguish between students' talents and comprehension levels. As a result, this study emphasizes the need for revision to ensure that the question is more closely aligned with the learning objectives and accurately tests students' knowledge and skills in the subject matter.

Overall, the results show that Gemini generates high-quality questions, with the majority demonstrating acceptable discrimination levels. This highlights the potential of generative AI techniques in creating successful assessment materials, while also identifying areas for refinement and enhancement to improve assessment accuracy and dependability.

Our findings underlined the exciting possibility of using quizzes generated by Gemini, a generative AI, to assess the competence of medical laboratory trainees. This investigation provided useful insights into the capabilities of AI in teaching, notably in the field of medical microbiology. The exam acted as a thorough evaluation tool, assessing students' ability to identify bacteria in micrographs, evaluate data, and display subject area knowledge.

Our interaction with Gemini was both entertaining and illuminating. Despite limitations that necessitated occasional human intervention, Gemini demonstrated proficiency in developing a medical microbiology case study and producing pertinent questions. While it did not meet all our objectives, generative AI performed satisfactorily, indicating intriguing applications in medical education. The use of AI into medical education

Table 2. Question analysis of the pilot test.

Question description	Discrimination	Difficulty %	Graded attempts	Average score
1. Which image (s) show bacteria commonly associated with meningitis?	0.69	23.08	13	0.24
2. Based on the images, what is the most likely cause of meningitis in this patient?	0.14	7.7	13	0.08
3. Which of the following statements is TRUE about the bacteria in Image 1?	0.69	53.85	13	0.54
4. The presence of white blood cells in the CSF is indicative of:	0.57	84.62	13	0.85
5. Which of the following is the most appropriate treatment for bacterial meningitis?	−0.14	92.31	13	0.93

has great promise, giving new opportunities to improve teaching and learning processes. Recent research of medical students offered light on their perception of AI's potential in medical teaching. The findings showed a necessity for courses covering fundamental AI principles such as ethics, constraints, and consistency [44]. This emphasizes the need of introducing AI education into medical curriculum to provide future healthcare practitioners with the information and abilities they need to use AI effectively in their practice. However, the issues regarding AI bias and misleading information remain valid concerns.

In summary, our findings highlight AI's transformative potential in medical education, paving the path for novel ways to teaching and learning. By using the capabilities of AI tools like Gemini and resolving pertinent ethical and practical concerns, we may realize the full promise of technology to better medical education and, eventually, improve patient care.

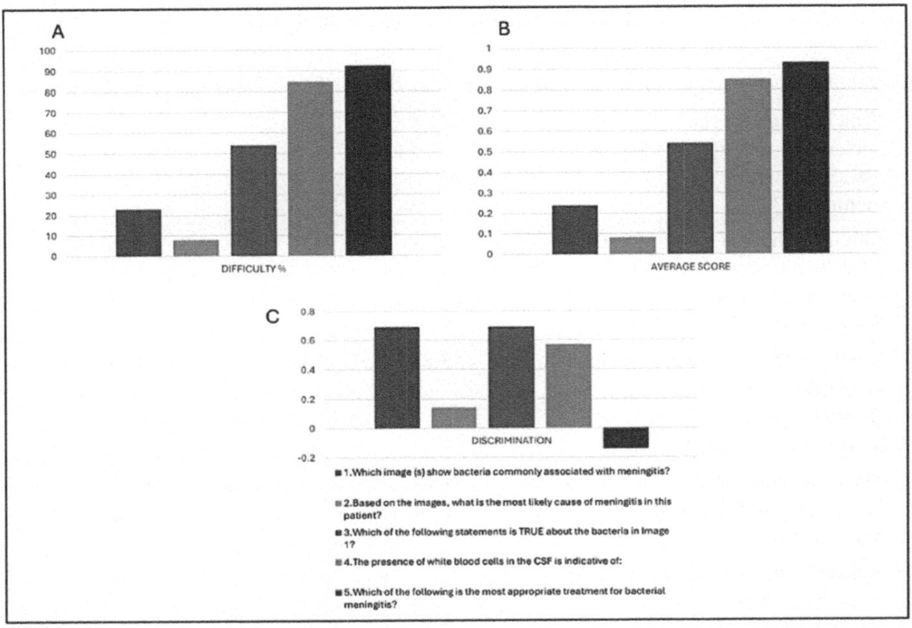

Fig. 3. Question analysis of the pilot test where the percentage of difficulty (A), the average score of each question (B) and the discrimination (C) are depicted.

5 Conclusion

Based on our findings, generative AI shows promise in improving laboratory abilities among medical laboratory students through the creation of personalized quizzes. Our investigation found that when asked, generative AI, as proven by Gemini, was able to generate questions and case studies that fit our expectations to a satisfactory degree. These generated resources have the potential to be useful additions to individualized teaching approaches.

However, it is vital to note that generative AI has limitations. One significant limitation is its limited ability to provide certain types of responses, which may limit its usefulness in some educational environments. Concerns about the consistency of AI-generated content remain valid, as changes in output quality may have an impact on the usefulness of educational materials created by these systems. Despite these limitations, our findings highlight the potential for generative AI to complement and improve instructional processes in medical laboratory science. Moving forward, it will be critical to further investigate the potential and limitations of generative AI in educational contexts, as well as address concerns about content consistency and quality assurance. By doing this, we can exploit our strengths of generative AI to optimize teaching and learning experiences for students in the medical field.

6 Future Work

Future research in this area should center on:

- Longitudinal studies are being conducted to investigate the long-term influence of artificial intelligence-generated quizzes on student learning outcomes and performance in medical laboratory science before and after using the AI-generated assessment and to increase the number of students involved in the study.
- Developing AI algorithms to generate more diverse and sophisticated responses, which will overcome present content generating limits.
- Implementing rigorous quality control and validation methods to assure the consistency and accuracy of AI-generated educational materials.
- Investigating the use of generative AI tools alongside other educational technology to produce immersive and engaging learning experiences.

Overall, future research should seek to maximize the benefits of generative AI in medical education while resolving current limitations and constraints.

References

1. Ferruz, N., Schmidt, S., Höcker, B.: ProtGPT2 is a deep unsupervised language model for protein design. Nat. Commun. **13**, 4348 (2022). https://doi.org/10.1038/s41467-022-32007-7
2. Prepare for truly useful large language models. Nat. Biomed. Eng. **7**, 85–86 (2023). https://doi.org/10.1038/s41551-023-01012-6
3. Kasneci, E., et al.: ChatGPT for good? On opportunities and challenges of large language models for education. Learn. Individ. Differ. **103**, 102274 (2023). https://doi.org/10.1016/j.lindif.2023.102274
4. Kung, T.H., et al.: Performance of ChatGPT on USMLE: potential for AI-assisted medical education using large language models. PLOS Digit. Health. **2**, e0000198 (2023). https://doi.org/10.1371/journal.pdig.0000198
5. Nori, H., King, N., McKinney, S.M., Carignan, D., Horvitz, E.: Capabilities of GPT-4 on medical challenge problems, http://arxiv.org/abs/2303.13375 (2023). https://doi.org/10.48550/arXiv.2303.13375
6. Burk-Rafel, J., Santen, S.A., Purkiss, J.: Study behaviors and USMLE step 1 performance: implications of a student self-directed parallel curriculum. Acad. Med. J. Assoc. Am. Med. Coll. **92**, S67–S74 (2017). https://doi.org/10.1097/ACM.0000000000001916
7. Dubin, J.A., et al.: Using a google web search analysis to assess the utility of ChatGPT in total joint arthroplasty. J. Arthroplasty **38**, 1195–1202 (2023). https://doi.org/10.1016/j.arth.2023.04.007
8. Yang, Z., Liu, Y., Ouyang, C., Ren, L., Wen, W.: Counterfactual can be strong in medical question and answering. Inf. Process. Manag. **60**, 103408 (2023). https://doi.org/10.1016/j.ipm.2023.103408
9. Weis, C.V., Jutzeler, C.R., Borgwardt, K.: Machine learning for microbial identification and antimicrobial susceptibility testing on MALDI-TOF mass spectra: a systematic review. Clin. Microbiol. Infect. **26**, 1310–1317 (2020). https://doi.org/10.1016/j.cmi.2020.03.014
10. Chiu, E.K.-Y., Chung, T.W.-H.: Protocol For Human Evaluation of Artificial Intelligence Chatbots in Clinical Consultations. https://www.medrxiv.org/content/10.1101/2024.03.01.24303593v1 (2024). https://doi.org/10.1101/2024.03.01.24303593

11. Sallam, M., Al-Salahat, K.: Below average ChatGPT performance in medical microbiology exam compared to university students. Front. Educ. **8** (2023). https://doi.org/10.3389/feduc.2023.1333415
12. Dunn, T.J., Kennedy, M.: Technology Enhanced Learning in higher education; motivations, engagement and academic achievement. Comput. Educ. **137**, 104–113 (2019). https://doi.org/10.1016/j.compedu.2019.04.004
13. Balkaya, S., Akkucuk, U.: Adoption and use of learning management systems in education: the role of playfulness and self-management. Sustainability **13**, 1127 (2021). https://doi.org/10.3390/su13031127
14. Coates, H., James, R., Baldwin, G.: A critical examination of the effects of learning management systems on university teaching and learning. Tert. Educ. Manag. **11**, 19–36 (2005). https://doi.org/10.1007/s11233-004-3567-9
15. Romero, C., López, M.-I., Luna, J.-M., Ventura, S.: Predicting students' final performance from participation in on-line discussion forums. Comput. Educ. **68**, 458–472 (2013). https://doi.org/10.1016/j.compedu.2013.06.009
16. Bernacki, M.L., Chavez, M.M., Uesbeck, P.M.: Predicting achievement and providing support before STEM majors begin to fail. Comput. Educ. **158**, 103999 (2020). https://doi.org/10.1016/j.compedu.2020.103999
17. Chan, Y.M.: Video instructions as support for beyond classroom learning. Procedia Soc. Behav. Sci. **9**, 1313–1318 (2010). https://doi.org/10.1016/j.sbspro.2010.12.326
18. Arias, M., Creus, C., Gascón, A., Godoy, G.: Learning theory through videos: a teaching experience in a theoretical course based on self-learning videos and problem-solving sessions. In: CSEDU 2011 - Proceedings of the 3rd International Conference on Computer Supported Education, Volume 2, Noordwijkerhout, Netherlands, 6–8 May 2011, pp. 93–98 (2011). https://doi.org/10.5220/0003333400930098
19. Riestra-González, M., Paule-Ruíz, M.delP., Ortin, F.: Massive LMS log data analysis for the early prediction of course-agnostic student performance. Comput. Educ. **163**, 104108 (2021). https://doi.org/10.1016/j.compedu.2020.104108
20. Santos, R.M., Henriques, R.: Accurate, timely, and portable: course-agnostic early prediction of student performance from LMS logs. Comput. Educ. Artif. Intell. **5**, 100175 (2023). https://doi.org/10.1016/j.caeai.2023.100175
21. Macfadyen, L.P., Dawson, S.: Mining LMS data to develop an "early warning system" for educators: a proof of concept. Comput. Educ. **54**, 588–599 (2010). https://doi.org/10.1016/j.compedu.2009.09.008
22. Fonseca, D., Martí, N., Redondo, E., Navarro, I., Sánchez, A.: Relationship between student profile, tool use, participation, and academic performance with the use of Augmented Reality technology for visualized architecture models. Comput. Hum. Behav. **31**, 434–445 (2014). https://doi.org/10.1016/j.chb.2013.03.006
23. Dede, C., Richards, J., Saxberg, B.: Learning Engineering for Online Education: Theoretical Contexts and Design-Based Examples. Routledge, New York (2018)
24. Patlins, A., Kunicina, N., Ribickis, L.: Information tools for education of electrical engineers. In: Proceedings of the 6th IEEE International Conference on Intelligent Data Acquisition and Advanced Computing Systems, pp. 660–665 (2011). https://doi.org/10.1109/IDAACS.2011.6072852
25. Zhiravetska, A., Kunicina, N., Berzina, K., Patlins, A.: Flexible approach to course testing for the improvement of its effectiveness in engineering education. In: 2015 IEEE 8th International Conference on Intelligent Data Acquisition and Advanced Computing Systems: Technology and Applications (IDAACS), pp. 955–959 (2015). https://doi.org/10.1109/IDAACS.2015.7341445

26. Zawacki-Richter, O., Marín, V.I., Bond, M., Gouverneur, F.: Systematic review of research on artificial intelligence applications in higher education – where are the educators? Int. J. Educ. Technol. High. Educ. **16**, 39 (2019). https://doi.org/10.1186/s41239-019-0171-0
27. Moore, S., Nguyen, H.A., Bier, N., Domadia, T., Stamper, J.: Assessing the quality of student-generated short answer questions using GPT-3. In: Hilliger, I., Muñoz-Merino, P.J., De Laet, T., Ortega-Arranz, A., Farrell, T. (eds.) EC-TEL 2022. LNCS, vol. 13450, pp. 243–257. Springer, Cham (2022). https://doi.org/10.1007/978-3-031-16290-9_18
28. Vaishya, R., Javaid, M., Khan, I.H., Haleem, A.: Artificial Intelligence (AI) applications for COVID-19 pandemic. Diabetes Metab. Syndr. **14**, 337–339 (2020). https://doi.org/10.1016/j.dsx.2020.04.012
29. Sridhar, P., Doyle, A., Agarwal, A., Bogart, C., Savelka, J., Sakr, M.: Harnessing LLMs in curricular design: using GPT-4 to support authoring of learning objectives, http://arxiv.org/abs/2306.17459 (2023). https://doi.org/10.48550/arXiv.2306.17459
30. Jauhiainen, J.S., Guerra, A.G.: Generative AI and ChatGPT in school children's education: evidence from a school lesson. Sustainability **15**, 14025 (2023). https://doi.org/10.3390/su151814025
31. Sarsa, S., Denny, P., Hellas, A., Leinonen, J.: Automatic generation of programming exercises and code explanations using large language models. In: Proceedings of the 2022 ACM Conference on International Computing Education Research - Volume 1, pp. 27–43. Association for Computing Machinery, New York (2022). https://doi.org/10.1145/3501385.3543957
32. MacNeil, S., Tran, A., Mogil, D., Bernstein, S., Ross, E., Huang, Z.: Generating diverse code explanations using the GPT-3 large language model. In: Proceedings of the 2022 ACM Conference on International Computing Education Research - Volume 2, pp. 37–39. Association for Computing Machinery, New York (2022). https://doi.org/10.1145/3501709.3544280
33. Waqas, A., et al.: Revolutionizing digital pathology with the power of generative artificial intelligence and foundation models. Lab. Invest. **103**, 100255 (2023). https://doi.org/10.1016/j.labinv.2023.100255
34. Peiffer-Smadja, N., et al.: Machine learning in the clinical microbiology laboratory: has the time come for routine practice? Clin. Microbiol. Infect. **26**, 1300–1309 (2020). https://doi.org/10.1016/j.cmi.2020.02.006
35. Smith, K.P., Kang, A.D., Kirby, J.E.: Automated interpretation of blood culture gram stains by use of a deep convolutional neural network. J. Clin. Microbiol. **56**, e01521-e1617 (2018). https://doi.org/10.1128/JCM.01521-17
36. Ferrara, E.: Fairness and bias in artificial intelligence: a brief survey of sources, impacts and mitigation strategies. Sci. **6**, 3 (2023). https://doi.org/10.3390/sci6010003
37. Gichoya, J.W., et al.: AI pitfalls and what not to do: mitigating bias in AI. Br. J. Radiol. **96**, 20230023 (2023). https://doi.org/10.1259/bjr.20230023
38. Roselli, D., Matthews, J., Talagala, N.: Managing bias in AI. In: Companion Proceedings of the 2019 World Wide Web Conference, pp. 539–544. Association for Computing Machinery, New York (2019). https://doi.org/10.1145/3308560.3317590
39. Xu, Z., Jain, S., Kankanhalli, M.: Hallucination is inevitable: an innate limitation of large language models http://arxiv.org/abs/2401.11817 (2024). https://doi.org/10.48550/arXiv.2401.11817
40. Ji, Z., Yu, T., Xu, Y., Lee, N., Ishii, E., Fung, P.: Towards mitigating LLM hallucination via self reflection. In: Bouamor, H., Pino, J., Bali, K. (eds.) Findings of the Association for Computational Linguistics: EMNLP 2023, pp. 1827–1843. Association for Computational Linguistics, Singapore (2023). https://doi.org/10.18653/v1/2023.findings-emnlp.123
41. Measuring and Reducing LLM Hallucination without Gold-Standard Answers via Expertise-Weighting, https://arxiv.org/html/2402.10412v1. Accessed 09 May 2024

42. Galitsky, B.A.: Truth-O-Meter: Collaborating with LLM in Fighting its Hallucinations, https://www.preprints.org/manuscript/202307.1723/v1 (2023). https://doi.org/10.20944/preprints202307.1723.v1
43. Quick Search - Public Health Image Library (PHIL). https://phil.cdc.gov/QuickSearch.aspx?key=true. Accessed 04 May 2024
44. Kimmerle, J., Timm, J., Festl-Wietek, T., Cress, U., Herrmann-Werner, A.: Medical Students' Attitudes toward AI in Medicine and their Expectations for Medical Education, https://www.medrxiv.org/content/10.1101/2023.07.19.23292877v3 (2023). https://doi.org/10.1101/2023.07.19.23292877

Taxonomy of Intelligent Attendance Systems

Rasha Hasan(✉)

Department of Information Technology, Liwa College, Abu Dhabi, UAE
rasha.hasan@lc.ac.ae, r.g.hasan@gmail.com

Abstract. Intelligent attendance systems play an essential role in enhancing human well-being within cognitive education frameworks. These systems include modern technology to facilitate attendance tracking processes, minimizing administrative burdens and maximizing instructional time. By automating attendance-related tasks, educators can allocate more resources towards personalized learning experiences addressed to individual cognitive needs. Moreover, intelligent attendance systems enforce a sense of accountability and punctuality among learners, instilling valuable time-management skills essential for academic and professional success. Beyond efficiency gains, these systems contribute to a positive learning environment by providing trust and transparency between students and educators. By optimizing attendance management, intelligent systems allow educators to focus on student development, enforcing a conducive atmosphere for cognitive growth and well-being within educational settings. In this paper, we explore intelligent attendance systems that are proposed for use in a variety of schools, universities, and other educational institutions that aim to enhance cognitive education.

Keywords: Intelligent attendance system · cognitive education · Well-being

1 Introduction

Educational institutions insist on the importance of taking attendance as it impacts students' performance as per several researches done in this context. For example, Sandberg et al. in [1] propose new research questions for the study of attendance, absenteeism, and preventive measures in international and comparative research. Keppens et al. in [2] address this issue by comparing administrative attendance data collected by schools with self-reported attendance data from the same group of students. Hazza et al. in [3] highlight the importance of class attendance in a four-year institution and that high school academic performance acts as a foundation for performance in a higher educational institute.

In modern educational settings, the issue of student attendance overhead poses a significant challenge for both educators and learners alike. Traditional

A. Basiouni and C. Frasson (Eds.): BBGI 2024, CCIS 2162, pp. 145–153, 2024.
https://doi.org/10.1007/978-3-031-65996-6_12

methods of attendance tracking often consume valuable instructional time, diverting attention from the primary objective of delivering high-quality educational content. Research by Smith and Johnson [4] underscores the negative effects of manual attendance-taking methods on instructional time, highlighting the need for more efficient alternatives. By deploying technology, educators can facilitate the attendance process, saving valuable minutes during each class session. This not only relieves educators of administrative burdens but also allows them to allocate more time and energy towards crafting engaging lectures, facilitating meaningful discussions, and providing personalized support to students.

Moreover, the integration of technology for attendance tracking holds promising implications for student well-being. According to a study conducted by Garcia et al. [5], the implementation of automated attendance systems is accompanied by a reduction in student stress levels and an enhanced sense of autonomy. By eliminating the need for manual roll calls or sign-in sheets, technology-driven attendance tracking fosters a more relaxed and inclusive learning environment, where students can focus on their academic pursuits without unjustifiable administrative distractions.

However, advancements in technology offer promising solutions to reduce this burden while simultaneously enhancing the overall learning experience. This paper provides a taxonomy of available intelligent attendance systems used in educational settings to reduce the lecture load on educators, thus enabling them to channel their efforts toward enriching the quality of instruction and fostering a conducive learning environment.

2 Taxonomy of Technological Attendance Systems

We conducted a literature review of available intelligent attendance systems, and we classified them as per the main technology used in them:

2.1 Biometrical Attendance Systems

A list of works approached the attendance system topic using bio-metrics as it is a unique trace that distinguishes attendees.

Face recognition - The face recognition approach was one bio-metric instance to be used, for example, [6] introduces an innovative approach to automatic attendance management systems by integrating real-time face detection algorithms with an existing Learning Management System (LMS). This system offers instructors a supplementary tool that automatically registers students attending lectures, utilizing machine learning algorithms to track facial changes over time. The method promises reduced time consumption compared to traditional methods while maintaining non-intrusiveness. Paradeep et al. in [7] focus on real-time video-based face recognition, acknowledging challenges such as image quality and variability in real-world conditions. The work emphasizes the need for robust face recognition algorithms to ensure accuracy in recognition systems.

Priya el al. in [8] emphasize the advantages of using face recognition for attendance management, addressing issues like fake attendance through techniques such as illumination invariant and Viola and Jones algorithm. Two works, [9,10] both propose automatic attendance management systems based on face recognition technology, highlighting their efficiency and reliability. However, they differ in their implementation details and target audience.

Fingerprint - The fingerprint as bio-metric was also used by some proposed systems, for example, [11] discusses the pivotal role of class attendance in student learning and proposes a fingerprint recognition system integrated into a portal for efficient attendance management. Tested on fifty students, the system achieved 98% accuracy, demonstrating its feasibility for large-scale deployment. Shoewu et al. in [12] address rising security concerns in Nigerian campuses, proposing a bio-metric hostel access control system to curb theft and unauthorized entry, aiming to replace manual attendance tracking methods.

2.2 Wireless-Communication-Based Attendance Systems

Among wireless communication technologies, the ones that could contribute to the attendance systems are those of short-range communication. For example, Near Field Communication, and Radio Frequency Identification.

Near Field Communication - Numerous research explored the deployment of Near Field Communication (NFC) into attendance systems. Among these, the studies by Nasir et al. [13,14] stand out for their utilization of Near-Field Communication (NFC) technology, showing its potential to revolutionize traditional attendance management practices. Nasir et al. [13] embark on a comprehensive review of existing research, aiming to enhance manual attendance processes by integrating NFC technology into the system, thereby enforcing efficiency and accuracy. Similarly, [14] introduces a cutting-edge smart attendance solution, the brainchild of technological advancements, which not only streamlines the attendance-taking process but also significantly reduces time investment and improves accuracy compared to conventional methods.

Radio Frequency Identification - Several studies have explored the application of Radio Frequency Identification (RFID) technology in attendance systems, each offering unique insights and contributions to the field. Baviskar et al. [15] present an Automatic Attendance System that deploys RFID tags, augmenting it with functionalities such as parent notifications and test marks reporting via GSM and SMS, thereby enhancing communication and accountability within educational settings. Similarly, Izang et al. [16] introduce BrasApp, an innovative mobile application that is based on RFID tags embedded in identity cards for seamless attendance tracking, extending its utility to encompass various school activities and even cafeteria management, exemplifying the multifaceted applications of RFID technology in educational environments. On a parallel trajectory,

Ohanu et al. [17] discloses an advanced RFID student monitoring system that employs passive RFID technology for classroom attendance tracking, further fortified by the integration of bio-metric thumb detection for heightened security measures, underscoring the importance of comprehensive solutions to address the evolving needs of educational institutions. In a parallel discourse, Almansor et al. [18] argue for the adoption of RFID-based attendance systems as a solution to irregular attendance concerns merging both educational institutions and workplaces, benefiting from the advantages of RFID technology in terms of its ease of use, rapidity, and enhanced security features, thus positioning it as a possible alternative to traditional attendance methods.

2.3 Smartphones Attendance Systems

Numerous of research works have explored the innovative utilization of smartphones and Short Message Service (SMS) technology to enhance attendance tracking processes, offering diverse insights and contributions to the field. For instance, Shraddha et al. [19] introduce the Mobile Phone-Based Attendance System (MPBAS), a groundbreaking solution that allows lecturers to take attendance using smartphones, thereby enhancing efficiency and providing greater student awareness of their attendance records. Similarly, Islam et al. [20] propose a comprehensive attendance management system wherein teachers use a dedicated mobile application to record attendance, calculate attendance percentages, and dispatch SMS notifications to parents, thereby facilitating real-time communication and accountability. Building upon this foundation, Idoko et al. [21] stress the ease of access and accuracy provided by attendance tracking through mobile applications, inviting the widespread adoption of such solutions to ease administrative tasks and improve overall efficiency. On the other hand, Chianga et al. [22] introduce an innovative Android-based attendance tracking system merging the capabilities of Global Positioning System (GPS) and Near-Field Communication (NFC) technologies for automated attendance recording, exemplifying the seamless integration of cutting-edge technologies. Lastly, Fatheenursyaza et al. [23] present the Student Attendance Monitoring System (SAMS), as an integrated solution supplemented with SMS notifications to inform parents about their children, thereby fostering greater parental involvement and accountability.

2.4 Blockchain Attendance Systems

The aforementioned works have not taken into consideration the security of the attendance system, whereas some other works did consider this aspect. For example, the integration of blockchain technology with various attendance management systems has emerged as a promising alternative for enhancing data security and reducing administrative burdens. Zhang et al. [24] propose a novel approach where blockchain is integrated with face recognition technology to create a tamper-proof attendance system, thereby ensuring data integrity and reducing the administrative workload associated with attendance tracking. In contrast, Balint et al. [25] advocate for the utilization of security cameras in conjunction with blockchain technology for attendance management, emphasizing the importance of implementing smart contracts to guarantee the validity of attendance data. Both studies use blockchain's role in providing secure data storage solutions, thereby mitigating concerns regarding data tampering and unauthorized access. Expanding upon this discourse, Geetha et al. [26] introduce a comprehensive web-based application that combines face recognition technology with blockchain to automate attendance tracking processes, effectively addressing issues related to administrator workload and the potential for data forgery. While Zhang et al. [24] primarily focus on the real-time marking of attendance, Balint et al. [25] and Geetha et al. [26] place greater emphasis on secure data storage mechanisms and automated monitoring functionalities. Despite the differences between the last three works, all do demonstrate blockchain's immense potential in enhancing attendance management systems' security and privacy.

2.5 Internet of Things-Based Attendance Systems

As the Internet of Things (IoT) trend started, it was adapted to serve the continuous attempts for a good attendance system. each offering unique insights and approaches to address the evolving challenges in educational environments. For example, Alotaibi et al. [27] searched about developing a robust attendance system tailored for blended learning environments at Taif University, with a primary emphasis on integrating the Internet of Things (IoT) technology and the Blackboard system to streamline attendance tracking processes and enhance data accuracy. In contrast, Banu et al. [28] tackle the issues of student attendance fraud and data manipulation by proposing an innovative IoT-based system equipped with fingerprint authentication mechanisms to ensure the integrity of attendance records and mitigate the risks associated with fraudulent activities. Additionally, Systems et al. [29] advanced in exploring the application of IoT technology in student attendance management, to improve data collection methodologies and enhance personnel efficiency, while considering nuanced factors such as student personality and psychology to optimize system performance. Meanwhile, Dania et al. [30] presents an attendance system addressed for smart classrooms, which uses Node-MCU and Finger-Spot technologies for data collection and integration with existing classroom management systems, thereby facilitating a robust and technologically advanced learning environment. While each of these works shares a common goal of enhancing attendance systems through technological innovations, they diverge in their approaches, spanning from security and fraud prevention measures to sophisticated data management strategies and integration with established educational platforms (e.g., blackboard). Collectively, these endeavors underscore the multifaceted nature of attendance system development and the diverse array of technological solutions available to address the complex challenges faced by educational institutions worldwide.

2.6 Management Attendance Systems

The aforementioned technologies result in collecting attendance data that still needs to be fed to a database and be subject to data analysis and management. A research conducted by Arvind et al. [31] centered on optimizing the management of higher education students through the implementation of a user-friendly web-based system, with a key emphasis on efficient data storage capabilities to accommodate the vast amount of student-related information. In contrast, the study conducted by Bharambe et al. [32] highlights the global concerns surrounding student attendance consistency, arguing for the adoption of computerized attendance systems to replace traditional manual methods. Expanding on this discourse, the research by Apandbharai et al. [33] spots light on the inherent challenges faced by class teachers in manually analyzing attendance data, particularly in school settings, and proposes the development of a web-based solution to address these specific needs. Furthermore, the study led by Riyanto et al. [34] shifts the focus towards employee attendance management, aiming to facilitate data collection and reporting processes within organizational settings to enhance overall efficiency. Despite the diverse contexts and requirements addressed by each study, they all stress the important role of digital solutions in attendance management, whether within educational institutions or business operations, with the goal of augmenting performance and productivity while reducing administrative burdens.

3 Conclusion

This research paper has provided a comprehensive taxonomy of the diverse intelligent approaches available for attendance tracking in educational institutions. From the integration of Near-Field Communication (NFC) and Radio Frequency Identification (RFID) technologies to the utilization of smartphones, the Internet of Things, and blockchain, the landscape of attendance management systems is characterized by innovation and ingenuity. Through an examination of various studies, it is evident that these technological solutions offer unique benefits, ranging from enhanced efficiency and accuracy to improved data security and automated monitoring. Moreover, the exploration of IoT integration, biometric authentication, and smart classroom solutions emphasize the dynamic nature of attendance tracking methodologies and their potential to transform traditional administrative processes. While each technological approach brings its own set of advantages and challenges, the overarching goal remains consistent: to optimize the attendance-taking process and facilitate the educational experience for both educators and students. By deploying these technologies, educational institutions can reduce administrative tasks, mitigate attendance fraud, and promote greater accountability and communication among stakeholders. However, it is essential to recognize that the adoption of these technologies requires careful consideration of factors such as cost, implementation complexity, and data privacy concerns. By embracing technological advancements and allowing collaboration between academia, industry, and policymakers, we can continue to enhance attendance tracking methodologies and contribute to the overall improvement of educational outcomes. In the end, the diversity of technological approaches to attendance management reflects the ever-evolving nature of education and the ongoing quest for efficiency, effectiveness, and innovation in educational institutions worldwide. In our future work, we plan to analyze the benefits and challenges of each of these systems, to easier refer the reader to an attendance system that better matches his needs.

References

1. Sandberg, S.K., Fredriksson, U.: Comparative perspectives on school attendance, absenteeism, and preventive measures in Europe and beyond, Taylor and Francis Online (2023)
2. Keppens, G., Spruyt, B., Dockx, J.: Measuring school absenteeism: administrative attendance data collected by schools differ from self-reports in systematic ways, Front. Psychol. **10**, 2623 (2019)
3. Al Hazaa, K., et al.: The effects of attendance and high school GPA on student performance in first-year undergraduate courses. Cogent Educ. **8**(1), 1956857 (2021)
4. Smith, A., Johnson, B.: Streamlining attendance tracking: leveraging technology in educational settings. J. Educ. Technol. **45**(2) (2018)
5. Garcia, M., et al.: The impact of automated attendance systems on student well-being: a comparative study. J. Educ. Psyc. **55**(4) (2020)
6. Karuppiah, A.B., Raja, R.R., Jeyalakshmi, M., Shiny, L.J., Devi, B.S.: Online attendance system. IJERT (2017)
7. Pradeep, D., Bhuvaneswari, A., Nandhini, M., Roshini Begum, A., Swetha, N.: Survey on attendance system using face recognition. In: Ranganathan, G., Bestak, R., Fernando, X. (eds.) Pervasive Computing and Social Networking, pp. 407–420. Springer, Singapore (2023). https://doi.org/10.1007/978-981-19-2840-6_32
8. Wagh, P.S., Wagh, P.S., Patil, S.R.: Attendance system based on face recognition using eigen face and PCA algorithms. In: International Conference on Green Computing and Internet of Things (ICGCIoT) (2015)
9. Bhattacharya, S., Nainala, G.S., Das, P., Routray, A.: Smart attendance monitoring system (SAMS): a face recognition based attendance system for classroom environment. In: IEEE 18th International Conference on Advanced Learning Technologies (2018)
10. Makkar, K.: Automation Attendance Systems, Technical report, Computer and Communication Engineer, Manipal University Jaipur, Jaipur, India (2023)
11. Badejo, J.A.: Integrating automated fingerprint-based attendance into a university portal system. In: International Conference on Computational Science and Computational Intelligence, pp.1016–1020 (CSCI) (2017)
12. Oluwagbemiga, O.S.: Development of a fingerprint-inspired hostel access control. AJERD **5**(2), 11–18 (2022)
13. bin Mohd Nasir, M.A.H., bin Asmuni, M.H., Salleh, N., Misra, S.: A review of student attendance system using near-field communication (NFC) technology. In: Gervasi, O., et al. (eds.) ICCSA 2015. LNCS, vol. 9158, pp. 738–749. Springer, Cham (2015). https://doi.org/10.1007/978-3-319-21410-8_56
14. Shoewu, O.O., et al.: Development of a smart attendance system using near field communication (SMAT-NFC). Global J. Eng. Technol. Adv. **12**(02), 121–139 (2022)

15. Baviskar, S.V., Dighe, D.D.: Review of RFID based attendance system. Int. J. Adv. Res. Innovative Ideas Educ. **3**(5), 116–123(2017)
16. Izang, A.A., Ajaegbu, C., Ajayi, W., Omotunde, A.A., Enike, V.O., Ifidon, B.O.: Radio frequency identification based student attendance system. Comput. Sci. Eng. **27**(02), 111–117 (2022)
17. Chibuike, O., Oluchi, U., Ogbuefi, U., Tole, S.: Implementation of a radio frequency identification and detection technology based digital class attendance system for university students. Indonesian J. Electr. Eng. Comput. Sci. **32**(11), 1206–1214 (2023)
18. Lim, T., Sim, S., Mansor, M.: RFID Attendance System. In: IEEE Symposium on Industrial Electronics Application (2009)
19. Chawhan, S.S. et al.: Mobile phone based attendance system. IOSRJCE **10**, 48–50 (2013)
20. Islam, M.M., Hasan, M.K., Billah, M.M., Uddin, M.M.: Development of smartphone-based student attendance system. In: 2017 IEEE Region 10 Humanitarian Technology Conference (R10-HTC), pp. 230–233 (2017)
21. Ugbama, J.: Tracking students attendance using a mobile based system. IJLTEMAS **9**(6) (2020)
22. Chianga, T.W.: Development and evaluation of an attendance tracking system using smartphones with GPS and NFC. Appl. Artif. Intell. **1** (2022)
23. Bakhri, F., Ekhsan, H.M., Hamid, J.N., : Students attendance monitoring system with SMS notification. JCRINN **5**(1) (2020)
24. Zhang, Q.: Attendance system based on blockchain and face recognition. In: 2022 International Conference on Smart Applications, Communications and Networking (SmartNets), pp. 1–6 (2022). IEEE
25. Balint, K.: The connection of a blockchain with students attendance register based on security cameras. In: 2021 IEEE 19th International Symposium on Intelligent Systems and Informatics (SISY), pp. 67–70 (2021)
26. Geetha, S., Kanakaprabha, S., Devipriya, A., Brindha, D., Vetrimani, E.: Implementation of a blockchain based attendance tracking system. In: 2023 International Conference on Computer Communication and Informatics (ICCCI), pp. 1–5 01 (2023). IEEE
27. Alotaibi, S.: Attendance system based on the internet of things for supporting blended learning. In: 2015 World Congress on Internet Security (WorldCIS), pp. 78–78 (2015). IEEE
28. Santoso, B.: Design of student attendance system using internet of things (IOT) technology. In: 1st UPY International Conference on Applied Science and Education, p. 012064 (2018)
29. Xun, H., Zou, B., Duan, C.: Retracted: design of the student attendance management system based on the internet of things technology. Mobile Inform. Syst. **2022**(1), 1990530 (2023)
30. Eridani, D., Widianto, E.D., Windasari, I.P., Bawono, W.B.: Internet of things based attendance system design and development in a smart classroom. Indonesian J. Electr. Eng. Comp. Sci. **23**(3) (2021)
31. Lal, A., Bhutia, C., Pradhan, B., Sharma, R., Limboo, M.: A review on web-based attendance management system. Int. J. Sci. Res. (IJSR), 2319–7064 (2018)
32. Bharambe, S., Dixit, O., Gudadhe,S.S.: Survey - student attendance management system. Int. J. Adv. Res. Innovative Ideas in Educ. (2017)

33. Apandi, S.H., Mohamed, R.:Development of attendance management system: an experience, Technical Report Faculty of Computer Systems and Software Engineering, Universiti Malaysia Pahang, 26300 Gambang. Kuantan, Pahang, Malaysia (2013)
34. Riyanto, A., Smith, I.R.: Building an employee attendance system in company. In: IOP Conference Materials Science and Engineering Series (2018)

Enhancing Education and Well-Being Through Artificial Intelligence: Opportunities and Challenges

Faiza Qasmi(✉) and Syeda Kauser Fatima

Department of General Education, Liwa College, Al Ain, Abu Dhabi, United Arab Emirates
{faiza.qasmi,syeda.fatima}@lc.ac.ae

Abstract. Artificial Intelligence (AI) is reshaping the landscapes of education and personal well-being, offering innovative solutions that promise to revolutionize traditional practices. This research paper delves into the transformative impact of AI across these critical sectors, emphasizing its capacity to customize educational experiences and bolster health monitoring and intervention. In the educational sphere, the paper examines how AI technologies such as adaptive learning systems and AI-driven analytics can personalize instruction to fit the unique learning styles and paces of individual students. By analysing interaction data and learning outcomes, AI helps educators identify student strengths and weaknesses, enabling tailored educational pathways that enhance engagement and achievement. Furthermore, the paper explores AI's role in well-being, particularly its use in mental health applications where machine learning models predict mental health crises from patterns in user data. Additionally, AI's integration into physical health apps that track and analyse user activity and physiological data highlights its role in promoting healthier lifestyle choices and preventive healthcare practices. Despite these advancements, the deployment of AI is not without challenges. The paper addresses critical concerns related to data privacy, ethical dilemmas in AI decision-making, and the potential exacerbation of social inequalities through unequal access to AI technologies. These issues underscore the need for stringent ethical guidelines and policies to govern AI use. The paper concludes with recommendations for a collaborative approach among educators, healthcare professionals, and policymakers. This approach should focus on developing inclusive AI systems that ensure equitable benefits across all societal segments, thereby maximizing the potential of AI to serve as a force for good in education and personal well-being.

Keywords: Artificial Intelligence · AI Accessibility · Ethical Considerations in AI · Mental Health Technology · Personalized Learning

1 Introduction

In recent years, the rapid advancement of artificial intelligence (AI) technologies has heralded transformative changes across numerous sectors, including education and healthcare. As AI systems become more sophisticated, their integration into daily life and

A. Basiouni and C. Frasson (Eds.): BBGI 2024, CCIS 2162, pp. 154–164, 2024.
https://doi.org/10.1007/978-3-031-65996-6_13

institutional frameworks offers promising enhancements in efficiency, personalization, and accessibility [1]. Particularly in education, AI's potential to tailor learning experiences to individual needs suggests a revolution in how educational content is delivered and consumed [2] Similarly, in the realm of well-being, AI's capabilities extend to monitoring health, providing psychological support, and managing chronic conditions with unprecedented precision [4].

The significance of education and well-being in modern society cannot be overstated. Education not only empowers individuals with knowledge and skills but also plays a crucial role in economic development and social stability [5]. Well-being, encompassing both mental and physical health, directly influences quality of life and productivity, impacting societal progress [3]. AI's role in these areas, therefore, is not just a matter of technological advancement but is deeply tied to broader social implications and the potential for substantial human betterment.

This study explores how AI technologies are currently being applied to enhance educational outcomes and individual well-being. Through the lens of recent advancements and implementations, this study seeks to understand the extent to which AI can support personalized education and health interventions, thereby contributing to more inclusive and effective environments. However, the integration of AI also poses significant ethical challenges, including concerns related to privacy, data security, and the potential widening of existing social inequalities [6]. These issues necessitate a careful and thoughtful approach to the deployment of AI technologies. Hence, while AI presents a remarkable opportunity to enhance both education and well-being, it also requires rigorous scrutiny to ensure its benefits are realized ethically and equitably. This study aims to delineate these opportunities and challenges, providing a comprehensive overview that can guide policymakers, educators, and health professionals in leveraging AI responsibly.

The potential of artificial intelligence (AI) to revolutionize both educational systems and individual well-being is substantial, promising transformations that could lead to significant improvements in learning efficiency, personalized healthcare, and overall quality of life. In education, AI technologies enable personalized learning environments that adapt to the needs of individual students, potentially reducing learning gaps and offering a more inclusive educational experience. This customization extends to well-being, where AI-powered applications provide tailored health advice, monitor mental health, and support chronic disease management with remarkable precision. However, the deployment of AI is not without its challenges. Critical issues such as data privacy, algorithmic bias, and the digital divide pose significant hurdles. These technologies rely on vast amounts of personal data, raising concerns about privacy and security. Furthermore, if not carefully managed, AI systems can perpetuate existing biases or create new forms of discrimination, potentially exacerbating inequalities in both education and health outcomes. Thus, while AI holds promising potential to enhance education and well-being significantly, it is imperative to address these challenges through stringent ethical standards, robust regulatory frameworks, and continuous monitoring to ensure fair and equitable benefits for all individuals. The scope of this research encompasses the evaluation of artificial intelligence (AI) applications within the domains of education and individual well-being, focusing on how AI can personalize and enhance learning experiences and health management. The objectives include identifying effective AI-driven strategies that improve educational outcomes and promote mental and physical health, as well as addressing the ethical, privacy, and accessibility challenges that arise with AI integration. Ultimately, the research aims to provide actionable insights and recommendations for policymakers, educators, and healthcare professionals to optimize the benefits of AI while mitigating its risks.

This research paper extensively explores the application of Artificial Intelligence (AI) within the realms of education and personal well-being, aiming to uncover and analyse the nuanced implications of AI technologies in these domains. In the educational sector, the scope includes the investigation of AI-driven adaptive learning systems, intelligent tutoring systems, and data analytics tools that personalize the learning experience by adapting to individual learner profiles and needs. The study assesses the effectiveness of these systems in improving student engagement, retention, and academic performance. Additionally, it explores AI's potential to democratize education by providing high-quality, personalized learning experiences to underserved populations. In the context of personal well-being, the research focuses on AI's role in mental health applications, such as predictive analytics used to forecast mental health episodes, and physical health applications, including AI-powered fitness apps and health monitoring devices that suggest personalized health interventions. The paper also critically examines the challenges and risks associated with AI integration in these sectors, such as privacy concerns, ethical dilemmas, and the potential for increased social inequalities due to disparate access to technology. Through this comprehensive examination, the research aims to provide

Table 1. An overview of the importance of education and well-being in modern society

Aspect	Importance in Society
Education	
Economic Growth	Education is a key driver of economic development, enhancing productivity and increasing potential for technological advancements
Social Stability	Educated populations tend to have lower rates of social issues like crime and poverty. Education promotes civic participation and social cohesion
Personal Empowerment	Provides individuals with the knowledge and skills necessary to pursue personal goals and improve their life chances
Well-being	
Workforce Productivity	Well-being directly impacts workforce productivity. Healthy individuals are more capable of contributing effectively to their professional roles
Public Health Costs	Improved well-being reduces overall public health costs by decreasing the prevalence of disease and the need for medical intervention
Quality of Life	Enhancing well-being improves overall quality of life, influencing happiness, satisfaction, and mental health

actionable insights and recommendations for effectively integrating AI in ways that are ethically sound and universally beneficial (Table 1).

2 Aims and Problem Statement

The overarching aim of this research is to critically analyse the transformative impact of AI on education and personal well-being, with a specific focus on how AI can be harnessed to personalize learning and support health. Despite AI's promising applications, some significant challenges and risks need careful consideration to ensure these technologies benefit all segments of society equitably.

2.1 Problem Statement

While AI offers revolutionary possibilities in enhancing educational outcomes and improving health monitoring and intervention, its deployment raises several critical issues. These include concerns over data privacy, ethical dilemmas around AI decision-making, and the risk of widening social inequalities due to uneven access to advanced technologies. There is a pressing need to address these challenges to prevent potential negative impacts on society.

2.2 Research Objectives

- To investigate the effectiveness of AI-powered adaptive learning systems and intelligent tutoring in personalizing education—assessing how these technologies can cater to diverse learning needs and improve engagement and educational outcomes.
- To explore AI's role in enhancing personal well-being—focusing on AI applications in mental health prediction and physical health monitoring and evaluating their effectiveness in promoting healthier lifestyles and preventive healthcare.
- To identify and analyse the ethical, privacy, and societal challenges associated with the integration of AI in education and health sectors—examining current practices, potential risks, and the impact of AI on data security and personal privacy.
- To develop recommendations for policymakers, educators, and healthcare providers—proposing strategies for the responsible deployment of AI that ensures equitable benefits and mitigates risks of exacerbating social inequalities.

3 Background

Artificial intelligence (AI) has evolved significantly since its inception in the mid-20th century when the term was first coined at the Dartmouth Conference in 1956. Initial progress focused on symbolic approaches, aiming to encode human knowledge and reasoning explicitly. By the 1980s, the advent of machine learning shifted AI research towards data-driven methods, where algorithms learn from data rather than from predefined rules. This shift was powered by increases in computational power and data availability, leading to the AI boom observed today [7].

3.1 Current Trends in AI Within the Educational Sector

In the educational sector, artificial intelligence (AI) is catalysing profound changes, notably through personalized learning, automation of administrative tasks, and the development of Intelligent Tutoring Systems (ITS). AI-powered personalized learning platforms are significantly enhancing the way educational content is tailored and delivered, adapting to individual students' learning styles and needs to optimize engagement and efficacy [2] Moreover, AI is streamlining administrative operations such as enrolment and grading, freeing educators from time-consuming tasks and allowing them to focus more on teaching and less on bureaucracy [4] Additionally, ITS are revolutionizing student interaction by providing customized tutoring and feedback, particularly beneficial in subjects requiring step-by-step learning approaches like mathematics and science, thereby replicating the benefits of one-on-one instruction [8] These AI-driven innovations are not only improving educational outcomes but also reshaping the traditional educational environment to be more efficient and responsive to student needs.

3.2 AI in Education

Artificial Intelligence (AI) is playing a transformative role in enhancing educational experiences through the implementation of personalized learning and adaptive learning platforms. These technologies are reshaping the educational landscape by making learning more responsive to the needs of individual students. AI enables personalized learning by tailoring educational content to match the unique needs, skills, and learning paces of individual students. This is achieved through the analysis of data from student activities and performance, allowing educational software to adjust content difficulty, suggest targeted resources, and even modify learning objectives to better suit the learner. This form of customization helps to optimize learning outcomes by ensuring that each student receives support tailored to their specific requirements [9].

Adaptive learning platforms utilize AI to dynamically adjust the learning paths of students as they interact with content. These systems assess student responses and performance in real-time, using this data to direct learners to appropriate resources and activities. This adaptive approach not only enhances learning efficiency but also keeps students engaged by presenting them with challenges that are neither too easy nor too difficult. The goal of these platforms is to create a fully individualized learning experience that can improve both knowledge acquisition and retention [10].

3.3 AI in Education: Improving Accessibility

Artificial Intelligence (AI) significantly enhances accessibility in education by providing tools that accommodate students with disabilities and by extending educational opportunities globally through online platforms. AI technologies such as speech-to-text and text-to-speech are pivotal in making learning accessible to students with disabilities. These tools allow students who have visual impairments or learning disabilities such as dyslexia to access educational content more easily. For example, speech-to-text software can help students with mobility or visual impairments by transcribing lectures in real-time, while text-to-speech software can aid those with reading difficulties by vocalizing written text. Additionally, AI can personalize learning accommodations, adjusting content delivery based on the specific needs of each student, thus ensuring a more inclusive learning environment [11].

AI-driven online learning platforms are breaking geographical barriers by providing high-quality education to students regardless of their location. These platforms use AI to deliver personalized learning experiences akin to those found in traditional classroom settings, including interactive tasks, automated feedback, and adaptive assessments. This global reach not only democratizes education but also allows for a diverse learning environment where students from different cultures and backgrounds can interact and learn from each other [12].

3.4 Teacher Support and Administrative Efficiency

AI technologies are increasingly utilized to grade student assignments and assessments, significantly reducing the time teachers spend on these tasks. By automating the grading process, teachers can dedicate more time to instructional activities and student interaction. AI systems can provide not only quick grading but also detailed feedback on student submissions, identifying areas of strength and weakness. This instant feedback is invaluable as it helps students learn and improve more effectively. Furthermore, AI can handle subjective responses by learning grading patterns from previously graded work, ensuring consistency and objectivity in evaluations [13].

AI is also streamlining school operations by automating administrative tasks such as student enrolment, attendance tracking, and schedule management. These systems can analyse data to optimize school logistics, predict staffing needs, and even manage resources more efficiently. For instance, AI can forecast enrolment trends, aiding schools in planning and resource allocation. This automation not only reduces the burden on administrative staff but also improves the accuracy and efficiency of school operations, allowing for better management of institutional resources [14].

3.5 AI in Well-Being: Mental Health Support

AI-powered mental health apps and chatbots are increasingly popular tools for delivering initial counselling and ongoing mental health support. These AI systems are designed to interact with users conversationally, providing immediate, confidential, and accessible support. They can guide users through therapeutic techniques such as cognitive-behavioural therapy (CBT) exercises, mindfulness practices, and stress management strategies. Additionally, these apps are equipped to monitor changes in mood or behaviour over time, helping users and their healthcare providers track well-being and adjust treatment plans accordingly. Such tools are particularly useful in providing first-line support and can act as a bridge to professional help for those reluctant to seek face-to-face counselling [15].

Predictive analytics in mental health utilizes AI to analyse various data points from an individual's behaviour and interaction patterns to identify those at risk of mental health disorders before severe symptoms manifest. This AI capability involves collecting data from a range of sources, including social media usage, mobile device activity, and even speech patterns. By analysing these data, AI models can detect subtle changes that may indicate mental health issues, such as depression or anxiety, allowing for earlier intervention and support. This proactive approach can significantly improve outcomes by ensuring that individuals receive help at an early stage [16].

4 Ethical Considerations and Challenges

The integration of artificial intelligence (AI) in sectors such as education and health care bring with it several ethical considerations and challenges that need careful attention. Privacy concerns are paramount, as AI applications often involve the processing and storing of vast amounts of sensitive personal data. Ensuring the security of this data and safeguarding the privacy of individuals is critical, as breaches can lead to significant personal and societal harm. Another major ethical issue is equity and access; AI-driven tools must be designed and deployed in ways that do not exacerbate existing inequalities. This means ensuring that these technologies are accessible across different demographics, including those who may not have advanced technological infrastructure, and adapting AI tools to cater to diverse cultural and socioeconomic backgrounds. Additionally, there is the issue of dependency and decision-making, where there is a risk that individuals or institutions may become over-reliant on AI for making crucial decisions in educational and healthcare settings. This dependency could potentially undermine human expertise and judgment, making it essential to maintain a balance where AI complements rather than replaces human decision-making processes.

5 Case Studies and Practical Applications

One notable success is the use of AI-driven personalized learning platforms in K-12 schools in the United States. These platforms adapt to individual student learning styles and paces, significantly improving engagement and academic performance. A study conducted by [17] two years of implementing these AI systems. In the realm of well-being, AI has successfully been implemented in remote patient monitoring systems. These systems use AI to analyse patient data in real time, providing healthcare professionals with actionable insights. For example, an AI system used in a pilot study in Toronto was able to predict diabetic emergencies, thereby reducing hospital admissions by 32% [19].

Despite these successes, there have been notable failures. An example is an AI-based system implemented in a European country intended to streamline healthcare appointment scheduling. The system failed to consider local dialects and cultural nuances, leading to significant misunderstandings and a public backlash [20] Another challenge was faced in an AI tutoring system intended for university students, which ended up demotivating students due to its inability to adapt to higher cognitive questions, reflecting the limitations of current AI in handling complex, nuanced academic interactions [18] (Table 2).

Table 2. Literature Review

Title	Authors	Year	Methodology	Results	Implications
AI in Personalized Learning [21]	Xu and Z	2024	Quantitative analysis of student performance data	AI adaptive systems improved student learning outcomes by 30%	Suggests that AI can significantly enhance individualized learning plans
AI for Early Detection of Neurodegenerative Diseases [22]	Philippe et al	2022	Analysis of neuroimaging data	AI accurately identified early-stage Alzheimer's in 85% of cases	Indicates AI's critical role in early diagnosis and potential treatment adjustments
AI-Enhanced Cognitive Behavioural Therapy [23]	Huang et al	2022	Mixed-methods study integrating qualitative and quantitative data	Participants reported a 40% reduction in depressive symptoms	Demonstrates AI's potential in enhancing traditional therapy methods
AI's Impact on Mental Health Monitoring [24]	Jurado et al	2020	Longitudinal study with a control group	Use of AI predictive analytics reduced emergency mental health incidents by 25%	Highlights the potential of AI in preventive mental health care
Ethical Considerations in AI Health Apps [25]	Ravì et al	2016	Qualitative interviews with stakeholders and ethicists	Identified privacy concerns and lack of transparency as main ethical issues	Calls for stricter regulations and transparency in AI applications in healthcare
Personalized AI in Online Learning Environments [20]	Mathur, P. et al	2022	Data mining of user interaction logs	Custom AI algorithms increased learner retention rates by 50%	Underlines the importance of personalized approaches in online education

(*continued*)

Table 2. (*continued*)

Title	Authors	Year	Methodology	Results	Implications
AI and Equity in Education [26]	Gray et al	2024	Case studies from diverse socioeconomic school districts	AI tools were less effective in low-income districts due to fewer resources	Indicates a need for policy to ensure equitable AI access and support in education
Predictive AI in Diabetes Management [27]	DeAngelis et al	2012	Randomized controlled trial	AI models predicted diabetic episodes with 95% accuracy	Supports the development of AI-driven proactive healthcare solutions
The Role of AI in Streamlining Education [28]	Aasim et al	2024	Survey and analysis of educational outcomes	Schools using AI reported a 20% increase in administrative efficiency	Highlights the potential for AI to optimize non-teaching aspects of education

6 Methodology and Data Analysis

The research methodology for this study involves a comprehensive investigation into the impact of artificial intelligence (AI) on education and well-being. Initially, an extensive literature review will identify current AI implementations and their outcomes. This will set the groundwork for a detailed qualitative analysis, utilizing case studies across varied educational and healthcare settings globally. These case studies will include interviews with key stakeholders such as developers, users, and administrators, as well as observational data and document reviews to explore AI's operational nuances and its effects on educational performance and well-being.

Further, the study will employ semi-structured interviews and focus groups with educators, students, healthcare professionals, and patients to capture personal experiences and perceptions. This qualitative approach will highlight the human aspects of AI interaction, providing depth that quantitative methods cannot achieve. Thematic analysis will be used to identify patterns and themes in the data, offering insights into the advantages, challenges, and ethical implications of AI in these sectors. Combining statistical analysis with qualitative narratives, this methodology aims to deliver a holistic understanding and actionable recommendations for the ethical integration of AI in education and healthcare.

7 Conclusion

The integration of artificial intelligence (AI) in the education and well-being sectors has demonstrated significant potential to enhance learning experiences and improve health outcomes. Through personalized learning platforms, AI has facilitated adaptive educational environments that cater to individual learning needs, thereby optimizing the educational process. In health care, AI's role in diagnostics, treatment personalization, and patient management has been pivotal, offering more efficient and targeted care. However, the journey of AI integration has also uncovered substantial challenges, particularly concerning privacy, equity, and dependency on technology, which necessitates cautious and thoughtful implementation.

8 Future Outlook

Looking forward, the future of AI in these sectors appears promising but requires a balanced approach. Continued advancements in AI technology are expected to further refine and expand its capabilities, potentially offering even more sophisticated tools for education and health care. However, to fully harness these advancements, it is crucial to address the ethical considerations and access disparities associated with AI technology. Ensuring robust privacy protections, equitable access, and enhancing human-AI collaboration will be essential. By addressing these challenges, AI can be more effectively integrated into societal frameworks, ultimately leading to more enriched and productive educational and health outcomes. The ongoing development and refinement of AI applications will likely continue to transform these sectors, making continuous evaluation and adaptation a necessity for future success.

References

1. Singareddy, S., et al.: Artificial intelligence and its role in the management of chronic medical conditions: a systematic review. Cureus **15**(9), e46066 (2023). https://doi.org/10.7759/cureus.46066
2. Polat, H.: Transforming education with artificial intelligence: shaping the path forward (2023)
3. Abdulmalek, S., et al.: IoT-based healthcare-monitoring system towards improving quality of life: a review (2022). https://doi.org/10.3390/healthcare10101993
4. Fountis, A., Lemonakis, C.: Artificial Intelligence (AI) in Education—Current Trends (2024). https://doi.org/10.1007/978-981-99-8976-8_18
5. Voskoglou, M.: Artificial intelligence and digital technologies in the future education (2023). https://doi.org/10.32388/07VE29
6. Siau, K., Wang, W.: Artificial Intelligence (AI) ethics: ethics of AI and ethical AI. J. Database Manag. **31**, 74–87 (2020). https://doi.org/10.4018/JDM.2020040105
7. Kaplan, A., Haenlein, M.: Siri, Siri, in my hand: Who's the fairest in the land? On the interpretations, illustrations, and implications of artificial intelligence. Business Horizons **62** (2018). https://doi.org/10.1016/j.bushor.2018.08.004
8. Al-aqbi, A., Saedi, A., Saleh, B.: The effect of the intelligent tutoring systems on the education, pp. 683–698 (2019). https://doi.org/10.36302/intel.v0i27.32

9. Costa, R., Tan, Q., Pivot, F., Zhang, X., Wang, H.: Personalized and adaptive learning: educational practice and technological impact. Texto Livre Linguagem e Tecnologia **14**, e33445 (2021). https://doi.org/10.35699/1983-3652.2021.33445
10. Taylor, D., Yeung, M., Bashet, A.Z.: Personalized and adaptive learning (2021). https://doi.org/10.1007/978-3-030-58948-6_2
11. Education, European, Weber, H., Elsner, A., Wolf, D., Rohs, M., Turner-Cmuchal, M.: Inclusive Digital Education (2022)
12. Krstić, L., Aleksić, V., Krstić, M.: Artificial intelligence in education: a review, 223–228 (2022). https://doi.org/10.46793/TIE22.223K
13. Zhao, T.: AI in educational technology (2023). https://doi.org/10.20944/preprints202311.0106.v1
14. Igbokwe, I.: Application of Artificial Intelligence (AI) in educational management. Int. J. Sci. Res. Publ. (IJSRP) **13**, 300 (2023). https://doi.org/10.29322/IJSRP.13.03.2023.p13536
15. Omarov, B., Narynov, S., Zhumanov, Z.: Artificial intelligence-enabled chatbots in mental health: a systematic review. Comput. Mater. Continua **74**, 5105–5122 (2022). https://doi.org/10.32604/cmc.2023.034655
16. Hahn, T., Nierenberg, A., Whitfield-Gabrieli, S.: Predictive analytics in mental health: applications, guidelines, challenges and perspectives. Mol. Psychiatry **22** (2016). https://doi.org/10.1038/mp.2016.201
17. Jian, M.: Personalized learning through AI. Adv. Eng. Innov. **5** (2023). https://doi.org/10.54254/2977-3903/5/2023039
18. Akinwalere, S., Ivanov, V.: Artificial intelligence in higher education: challenges and opportunities. Border Crossing **12**, 1–15 (2022). https://doi.org/10.33182/bc.v12i1.2015
19. Pulimamidi, R.: Enhancing healthcare delivery: AI applications in remote patient monitoring. Tuijin Jishu/J. Propuls. Technol. **44**, 3948–3954. https://doi.org/10.52783/tjjpt.v44.i3.2160
20. Mathur, P., et al.: Artificial intelligence in healthcare: 2021 year in review (2022). https://doi.org/10.13140/RG.2.2.25350.24645/1
21. Xu, Z.: AI in education: enhancing learning experiences and student outcomes. Appl. Comput. Eng. **51**, 104–111 (2024). https://doi.org/10.54254/2755-2721/51/20241187
22. Philippe, T.J., et al.: Digital health interventions for delivery of mental health care: systematic and comprehensive meta-review. JMIR Mental Health **9**(5), e35159 (2022). https://doi.org/10.2196/35159
23. Huang, C., Zhang, Z., Mao, B., Yao, X.: An overview of artificial intelligence ethics. IEEE Trans. Artif. Intell. **4**, 799–819 (2022). https://doi.org/10.1109/TAI.2022.3194503
24. Jurado, P., Moreno Guerrero, A., Marín-Marín, J.-A., Costa, R.: The term equity in education: a literature review with scientific mapping in web of science. Int. J. Environ. Res. Publ. Health **17**, 3526 (2020). https://doi.org/10.3390/ijerph17103526
25. Ravì, D., et al.: Deep learning for health informatics. IEEE J. Biomed. Health Inform. (2016). https://doi.org/10.1109/JBHI.2016.2636665
26. Gray, K., Yam, K.C., Zhen'an, A., Wilbanks, D., Waytz, A.: The Psychology of Robots and Artificial Intelligence (2024)
27. DeAngelis, K., Kawakyu, N.: Examining the pipeline into educational administration: an analysis of applications and job offers. Educ Admin Quart. **48**, 468–505 (2012). https://doi.org/10.1177/0013161X11436269
28. Aasim, D., et al.: 2024-xli-annual-meeting-of-the-indian-academy-of-neurosciences-and-international-conference-on-brain-chemistry-to. Ann. Neurosci. **30**, 1 (2024)

A Transformer-Based Generative AI Model in Education: Fine-Tuning BERT for Domain-Specific in Student Advising

Suha Khalil Assayed(✉), Manar Alkhatib, and Khaled Shaalan

Faculty of Engineering and Information Technology, The British University in Dubai, Dubai, UAE

sassayed@gmail.com, {manar.alkhatib,khaled.shaalan}@buid.ac.ae

Abstract. The Transformer model has inspired state-of-the-art generative NLP models such as the Bidirectional Encoder Representations from Transformers (BERT), Generative Pre-trained Transformer (GPT) and their variations models. Despite the fact that these training methods are responsible to have an effective language model, but the computational cost will be very expensive for performing any NLP tasks. Accordingly, the fine-tuning plays an essential role in improving the performance during the training process and reducing the computational cost. In this study we applied one of the pre-trained model from HuggingFace platform called a BERT-base-uncased model, which it's variant of BERT and we utilized a specific purpose dataset for high school advising. However, the data is collected from high school and universities websites as well as from educational experts. The data includes enquiries and answers about advising high school students toward their future. This transformer, takes the input as a pair from the context and the question, and the output defined with the start and end positions of the answer in the context. Accordingly, the collected dataset is converted into json file, and then we applied the PyTorch libraries for building both, training and inference models. The ROUGE metrics revealed that the model achieves a good performance in answering to the students' questions.

Keywords: Pre-trained · LLM · Transformer · BERT · GPT · Generative · Domain-Specific · NLP · Fine-Tuning · Conversational AI

1 Introduction

In 2017, the Transformer model was introduced by Vaswani et al. [1] in their paper "Attention is All You Need". It is unlikely the recurrent neural network model (RNN), it depends on self-attention mechanism, by enabling the parallel processing of all units in the input sequence without recurrent units. As each predicted output depends on the relationship between it and other elements in same sequence, this relationship can be determined by calculating attention scores for each element. This calculation is performed by comparing the query of one input to the keys of other inputs in same sequence. This comparison allows the model to determine the importance of this token when generating the output.

A. Basiouni and C. Frasson (Eds.): BBGI 2024, CCIS 2162, pp. 165–174, 2024.
https://doi.org/10.1007/978-3-031-65996-6_14

Interestingly, that the Transformer model with its attention mechanism has inspired state-of-the-art NLP models such as the Bidirectional Encoder Representations from Transformers (BERT), Generative Pre-trained Transformer (GPT) and their variations models.

Indeed, that both the GPT and BERT models follow the pre-training process and fine-tuning. The pre-training phase is an actual training of the language model, as in this phase the model learns from large corpora of text data collected from various resources including the Wikipedia articles, books, and other internet texts. For example, the GPT predicts the next token by given the previous tokens by applying the augmentation technique [2, 3]. Moreover, the BERT model computes the predictions of the masked tokens through multiple iterations with using forward and backward directions and the weights are adjusted accordingly. On the other hand, the fine-tuning process is justifying the pre-trained model to meet a specific task within a particular domain such as text classification [4], sentiment analysis [5] and question answering [6].

The main difference between BERT and GPT model, is that BERT is a multiple layers of encoders, and each encoder has a multi head self-attention mechanisms [1] and it works in both directions. Whereas, the GPT is unlike BERT model; it's a unidirectional and autoregressive language model, that uses only the decoder component of the Transformer. It generates the text from left to right, using the previous words to predict the next word. Since, the BERT is a bidirectional model that can use the left and right tokens for the predictions, accordingly it can perform well in long sequences with capturing the semantic meaning of the words by generating the contextual word embedding, as each word can have different meaning in other sentence. Henceforth, this model can work effectively based on the Masked Language Model (MLM) by teaching the model to predict the masked or the hidden tokens based on the context that surrounded the tokens from left and right. Interestingly, some tasks such as classifications and question answering, that need to extract a relevant information from the input text to generate the accurate answer or label, can perform well in such models. However, in this study we applied one of the pre-trained model from HuggingFace platform called a BERT-base-uncased model, which it's variant of BERT and we used our specific purpose dataset accordingly.

2 Related Work

Due to the high computationally cost in using the pre-trained large language model (LLM), researchers and developers are inspired to work on fine tuning the pre-trained models to develop state-of-the-art NLP application and tasks from different industries. For example, Aparicio et al. [7] used a fine-tuned model called BioFinBERT to perform financial sentiment analysis by using a financial textual database. Furthermore, the health and medical industries as well are given more attention by researchers and developers in building applications by fine-tuning large language models [8, 9].

On the other side, some authors used the fine-tuning models in educational fields from different perspectives. For example, Sung et al. [10] performed a fine-tuning a pre-trained self-attention language model, using the Bidirectional Encoder Representations from Transformers (BERT) in applying it to short answer grading. Interestingly, that

Beheitt & Hmida [11] trained language model GPT-2 to generate Arabic poems. Despite the importance role of student's guidance in high schools, but limited studies are adopted the pre-trained models to high school students particularly. To bridge this gap, in this study we fine-tuned the BERT model by using a specialized dataset focused on student guidance domain.

3 Bidirectional Encoder Representations from Transformers (BERT) Model

BERT [1] is the first language model that adopted the self-attention mechanism by using the bidirectional Transformers and compares the weights of input sequences all together and it's trained by Google. However, BERT is effective in understanding languages as well as in interpreting sentences [12], as it considers both directions (left to right and right to left) in capturing the context of the tokens within a given sentence.

3.1 BERT Architecture

The original Transformer model consists of both components the encoder and the decoder. The encoder part is responsible in understanding the contexts of the words in the inputs as well as the semantic in the languages. Whereas the decoder is generating the output based on the NLP tasks such as text classifications or question answering. However, the BERT has only the encoder part of the Transformer architecture. It consists multiple layers of encoders, and each encoder has a multi head self-attention mechanisms.

The architecture of the BERT depends on the model as there are two versions of the BERT. The BERT Base has 12 layers of encoders and 110 million parameters and BERT- Large has 24 layers of encoders with 340 million of parameters. BERT accepts the input sequences tokens in an embedding representation in three kinds of embeddings. The first is *position embeddings*, which use it to define the position of tokens in the sentence, in order to overcome the limitation in the Transformer, because it's unlike

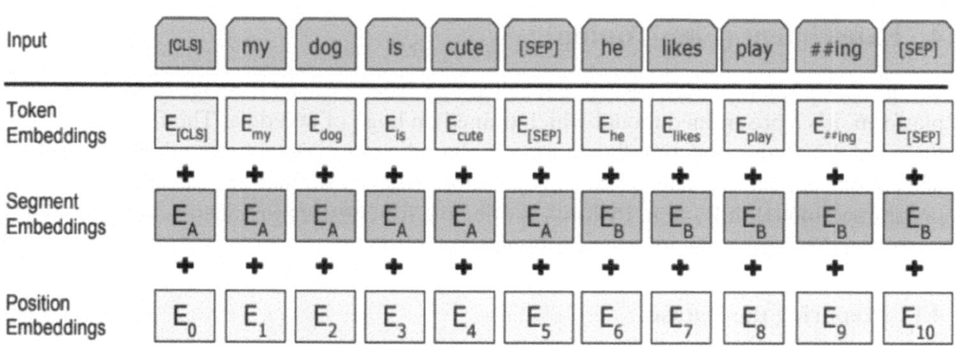

Fig. 1. The three embeddings input in BERT model. Note. From "Learning text embeddings on virus sequences for candidate drug discovery by LANZILLOTTA 2019"

the RNN models which tokens are processed in sequence [13]. The second is *segment embeddings,* which is responsible to distinguish between the sentences, since BERT receives multiple sentences at the same time, which make it hard to recognize the order between them. Finally, the *token embedding*, which is a numeric representation of each token based on Bert token vocabulary. Figure 1 illustrates the three embeddings input.

3.2 Fine-Tuning process

As we mentioned earlier that BERT is one of the deep neural network with multiple layers of encoders, which training a model with millions of parameters. However, BERT trains the data by using one of the below options:

- Masked Language Modeling: It's round 15% of the tokens are masked randomly in order to prevent the model from memorizing the masked tokens, the goal is predicting the blanks in the sentence [14]. For example, the sentence: IELTS score is—test for applying to UK universities. The blank can be predicted by using computing the probability score over the entire vocabulary list.
- Next Sentence Prediction (NSP): Training the model to predict the relationship between sentences [15] whether two sentences are related together or not?

Despite the fact that these training methods are responsible to have an effective language model, but the computational cost will be very expensive for performing any NLP tasks. Accordingly, the fine-tuning plays an essential role in improving the performance during the training process and reducing the computational cost. The process of fine-tuning in question answering tasks works by having a question and a context that includes the answer of the question. Both the context segments and the question are tokenized. However, the first token is usually used as a special token <CLS> and the sequences are separated with another special token <SEP>. Then the BERT determines the correct answer from the context by identifying the first and the end tokens of the answer.

Moreover, the fine-tuning involves as well hyperparameters tuning such as learning rate, batch size as well as optimization algorithm for improving the performance of the task.

4 Experiment (Fine-Tuning)

We used a variant of BERT base model called bert-base-uncased from the Hugging Face platform, it's a pre-trained model which trained on huge of text data. The fine-tuning in this model includes updating the parameters based on our domain of students advising dataset. We used various functions and operations from PyTorch libraries to fine-tune the pre-trained model in Python. PyTorch is effective for constructing deep neural network models and is applicable in many different areas [16].

4.1 Preparing the Dataset

The dataset in this study includes 5,000 question-answer pairs collected from high schools and universities websites as well as from educational experts. The data is converted into JSON file using the below Python library json.

import json
csv_to_json (csv_file, json_file)

4.2 Preprocessing the Data

This process includes different tasks, including the tokenization for both the contexts and the questions, besides of using the special tokens < CLS> & < SEP>. The <CLS> is a (classification token) used to identify the beginning of the input token before it's fed into the model. Whereas the <SEP> is used for separating the texts.

On the other hand, padding process is part in preprocessing the data as well, which can make all sequences in the same size. The model uses the attention mask to identify the actual tokens from the padding token by using a binary indicator (0, 1).

4.3 Training the Model

The bert-base-uncased is loaded into the system from the Hugging Face [17] platform using the Transformers library as follows:

from transformers import BertForQuestionAnswering, BertTokenizer

The "BertForQuestionAnswering" takes the input as a pair from the context and the question, and the output defined with the start and end positions of the answer in the context.

Then the training parameters are defining with Adam optimizer for updating the parameters during the training, with assigning the (0.00005) to the learning rate. The data is divided into six batches within 2 epochs only. This training took approximately 7 h to be completed within each epoch, although, the training model was executed using an Intel Core i7-1065G7 processor and 16.0 GB of the RAM.

The below Table 1 displays the performance of the training process in terms of calculating the loss score.

Table 1. The loss score during fine-tuning

Processor: Intel Core i7-1065G7 RAM: 16 GB	Epochs	Loss score	Time
	Epoch 1/2	Average Loss: 5.9181	8 h
	Epoch 2/2	Average Loss: 5.9151	7 h

4.4 Inference Model

The inference model is unlike the training model; this model generates responses for new data that which was not part of the training dataset. In this study, we utilized the PyTorch for fine-tuning the re-trained model "bert-base-uncased" as well the inference model. Since, PyTorch includes effective libraries for building and fine-tuning the neural network models effectively [16].

However, during the inference model, the input data including both the context and the questions are tokenized as depicted in the below code. Then, the model predicts the probability of the answer span which includes the answer in the sentence by determining the start and the end position of the span. However, the below code is used for implementing this process:

```
inputs = tokenizer.encode_plus(question, context, return_tensors="pt")
input_ids = inputs["input_ids"]
attention_mask = inputs["attention_mask"]
start_index = torch.argmax(start_logits, dim=1).item()
end_index = torch.argmax(end_logits, dim=1).item()
answer_tokens = input_ids[0][start_index : end_index + 1]
answer = tokenizer.decode(answer_tokens)
```

5 Results and Discussion

The proposed model is tested with using ten unseen questions that was not used during the training phase as shown in Table 2. The input data for the BERT model for question answering tasks are included both the context and the question. However, the context is represented by the paragraph or the sentence that has the answer that will be extracted. The below is an example of testing the model.

```
context = "Universities in the UAE have initiated reductions on tuition fees for the upcoming academic year. These reductions extend up to 50% "
question = "I need a discount in tuition in UAE"
answer = predict_answer(model, tokenizer, context, question)
print ("Answer:", answer)
```

However, the average of metrics scores for the (10) generated answers in all models are calculated. The results show that the average ROUGE-L scores are 56%, 50%, and 51% for precision, recall and F1-score, respectively, as depicted in Table 3.

Nevertheless, the ROUGE performance metrics has some limitations in comparing the answers between the reference text and the chatbot. As human references might provide different perspectives comparing with those generated by the chatbot, even though both answers are correct.

Interestingly, the ROUGE metrics revealed that the model achieves a good performance in answering to the questions, specifically in terms of understanding the semantics of the words. This achievement is due to the embedding representations that BERT accepts during the input process. However, applying the BERT model depends on the tasks [18], since some tasks might be easier and more flexible to use the sequential model rather than Transformer architecture.

Table 2. Evaluating the model with new unseen of students enquiries.

Chatbot- BERT (bert-base-uncased)				
Student's enquiry		Precision	Recall	F1
1.	what are the steps apply to New york university	to apply to nyu use first the commonapp and be sure to review your personalized list with a counselor and your family or an adult you trust remember to work on your college essay, supplemental		
		0.22	0.22	0.22
2.	I need discount in tuition in UAE	universities in the uae have initiated reductions on tuition fees for the upcoming		
		0.46	0.5	0.48
3.	What is the common app	common application is a widely accepted application platform the common application		
		0.45	0.33	0.38
4.	What is the difference between AP and IB	the dp core, comprising theory of knowledge (tok), creativity, activity, service (cas) and the extended essay. it is is a two - years program - high school curriculum for students aged 16 to 19 (grade 11 & 12		
		0.28	0.36	0.32
5.	What are the demanded majors in the market	emphasis on environmental and ecological economics. data scientists and ai professionals are in high demand across various industries, including healthcare, finance, tech companies		

(*continued*)

Table 2. (*continued*)

		0.39	0.6	0.47
6.	Should I take IELT test or TOEFL	ielts or toefl scores		
		0.75	0.42	0.54
7.	Where can I study bachelor medicine degree in UAE	you can study medicine in united arab emirates university		
		0.88	0.72	0.79
8.	How many universities should I apply to	apply to a mix of safety, match, and reach schools		
		0.7	0.7	0.7
9.	Why should I take AP exam	whereas the ap exams used for college creditit is is a two - years		
		0.46	0.35	0.4
10.	What is the MCAT test	mcat is the medical college admission test you should take it after completing your prerequisite courses. use mcat prep		
		0.46	0.35	0.4

Table 3. The average score of the ROUGE-L in fine-tuning the Bert model

ROUGE-L metric		
Precision	Recall	F1-score
0.56	0.5	0.51

6 Conclusion

This study discusses fine-tuning the pre-trained model BERT called "bert-base-uncased", by using a question answering transformer and our collected dataset. We used the Hugging Face platform to upload the transformer "BertForQuestionAnswering". This transformer, takes the input as a pair from the context and the question, and the output defined with the start and end positions of the answer in the context. Accordingly, the high school collected dataset is converted into json file, and then we applied the PyTorch libraries for building both, training and inference models.

Nevertheless, the BERT model is expected to receive a context text in the inference mode in each running time in order to generate the answer. However, applying the BERT model depends on the tasks, since some tasks might be easier and more flexible to use a machine learning model [19, 20] rather than Transformer architecture [21].

References

1. Vaswani, A., et al.: Attention is all you need. Adv. Neural Inf. Process. Syst. **30** (2017)
2. Shorten, C., Khoshgoftaar, T.M., Furht, B.: Text data augmentation for deep learning. J. Big Data **8**(1), 101 (2021)
3. Gillioz, A., Casas, J., Mugellini, E., Abou Khaled, O.: Overview of the transformer-based models for NLP tasks. In: 2020 15th Conference on Computer Science and Information Systems (FedCSIS), pp. 179–183. IEEE, September 2020
4. Yu, S., Su, J., Luo, D.: Improving BERT-based text classification with auxiliary sentence and domain knowledge. IEEE Access **7**, 176600–176612 (2019)
5. Truong, T.L., Le, H.L., Le-Dang, T.P.: Sentiment analysis implementing BERT-based pre-trained language model for Vietnamese. In: 2020 7th NAFOSTED Conference on Information and Computer Science (NICS), pp. 362–367. IEEE, November 2020
6. Ngai, H., Park, Y., Chen, J., Parsapoor, M.: Transformer-based models for question answering on COVID19. arXiv preprint arXiv:2101.11432 (2021)
7. Aparicio, V., Gordon, D., Huayamares, S.G., Luo, Y.: BioFinBERT: finetuning large language models (LLMs) to analyze sentiment of press releases and financial text around inflection points of biotech stocks. arXiv preprint arXiv:2401.11011 (2024)
8. Xie, K., et al.: Generalization of finetuned transformer language models to new clinical contexts. JAMIA Open **6**(3), ooad070 (2023)
9. Yang, F., Wang, X., Ma, H., Li, J.: Transformers-sklearn: a toolkit for medical language understanding with transformer-based models. BMC Med. Inform. Decis. Making **21**(2), 1–8 (2021)
10. Sung, C., Dhamecha, T.I., Mukhi, N.: Improving short answer grading using transformer-based pre-training. In: Isotani, S., Millán, E., Ogan, A., Hastings, P., McLaren, B., Luckin, R. (eds.) AIED 2019, Part I. LNCS (LNAI), vol. 11625, pp. 469–481. Springer, Cham (2019). https://doi.org/10.1007/978-3-030-23204-7_39
11. Beheitt, M.E.G., Hmida, M.B.H.: Automatic Arabic poem generation with GPT-2. In: ICAART, no. 2, pp. 366–374 (2022)
12. Sur, C.: RBN: enhancement in language attribute prediction using global representation of natural language transfer learning technology like Google BERT. SN Appl. Sci. **2**(1), 22 (2020)
13. Lanzillotta, S.: Learning text embeddings on virus sequences for candidate drug discovery (2020)
14. Song, K., Tan, X., Qin, T., Lu, J., Liu, T.Y.: MPNet: masked and permuted pre-training for language understanding. Adv. Neural Inf. Process. Syst. **33**, 16857–16867 (2020)
15. Shi, W., Demberg, V.: Next sentence prediction helps implicit discourse relation classification within and across domains. In: Proceedings of the 2019 Conference on Empirical Methods in Natural Language Processing and the 9th International Joint Conference on Natural Language Processing (EMNLP-IJCNLP), pp. 5790–5796, November 2019
16. Imambi, S., Prakash, K.B., Kanagachidambaresan, G.R.: PyTorch. In: Kolla Bhanu Prakash, G.R., Kanagachidambaresan (eds.) Programming with TensorFlow: Solution for Edge Computing Applications, pp. 87–104. Springer, Cham (2021). https://doi.org/10.1007/978-3-030-57077-4

17. Hugging Face: Hugging Face Transformers Documentation (n.d.). https://huggingface.co/docs/transformers/en/model_doc/bert
18. Assayed, S.K., Alkhatib, M., Shaalan, K.: A generative AI Chatbot in high school advising: a qualitative analysis of domain-specific Chatbot and ChatGPT (2023)
19. Assayed, S.K., Alkhatib, M., Shaalan, K.: Advising chatbot for high school in smart cities. In: 2023 8th International Conference on Smart and Sustainable Technologies (SpliTech), pp. 1–6. IEEE, June 2023
20. Assayed, S.K., Alkhatib, M., Shaalan, K.: Enhancing student services: machine learning chatbot intent recognition for high school inquiries. In: Al Marri, K., Mir, F.A., David, S.A., Al-Emran, M. (eds.) BUiD Doctoral Research Conference 2023: Multidisciplinary Studies. LNCS, vol. 473, pp. 243–254. Springer, Cham (2024). https://doi.org/10.1007/978-3-031-56121-4_24
21. He, J., et al.: TransFG: a transformer architecture for fine-grained recognition. In: Proceedings of the AAAI Conference on Artificial Intelligence, vol. 36, no. 1, pp. 852–860 (2022)

A Statistical Analysis to Investigate the Factors Affecting Generative AI Use in Education and Its Impacts on Social Sustainability Using SPSS

Mohammad Binhammad(✉) and Khaled Shaalan

Department of Computer Science, British University Dubai, Dubai, United Arab Emirates
m.hassan.y1994@gmail.com, khaled.shaalan@buid.ac.ae

Abstract. The emergence of generative AI, as a relatively new technological advancement in education, presents new opportunities, but its integration and effects on society remain uncertain. This research focuses on the key factors that affect generative AI in students' learning integration and its impact on social sustainability. The central problem is the lack of understanding regarding integrating generative AI in education and its broader social sustainability implications. It further employs online surveys targeting higher education students to gather quantitative data. The survey is designed to be composed of closed-ended questions that will focus on the factors of the IDT, SCT, and SDT theories as presented in the theoretical model. This will be done using descriptive analysis, internal consistency reliability, exploratory factor analysis, and multiple regression analysis using SPSS to find out the factors that define the use and adoption of generative AI and its effects on other social sustainability factors like education, diversity, and readiness. The study therefore assists in filling gaps within the literature on AI in education and is beneficial for students, policymakers, educators, and academics. It will highlight and shed light on policies and standards in the use of generative AI in education for the betterment of society. Besides, as the concept of generative AI is advancing in the future, this work will help to form the basis for further research and applications in the field of education while emphasizing the values of technological, pedagogical, and social responsibility.

Keywords: Generative AI · education · social sustainability · technology adoption · student engagement · educational equity

1 Introduction

The use of generative AI in learning is gradually being adopted because of the possibility of designing unique learning approaches and teaching methodologies (Chan & Hu, 2023). The use of generative AI in delivering content can help in such ways that learner needs can be met by generating content according to their learning style and foster social sustainability factors such as equity and community welfare, in the long run (Kioupi & Voulvoulis, 2019). However, some limitations such as the technicality of the intervention, training issues, ethical issues, and the issue of the digital divide cannot be overlooked

A. Basiouni and C. Frasson (Eds.): BBGI 2024, CCIS 2162, pp. 175–186, 2024.
https://doi.org/10.1007/978-3-031-65996-6_15

and must be attended to for proper implementation of the intervention (Michel-Villarreal et al., 2023). Furthermore, policymakers and educators will benefit from this research in understanding how to apply generative AI in education (Bahroun et al., 2023) to advance equity and education.

2 Problem Statement

As generative AI improves, schooling may suffer (Kshetri, 2024). Generative AI may change technical, instructional, and learning situations. This study focuses on adoption, justice, worker preparation, and societal values. This research optimizes the benefits and drawbacks of utilizing generative AI, student performance, and ethical and societal impacts. It further examines how generative AI influences student learning, social participation, and satisfaction using closed-ended surveys and SPSS. Generative AI adoption will be studied using Innovation Diffusion Theory's factors such as benefit, compatibility, and complexity. Additionally, based on learning from others, predicted consequences, and competency, SCT will evaluate generative AI. Self-determination theory, on the other hand, suggests that generative AI can motivate humans to achieve their positive psychological demands for autonomy, competence, and relatedness. To address these challenges, this research employs the following research questions:

1. What factors influence the adoption of generative AI in higher education?
2. How does generative AI integration impact student engagement and performance in courses?
3. What are the social sustainability implications of generative AI use in education?

3 Research Aim and Objectives

3.1 Aim

To explore the factors influencing generative AI adoption in higher education, its impact on student engagement and performance, and the social sustainability implications of generative AI use in education.

3.2 Objectives

1. Identify key factors influencing generative AI adoption in higher education through surveys for statistical insights.
2. Assess the impact of generative AI integration on student engagement and performance using pre- and post-test evaluations.
3. Investigate social sustainability implications by analyzing access to educational resources and inclusivity measures through SPSS-based quantitative analysis.

3.3 Research Hypotheses

1. Technological, pedagogical, and social aspects influence education's acceptance and deployment of generative AI.
2. Generative AI can personalize and adapt learning to learners' needs and skills, improving educational access, equity, and inclusion.
3. To integrate generative AI with social justice, fairness, and sustainability in education, stakeholders, especially marginalized and underprivileged groups, must participate in AI tool creation, deployment, and assessment.

4 Research Significance and Scope

This research may help to make people in general and students, in particular, aware of generative AI in education and its social implications. It covers essential areas, for instance, the factors that influence adoption in higher learning institutions, to enhance educational practices and for the development of evidence-based policies for educators and policymakers. Online questionnaires also assess social sustainability in learning and employment preparedness of higher learning institute students. The application of quantitative research methodology involving online surveys and SPSS analysis offers a broad perspective of education and policy choices.

5 Literature Review

Adaptive and transformative AI advances learning and academic achievement and reduces the achievement gap (Shukla, 2023). This literature review assesses its integration into learning processes and its impact on learners; it also identifies areas for future research (Paré & Kitsiou, 2017). Thus, the integration of existing literature is a helpful guide for teachers who would like to apply generative AI to their teaching and promote long-term social education for students (Langran et al., Langran et al., 2024). Focusing on expected outcomes, the study outlines the directions of the study regarding the themes listed in Table 1.

Specifically, generative AI like GANs, VAEs, and the transformer model has made it possible to develop individualized content for teaching, learning, and assessment in the form of textbooks, assignments, and feedback (ElSayary, 2024). This technology creates evaluation question banks on its own and adapts the speed of learning depending on the performance and engagement of a student (Lipton & Steinhardt, 2019). As for the early systems, they had no computational power and data to work with but modern developments in deep learning have boosted the generative AI education (Ruiz-Rojas et al., 2023). It provides multilevel teaching, enhances reading and writing abilities, and provides gaming and learning assistance in higher-level teaching (Rodak, 2023).

Table 1. Expected Outcomes and Research Hypothesis

Expected Outcomes	Hypothesis
• Development of comprehensive frameworks integrating technological, pedagogical, and social aspects to facilitate generative AI adoption in education • Development of reliable and scalable generative AI systems in education, promoting long-term sustainability	Hypothesis 1: Technological, pedagogical, and social aspects influence education's acceptance and deployment of generative AI
• Enhanced educational access, equity, and inclusion through personalized learning facilitated by generative AI • Reduction of algorithmic bias and prejudice in AI-generated educational content, ensuring fairness and inclusivity • Promotion of critical thinking, creativity, and social responsibility through generative AI in education	Hypothesis 2: Generative AI can personalize and adapt learning to learners' needs and skills, improving educational access, equity, and inclusion
• Increased involvement of marginalized and underprivileged groups in the creation, deployment, and assessment of AI tools in education • Mitigation of financial inequality, teacher shortages, and structural inadequacies hindering social sustainability in learning	Hypothesis 3: To integrate generative AI with social justice, fairness, and sustainability in education, stakeholders, especially marginalized and underprivileged groups, must participate in AI tool creation, deployment, and assessment

5.1 Theoretical Underpinnings: Factors Influencing Technology Adoption in Education

IDT, SCT, and SDT make it possible to explain the use of educational technology and generative AI in the teaching and learning process. The Acceptance of Innovation in IDT is determined by innovation, communication, and social systems. SCT focuses on both social and personal learning that is brought out by observational learning and social norms. Self-Determination Theory (SDT) postulates autonomy, competence, and relatedness. SCT focuses on social requirements and standards, whereas SDT focuses on inherent motivation as a result of psychological requirements. IDT is the focus of social system innovation and diffusion.

It is therefore a function of technological, pedagogical, and societal factors that define the educational adoption of generative AI. AI adoption and implementation entail credible, expansible AI systems, structures, and assets (Bahroun et al., 2023). To enable generative AI to complement teaching, curriculum, and assessment, Kong and Yang (2024) pointed out that these four concepts must be adapted. Stakeholder engagement, ethics, bias, diversity and inclusion, and accessibility are crucial to ensuring that generative AI is used fairly and ethically in educational settings (Ferrara, 2023). This pedagogical framework as illustrated in Fig. 1, is centered on aspects of how generative AI can be adopted in the learning environment, such as; foundational theory, curriculum enactment, engagement, evaluation, differentiation, student voice, ethics, and metacognition.

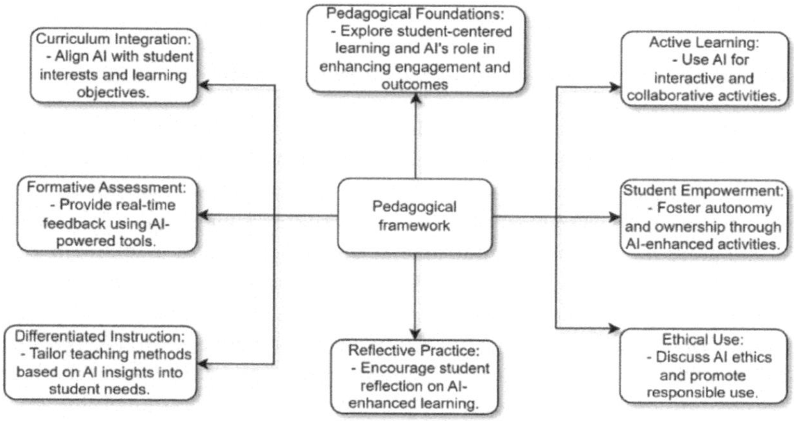

Fig. 1. Pedagogical Framework

5.2 Impact of Generative AI on Educational Outcomes

Incorporating generative AI in education can improve learning outcomes and skills, but the implementation of the technology must be done effectively, efficiently, and with proper evaluation (Kshetri, 2024). In particular, when learning is personalized according to one's interests, learning styles, and abilities, it enhances their level of engagement (Kong & Yang, 2024). Adaptability in material, pacing, and difficulty levels promotes learning, particularly evident in mathematics courses where low-achieving students show increased engagement and perseverance (Kong & Yang, 2024). Additionally, targeted feedback generated by generative AI aids student improvement by identifying strengths and weaknesses (McDonald et al., 2024). Compared to traditional evaluation methods, generative AI-based writing assistance leads to higher essay quality and coherence among university students (Ghimire, 2024). Moreover, generative AI fosters creativity, critical thinking, and problem-solving through varied and challenging learning experiences, as demonstrated in computer science courses (Ghimire, 2024).

5.3 Social Sustainability and Education

Education is essential for sustainable development, promoting social justice and inclusion (Gupta & Vegelin, 2016). It provides the knowledge and skills needed for fulfilling lives and addressing societal challenges. Socially sustainable education emphasizes equality, lifelong learning, and addressing barriers to education (Rieckmann, 2018). Equal opportunities in education are crucial for all children, including those from marginalized backgrounds (Egalite, 2016). Lifelong learning is vital for adapting to changes in the labor market and society. Technology, like generative AI, enhances access to learning and promotes equity (Alasadi & Baiz, 2023). Generative AI systems can customize learning and help individuals discover lifelong learning opportunities that match their interests and career goals.

5.4 Integration of Generative AI and Social Sustainability

For social sustainability, generative AI in education brings potential and problems. Learning techniques, accessibility, equity, and inclusion improve for students with impairments and academic struggles. It also recommends personalized courses and materials and tailors models to career goals to promote ongoing learning (Zhang et al., 2021). Nonetheless, bias and prejudice in the algorithm and AI-created content or assessment are likely to reproduce social injustice. Generative AI may also bring about the normalization of learning without regard to cultures (Anis, 2023). Bias mitigation, accountability, and stakeholder involvement in AI design and implementation are essential to solving these issues (Ferrara, 2023). AI in education should promote critical thinking, creativity, and social responsibility while tackling structural hurdles to social sustainability (Bahroun et al., 2023).

5.5 Literature Gaps

Current research on generative AI and learning has identified limitations and gaps, highlighting the need for more empirical and theoretical studies on its application in education and its sustainability implications. Table 2 provides a clear overview of how each research objective directly addresses specific literature gaps:

Table 2. Research Objectives and Research Gaps.

Literature Gap	Research Objective
Lack of comprehensive frameworks for addressing the multifaceted nature of generative AI adoption in education and limited studies on adopting generative AI in educational institutions, policies, and practices with comprehensive quantitative approaches	Objective 1: Identify key factors influencing generative AI adoption in higher education through surveys for statistical insights
Uncertainty regarding the long-term scalability of generative AI in education and social sustainability	Objective 2: Assess the impact of generative AI integration on student engagement and performance using pre- and post-test evaluations
Sparse literature on generative AI education experiences of disadvantaged and impoverished groups	Objective 3: Investigate social sustainability implications by analyzing access to educational resources and inclusivity measures

The literature on generative AI adoption in education has several shortcomings. First, adoption frameworks are lacking in addressing the many elements that affect it (Ivanov et al., 2024). In addition, research rarely uses quantitative methods to implement generative AI in educational institutions and policy. The primary research objective is to uncover critical adoption determinants through surveys for statistical insights. Second, generative AI in education's long-term scalability and societal sustainability are unknown. In learning situations and with varied learners, stability and generalization have not been well assessed. The second research aims to examine how generative AI integration affects student engagement and performance utilizing pre-and post-tests. Finally, there is little research on disadvantaged populations' generative AI education (Morris, 2021). Many studies ignore low-income, minority, and disadvantaged pupils in favor of university or K-12 teachers. The third study objective looks at social sustainability implications to ensure inclusivity and access to educational resources, especially for those affected by social injustice in education. (Bail, 2024).

6 Methodology

This study employs an exploratory and normative research approach to assess generative AI's potential in education and guide its responsible development. Exploratory analysis identifies trends and uncertainties in generative AI integration, while normative assessment evaluates its alignment with social justice, equity, and sustainability principles. Drawing on theories like IDT, SCT, and SDT, the study examines their relevance to generative AI adoption. The study aims to provide empirical evidence supporting theoretical propositions on generative AI adoption and its impact on education.

6.1 Theoretical Framework

This research takes into account more creative attributes such as relative advantage and compatibility, channels such as professional networks, and time including the stages of adoption. SCT's core concepts include observational learning, social norms, self-efficacy, and result expectations. SDT also fosters behavioral self-regulation by motivation, personality, autonomy, competence, and relatedness. Figure 2 uses Innovation Diffusion Theory (IDT), Social Cognitive Theory (SCT), and Self-Determination Theory (SDT) to propose the adoption process of generative AI in education. These theories help the research to grasp generative AI adoption and impact, enhancing educational efforts. Hypothesis 1 posits that IDT, SCT & SDT play a role in the acceptance of generative AI in education. It has the elements of advantages and compatibility, SCT self-efficacy observational learning, and SDT autonomy. Hypothesis two relates to the extent to which generative AI might transform learning with IDT time, SCT result expectancies, and SDT competence. Hypothesis 3 acknowledges stakeholder engagement with a focus on the disadvantaged in generative AI, social justice, and sustainability of education. This includes the establishment of an inclusive workplace, social justice, and business relations with AI communities.

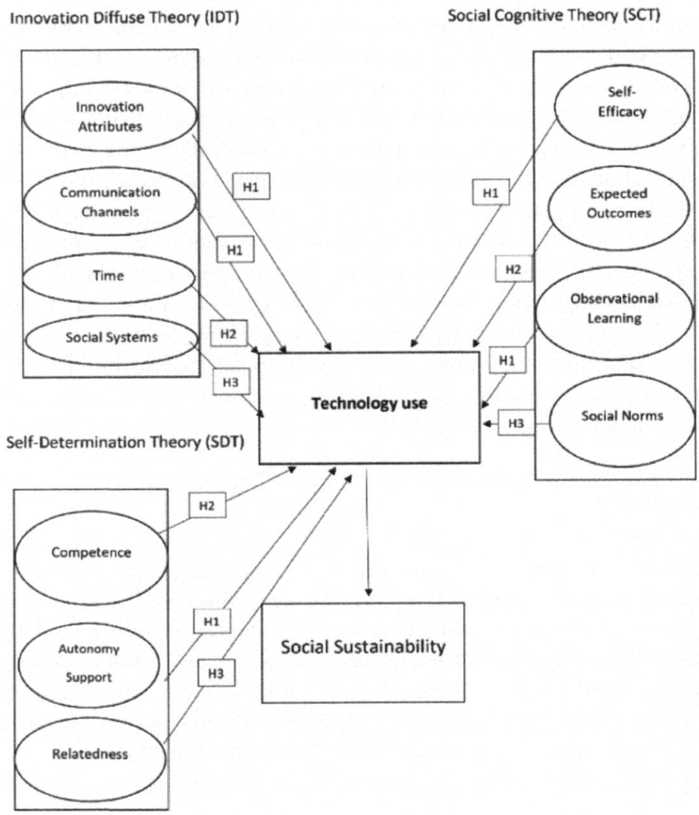

Fig. 2. Theoretical Framework

6.2 Data Collection and Analysis:

A comprehensive literature search and review was done to discover relevant research articles and synthesise important findings on generative AI in education and social sustainability. Google Scholar, IEEE Xplore, ACM Digital Library, ScienceDirect, and JSTOR were used. Keywords were "generative AI," "education," "social sustainability," "adoption factors," "student engagement," "performance," "equity," & "inclusion." The selected publications' whole texts were evaluated for methodological quality, research relevance, and field contribution. Key findings, methodologies, and theoretical frameworks were extracted and synthesised to understand current knowledge and indicate research gaps. The literature review selected, significant theories to form the research hypotheses and theoretical framework and guided research design, data collection, and analysis and helped contextualise the findings. Based on the theoretical paradigm with hypothesis, the quantitative analysis is conducted with the help of SPSS and a self-administered questionnaire designed for UAE university students. Descriptive statistics shall comprise frequency distribution, measure of central tendency, reliability using Cronbach's alpha, and exploratory factor analysis for concept validity. Hypothesis testing and relationship analysis are conducted with the help of t-tests, ANOVA, and regression analysis. Due to the sensitive nature of the study, several ethical considerations will be observed in the course of the research to protect the participants' rights, privacy, and anonymity. The participants will be asked to provide consent to participate in the study and all data collected will be anonymous and stored in a secure place.

7 Discussion

Data analysis has theoretical, practical, and policy implications and encompasses IDT-influenced adoption, SCT-influenced adoption, and SDT-influenced adoption. When addressing the issue of hypothesis gaps in research, generative AI also promotes the adaptability of content and equal access to education. Adoption, personalization, and integration improve innovation, self-efficacy, and autonomy for every theory, with social justice and fairness incorporated into AI. These ideas are backed by data, which would help provide a comprehensive view of AI implementation in education. Based on the analysis, AI equity, inclusiveness, and sustainability can be enhanced through IDT, SCT, and SDT. Hypothesis 1 examines the relationships between IDT innovation, communication, SCT and SDT self-efficacy, observational learning, and autonomy drive AI acceptance. Thus, Hypothesis 2 is that IDT time, SCT outcome expectancies, and SDT competence will impact customized learning. In Hypothesis 3, IDT's social structure incorporates disadvantaged groups, SCT's social norms are related to disadvantaged groups, and SDT's relatedness is concerned with disadvantaged groups. This integration addresses technological, pedagogical, and social aspects of AI adoption to enhance the fairness and diversity of education. Table 3 shows the hypotheses with their theoretical frameworks adopted: IDT, SCT, and SDT, as well as key aspects of each theory.

Table 3. Theoretical Framework and Key Factors

Hypothesis	Theoretical Framework	Key Factors
Technological, pedagogical, and social aspects influence education's acceptance and deployment of generative AI	IDT, SCT, SDT	Innovation Attributes, Communication Channels, Self-Efficacy, Observational Learning, Autonomy
Generative AI can personalize and adapt learning to learners' needs and skills, improving educational access, equity, and inclusion	IDT, SCT, SDT	Time, Outcome Expectations, Competence
To integrate generative AI with social justice, fairness, and sustainability in education, stakeholders, especially marginalized and underprivileged groups, must participate in AI tool creation, deployment, and assessment	IDT, SCT, SDT Generative	Social System, Social Norms, Relatedness

Generative AI may disrupt education by providing learners with personalized content, dynamic and easily adaptable content, and better instructional strategies. Thus, the study identified the adoption factors to reveal the patterns of generative AI adoption, analyzed the scalability of the results, and evaluated the social sustainability of the results in the context of education and society. For the improvement of education equality and inclusion, the study further implements generative AI technology for all the stakeholders and more so for excluded groups. The research achieved its objective and its assumptions to offer guidelines to not only students but also to policymakers, educators, and researchers on how to responsibly and efficiently implement generative AI in education, as well as how to evaluate the integration and impacts on student learning and social sustainability through empirical and theoretical analysis.

8 Conclusion

Generative AI in education has revolutionary potential for societal sustainability, as shown in this study. This study addresses critical gaps in the literature and provides valuable insights for educators, policymakers, and researchers by examining the key factors influencing generative AI adoption in higher education, its effects on student engagement and performance, and its social sustainability implications. The study found that technological, pedagogical, and social aspects affect education's generative AI adoption. Innovation Diffusion Theory (IDT), Social Cognitive Theory (SCT), and Self-Determination Theory (SDT) are utilised to explore the complex relationships that promote generative AI uptake in education. The study also illustrates that generative AI may tailor learning to individual learners' needs and talents, boosting educational access, equity, and inclusion. Generative AI-powered technologies can help educators create more interesting and effective learning environments for varied student groups and academic success. Therefore, it must be integrated with social justice, fairness, and sustainability in education, according to the research. The research further suggests involving all stakeholders, especially marginalised and underprivileged communities, as by including diverse perspectives and experiences, educational institutions can eliminate algorithmic bias and promote equity and inclusion. It also assists educators and administrators focus generative AI integration into teaching and learning and overcome acceptance barriers as well as policymakers to create responsible and ethical generative AI frameworks and norms for social sustainability and inclusivity in education. The discussion further underlines the need for generative AI and education collaboration and research. As technology improves, one must consider its long-term effects on children, educators, and society.

References

Alasadi, E.A., Baiz, C.R.: Generative AI in education and research: opportunities, concerns, and solutions. J. Chem. Educ. **100**(8), 2965–2971 (2023). https://pubs.acs.org/doi/abs/10.1021/acs.jchemed.3c00323

Anis, M.: Leveraging artificial intelligence for inclusive English language teaching: strategies and implications for learner diversity. J. Multidisc. Educ. Res. **12**(6) (2023). http://ijmer.s3.amazonaws.com/pdf/volume12/volume12-issue6(5)/9.pdf

Bahroun, Z., Anane, C., Ahmed, V., Zacca, A.: Transforming education: a comprehensive review of generative artificial intelligence in educational settings through bibliometric and content analysis. Sustainability **15**(17), 12983 (2023). https://www.mdpi.com/2071-1050/15/17/12983

Bail, C.A.: Can generative AI improve social science? Proc. Natl. Acad. Sci. **121**(21), e2314021121 (2024). https://www.pnas.org/doi/abs/10.1073/pnas.2314021121

Chan, C.K.Y., Hu, W.: Students' voices on generative AI: perceptions, benefits, and challenges in higher education. Int. J. Educ. Technol. High. Educ. **20**(1), 43 (2023). https://link.springer.com/article/10.1186/s41239-023-00411-8

Egalite, A.J.: How family background influences student achievement. Educ. Next **16**(2), 70–78. https://www.uccronline.it/wp-content/uploads/2012/06/201604educationnext.pdf

ElSayary, A.: Integrating Generative AI in Active Learning Environments: Enhancing Metacognition and Technological Skills (2024). https://www.iiis.org/CDs2024/CD2024Spring/papers/ZA265LA.pdf

Ferrara, E.: Fairness and bias in artificial intelligence: a brief survey of sources, impacts, and mitigation strategies. Science **6**(1), 3 (2023). https://www.mdpi.com/2413-4155/6/1/3

Ghimire, A.: Generative AI in Education From the Perspective of Students, Educators, and Administrators (2024). https://digitalcommons.usu.edu/etd2023/124/

Gupta, J., Vegelin, C.: Sustainable development goals and inclusive development. Int. Environ. Agreem. Polit. Law Econ. **16**, 433–448 (2016). https://link.springer.com/article/10.1007/s10784-016-9323-z

Ivanov, S., Soliman, M., Tuomi, A., Alkathiri, N.A., Al-Alawi, A.N.: Drivers of generative AI adoption in higher education through the lens of the Theory of Planned Behaviour. Technol. Soc. **77**, 102521 (2014). https://www.sciencedirect.com/science/article/pii/S0160791X24000691

Kioupi, V., Voulvoulis, N.: Education for sustainable development: a systemic framework for connecting the SDGs to educational outcomes. Sustainability **11**(21), 6104 (2019). https://www.mdpi.com/2071-1050/11/21/6104

Kong, S.C., Yang, Y.: A human-centred learning and teaching framework using generative artificial intelligence for self-regulated learning development through domain knowledge learning in K–12 settings. IEEE Trans, Learn, Technol. (2024). https://ieeexplore.ieee.org/abstract/document/10507034/

Kshetri, N.: The academic industry's response to generative artificial intelligence: an institutional analysis of large language models. Telecommun. Policy, 102760 (2024). https://www.sciencedirect.com/science/article/pii/S0308596124000570

Langran, E., Searson, M., Trumble, J.: Transforming teacher education in the age of generative AI. Explor. New Horiz. Gener. Artif. Intell. Teach. Educ. **2** (2024). https://www.learntechlib.org/primary/p/223928/ebook_223928.pdf#page=8

Lipton, Z.C., Steinhardt, J.: Troubling trends in machine learning scholarship: some ML papers suffer from flaws that could mislead the public and stymie future research. Queue **17**(1), 45–77 (2019). https://dl.acm.org/doi/abs/10.1145/3317287.3328534

McDonald, N., Johri, A., Ali, A., Hingle, A.: Generative artificial intelligence in higher education: evidence from an analysis of institutional policies and guidelines. arXiv preprint arXiv:2402.01659 (2024)

Michel-Villarreal, R., Vilalta-Perdomo, E., Salinas-Navarro, D.E., Thierry-Aguilera, R., Gerardou, F.S.: Challenges and opportunities of generative AI for higher education as explained by ChatGPT. Educ. Sci. **13**(9), 856 (2023). https://www.mdpi.com/2227-7102/13/9/856

Morris, R.N.: K-12 Economically Disadvantaged Students, Poverty, and Education: Ecological Narratives of Successful Raised-In-Poverty, Texas Educators (2021). https://scholarworks.sfasu.edu/etds/360/

Paré, G., Kitsiou, S.: Methods for literature reviews. In: Handbook of eHealth Evaluation: An Evidence-Based Approach [Internet]. University of Victoria. https://www.ncbi.nlm.nih.gov/books/NBK481583/

Rieckmann, M.: Learning to transform the world: key competencies in Education for Sustainable Development. Issues Trends Educ. Sustain. Dev. **39**(1), 39–59 (2018)

Rodak, M.Y.: Generative AI Writing Course Framework (2023). https://hcommons.org/deposits/item/hc:60047/

Ruiz-Rojas, L.I., Acosta-Vargas, P., De-Moreta-Llovet, J., Gonzalez-Rodriguez, M.: Empowering education with generative artificial intelligence tools: approach with an instructional design matrix. Sustainability **15**(15), 11524 (2023). https://www.mdpi.com/2071-1050/15/15/11524

Shukla, S.: Creative Computing and Harnessing the Power of Generative Artificial Intelligence. J. Environ. Sci. Technol. **2**(1), 556–579 (2023). https://jest.com.pk/index.php/jest/article/view/123

Zhang, Q., Lu, J., Jin, Y.: Artificial intelligence in recommender systems. Complex Intell. Syst. **7**(1), 439–457 (2021). https://link.springer.com/article/10.1007/s40747-020-00212-w

Predicting Student Adaptability to Online Education Using Machine Learning

Said A. Salloum[1,2](✉), Ayham Salloum[3], Raghad Alfaisal[4], Azza Basiouni[5], and Khaled Shaalan[6]

[1] Health Economic and Financing Group, University of Sharjah, Sharjah, UAE
ssalloum@sharjah.ac.ae
[2] School of Science, Engineering, and Environment, University of Salford, Salford, England
[3] College of Medicine, University of Sharjah, Sharjah, UAE
[4] Faculty of Computing and Meta-Technology, Universiti Pendidikan Sultan Idris, Perak, Malaysia
[5] Faculty of Information Technology, Liwa College, Abu Dhabi, UAE
azza.basiouni@lc.ac.ae
[6] Faculty of Engineering and IT, The British University in Dubai, Dubai, UAE
khaled.shaalan@buid.ac.ae

Abstract. In the wake of global shifts towards digital platforms, online education has become a cornerstone of modern learning environments. Understanding student adaptability in these settings is crucial for developing effective educational strategies and ensuring successful learning outcomes. While the transition to online education offers numerous benefits, it also poses significant challenges, particularly in terms of student engagement and adaptability. Identifying factors that influence adaptability can help educators tailor interventions to assist students who may struggle with online learning modalities. This study utilized a dataset from Kaggle, consisting of 1,205 students with features encompassing demographic information, technological access, and personal educational environments. A Random Forest classifier was employed within a One-vs-Rest strategy to predict three levels of student adaptability to online education. The model's performance was evaluated using accuracy, precision, recall, and F1-score metrics. The Random Forest model achieved an accuracy of 88.3%. It showed high precision and recall for the 'High' and 'Moderate' adaptability classes but lower performance in predicting 'Low' adaptability. The analysis also revealed that class duration, financial condition, and age were among the most significant predictors of adaptability. The findings underscore the potential of machine learning in identifying key factors affecting student adaptability, which can inform the design of personalized learning experiences and interventions in online education. These insights are pivotal for educational institutions aiming to enhance student engagement and reduce dropout rates in digital learning environments.

Keywords: Digital Learning · Educational Technology · Machine Learning · Online Education · Predictive Analytics · Student Adaptability · Student Engagement

A. Basiouni and C. Frasson (Eds.): BBGI 2024, CCIS 2162, pp. 187–196, 2024.
https://doi.org/10.1007/978-3-031-65996-6_16

1 Introduction

The rapid advancement of digital technologies and the increasing access to the internet have revolutionized many sectors, including education [1]. Online education has experienced substantial growth over the last decade, significantly transforming the traditional classroom setting to a more flexible and accessible virtual format [2]. This shift has been accelerated by global challenges such as the COVID-19 pandemic, which forced educational institutions worldwide to adopt remote learning strategies [3]. While online education offers numerous advantages such as flexibility, accessibility, and the ability to cater to diverse learning needs, it also presents unique challenges in student engagement, motivation, and adaptability [4].

Understanding how students adapt to online learning environments is crucial, as it affects their learning outcomes, satisfaction, and overall educational experience. Student adaptability in online education can be influenced by various factors, including individual learning styles, technological proficiency, and the quality of digital resources available [5].

Despite the increasing prevalence of online education, predicting student success and adaptability remains a significant challenge. Traditional indicators of academic performance, such as prior grades and test scores, may not fully capture a student's ability to adapt to and thrive in online learning environments. This gap highlights the need for innovative approaches to identify and support students who might struggle with online education [6].

This research aims to leverage machine learning techniques to predict the adaptability levels of students in online learning environments. By analyzing data on students' demographic backgrounds, technological access, and educational settings, the study seeks to develop predictive models that can help educators identify students at risk of poor adaptation and implement targeted interventions to improve their learning experiences. The rationale behind this research is rooted in the growing necessity for adaptive educational practices that accommodate the shift towards digital learning platforms. By applying machine learning models to educational data, this study aims to uncover underlying patterns and predictors of student adaptability that are not immediately apparent through traditional analysis methods. The contribution of this research lies in its potential to provide actionable insights that can inform the design of personalized learning experiences, thereby enhancing student engagement and success in online education. Furthermore, the findings could serve as a basis for developing automated support systems that dynamically adjust learning content and strategies based on individual student needs.

The remainder of this paper is organized as follows, Sect. 2 reviews the literature on online education, student adaptability, and the application of machine learning in educational settings. Section 3 describes the methodology, including data collection, preprocessing, model selection, and evaluation metrics. Section 4 presents the results of the machine learning models, including accuracy measures, feature importance analysis, and model evaluation. Section 5 discusses the implications of the findings, explores the limitations of the study, and suggests directions for future research. Section 6 concludes the paper by summarizing the key outcomes and their implications for educational practice and policy.

2 Literature Review

The landscape of online education has been extensively studied from multiple dimensions, including technological integration, pedagogical effectiveness, and student adaptability. Notably, research by [7] highlighted that students' adaptability to online learning is significantly influenced by both their self-regulation skills and the technological tools at their disposal. These findings underscore the complex interplay between student characteristics and the learning environment in determining educational outcomes in online settings.

Furthermore, a study by [8] explored how socio-economic factors influence the adaptability of students to online education. They found that students from lower socio-economic backgrounds often face greater challenges in adapting due to limited access to necessary technological resources. This aligns with findings from [9], who emphasized the critical role of accessibility to digital devices and reliable internet connectivity in students' success in online courses.

On the psychological and instructional front, Thompson et al. [10] investigated the impact of instructional design on adaptability. Their research demonstrated that courses designed with adaptive learning technologies that adjust to individual student needs can significantly enhance student engagement and adaptability. This adaptability not only contributes to immediate academic performance but also to long-term educational resilience.

While these studies provide valuable insights into factors affecting student adaptability in online education, there remains a gap in applying advanced predictive analytics to preemptively identify students who may struggle with online learning modalities. Most existing research focuses on post-hoc analysis of adaptability factors or relies on traditional statistical methods that do not fully exploit the potential of modern data science techniques. This study contributes to the field by employing machine learning algorithms to predict student adaptability levels based on a comprehensive set of variables, including demographic data, technology access, and educational backgrounds. Unlike traditional approaches, this predictive model allows for the identification of at-risk students before they encounter significant challenges, enabling proactive interventions. Furthermore, this research integrates feature importance analysis to identify which factors most significantly impact student adaptability, providing educators and policymakers with actionable insights to tailor educational resources and support mechanisms effectively.

3 Methodology

3.1 Data Source

The dataset used in this study is sourced from Kaggle [11]. It is titled "Students' Adaptability Level in Online Education" and includes data on 1,205 students. The dataset features a range of variables that describe demographic information, access to technology, and personal education-related factors. Key attributes include gender, age, education level, type of institution (government or non-government), IT background, geographic location, financial condition, internet type, network type, duration of classes, whether the student uses a self-learning management system, and the primary device used for online education. The target variable, 'Adaptivity Level,' classifies students into three categories: 'Low,' 'Moderate,' and 'High' based on their adaptability to online education.

3.2 Data Preprocessing

Data preprocessing involved several steps to prepare the dataset for modeling. Initially, the dataset was examined for missing values, and anomalies were addressed to ensure data integrity. Categorical variables such as gender, education level, and institution type were encoded using the Label Encoder method to transform them into numerical formats suitable for machine learning algorithms. The target variable 'Adaptivity Level' was also encoded from categorical to numerical values to facilitate the classification process.

Given the uneven distribution of classes in the dataset, Synthetic Minority Oversampling Technique (SMOTE) was utilized to address this imbalance. SMOTE helps in synthesizing new examples from the minority class, thereby balancing the class distribution and preventing the model from being biased towards the majority class. This technique is critical for improving model performance, particularly for underrepresented classes [12].

3.3 Model Selection

The Random Forest algorithm was selected for this study due to its robustness and effectiveness in handling both binary and multi-class classification problems. Random Forest operates by constructing a multitude of decision trees at training time and outputting the class that is the mode of the classes predicted by individual trees. This ensemble method is advantageous due to its ability to improve prediction accuracy and control over-fitting, making it highly reliable for complex classification tasks [13]. The One-vs-Rest (OvR) strategy was employed to adapt the Random Forest algorithm for multi-class classification tasks. In the OvR approach, a separate model is trained for each class to distinguish instances of that class from all other classes, which simplifies the multi-class problem into multiple binary classification problems. This method was chosen because of its scalability and ease of implementation, especially useful when dealing with a limited number of classes as in this dataset.

3.4 Evaluation Metrics

The performance of the predictive model was evaluated using several metrics: accuracy, precision, recall, and F1-score. Accuracy measures the proportion of correct predictions (both true positives and true negatives) among the total number of cases examined. Precision reflects the correctness achieved in positive prediction while recall, or sensitivity, measures the ability of the model to find all the relevant cases (true positives). The F1-score provides a balance between precision and recall by taking their harmonic mean, and it is particularly useful when the class distribution is uneven, as it accounts for both false positives and false negatives [14].

4 Results

4.1 Model Performance

The Random Forest model achieved a commendable overall accuracy of 88.38%, with precision, recall, and F1-scores as follows:

- **Class 0 (Low Adaptability):** Precision of 0.92, recall of 0.86, and F1-score of 0.89, reflecting strong predictive performance for students with lower adaptability.
- **Class 1 (Moderate Adaptability):** Achieved a precision of 0.93, recall of 0.91, and F1-score of 0.92, indicating excellent model accuracy for predicting moderate adaptability.
- **Class 2 (High Adaptability):** Showed a lower precision of 0.61 but a very high recall of 0.95, leading to an F1-score of 0.75. This suggests the model is highly sensitive to detecting students with high adaptability but at the cost of more false positives compared to other classes.

These results underscore the model's strength in identifying students who are more likely to adapt well to online education while highlighting areas for refinement in distinguishing between the adaptability levels more distinctly.

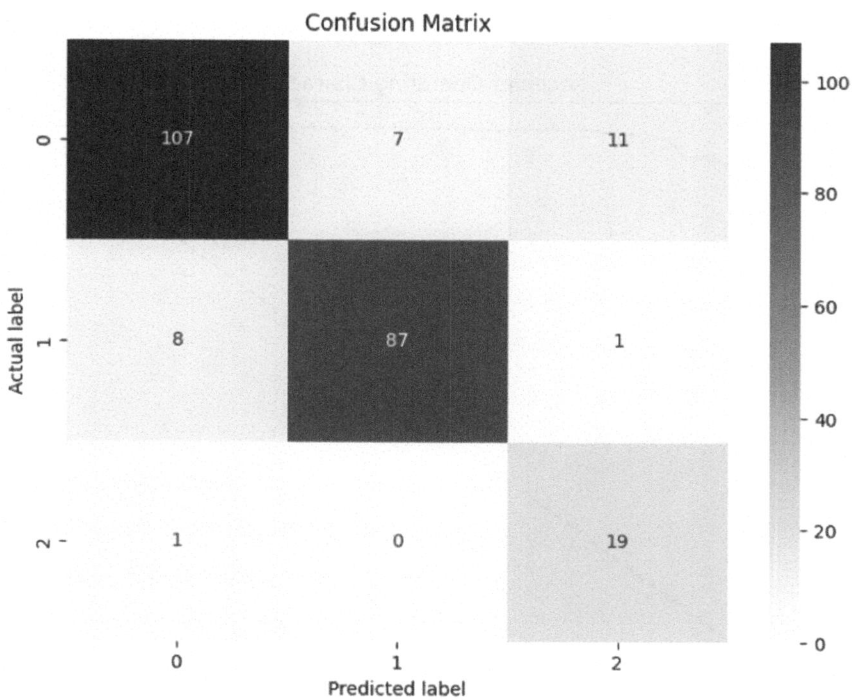

Fig. 1. The confusion matrix

4.2 Confusion Matrix

The confusion matrix (Fig. 1) further illustrates the model's performance across different adaptability levels. The matrix reveals that:

- Most students with low adaptability (107 out of 125) were correctly identified, although there were some misclassifications with students being predicted as moderate (7) and high (11) adaptability.
- The model was very effective in classifying moderate adaptability, correctly identifying 87 out of 96 students.
- For high adaptability, while only 19 students were correctly predicted, the model exhibited high sensitivity by capturing 95% of the high adaptability students, albeit with some over-prediction.

4.3 ROC Curve

The Receiver Operating Characteristic (ROC) curve (Fig. 2) and the area under the curve (AUC) provide insights into the model's discriminative ability. The mean ROC curve achieved an AUC of 0.98, indicating an excellent overall ability of the model to distinguish between the three classes of adaptability. This high AUC reflects the model's effectiveness in handling true positive rates against the false positive rates across different threshold settings.

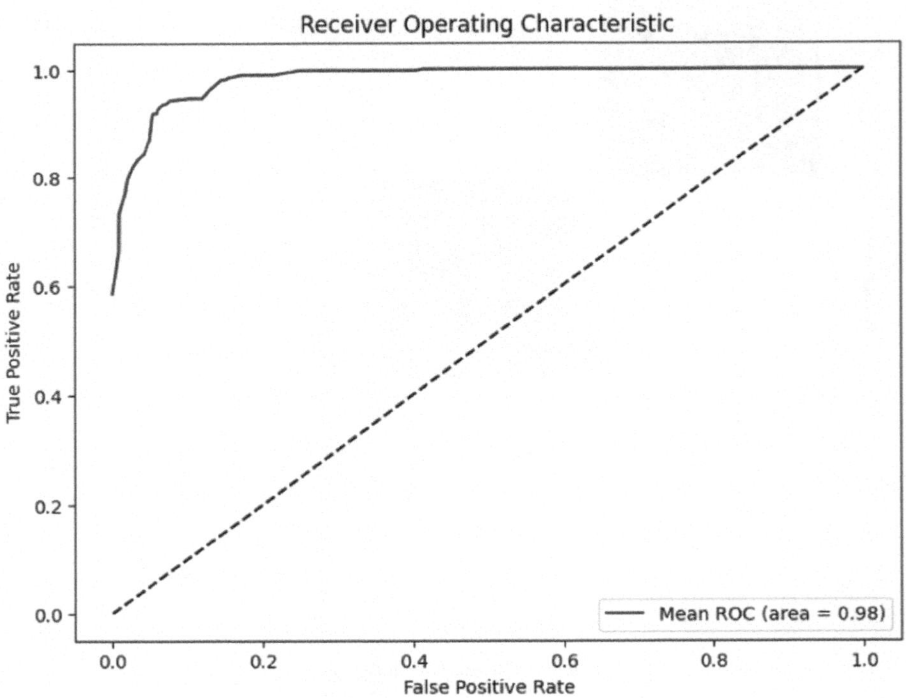

Fig. 2. ROC Curve

4.4 Feature Importances

Analysis of feature importances (Fig. 3) revealed that 'Class Duration' was the most significant predictor of adaptability, highlighting the impact of engagement time on student outcomes. 'Financial Condition' and 'Age' were also critical, suggesting socioeconomic factors and maturity level play substantial roles in adaptability to online learning. The influence of 'Gender' and 'Education Level' was less pronounced but still noteworthy, indicating demographic factors moderately affect adaptability outcomes.

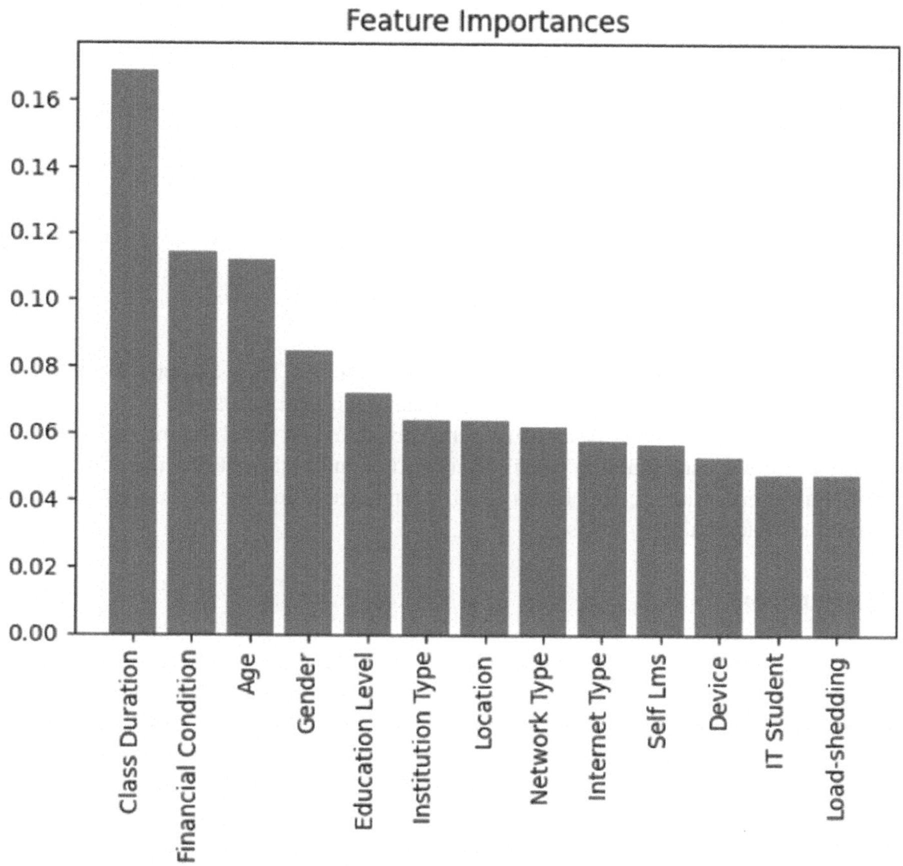

Fig. 3. Feature Importances

4.5 Age Distribution Across Adaptability Levels

The box plot of age distribution across adaptability levels (Fig. 4) shows that age groups across the adaptability levels do not vary widely, implying that while age is an important

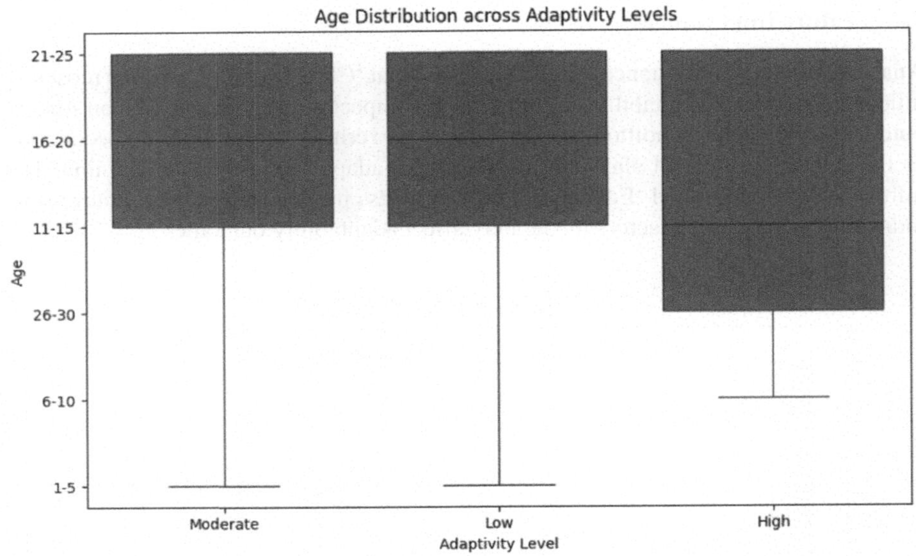

Fig. 4. Age Distribution across Adaptability Levels

factor, it does not single-handedly determine adaptability. This supports the model's reliance on a combination of features to predict adaptability accurately.

These results collectively demonstrate the robustness of the Random Forest model in predicting student adaptability to online education and highlight specific areas where educational interventions could be targeted to enhance student experiences based on their predicted adaptability levels.

5 Discussion

The results of the study reveal a nuanced understanding of how different factors contribute to student adaptability in online education. High performance in predicting moderate and low adaptability, with respective high precision and recall rates, suggests that the model is particularly effective at identifying students within these adaptability levels, which are critical for interventions aimed at preventing dropouts and disengagement. The relatively lower precision in the high adaptability class, coupled with high recall, indicates that the model tends to overpredict this category. While this might lead to unnecessary interventions for some students, it ensures that almost all students needing support are identified, aligning with the educational imperative to support every student's learning journey.

The importance of 'Class Duration' as a predictor underscores the significance of engagement time in online learning environments. Longer durations might imply more intense or interactive sessions that enhance adaptability, offering valuable insights for instructional design. The strong influence of 'Financial Condition' and 'Age' on adaptability suggests that socioeconomic factors and maturity significantly affect student experiences and outcomes in online education. These insights could inform policymakers and educators to tailor resources and support systems more effectively, ensuring equitable access to learning tools and support for students from varied economic backgrounds and age groups.

This study, while insightful, is not without limitations. The potential for biases in the dataset, such as sampling bias or data entry errors, cannot be overlooked and could affect the generalizability of the findings. Additionally, the use of SMOTE for addressing class imbalance introduces synthetic samples, which might not perfectly represent real-world scenarios. The model's overfitting is another concern, given the complexity of Random Forest algorithms, necessitating further validation and testing on independent data sets to ensure the robustness and applicability of the predictive model.

6 Conclusion

This research highlighted the capability of machine learning, specifically Random Forest models, to predict student adaptability in online education environments with high accuracy. Key features such as class duration, financial condition, and age were identified as significant predictors of adaptability, offering actionable insights for enhancing student engagement and success. The model's high sensitivity in detecting students at risk of low adaptability ensures that educational interventions can be timely and effectively targeted. Future research could explore several avenues to enhance the understanding and prediction of student adaptability. Integrating additional data sources such as real-time engagement metrics, biometric data, and qualitative feedback could enrich the model's predictive power and provide a more holistic view of student behavior and preferences. Experimenting with other machine learning models like neural networks or ensemble methods that combine multiple learning algorithms might also uncover deeper insights and improve prediction accuracy. Additionally, longitudinal studies tracking student adaptability over time could help in understanding long-term trends and effects of interventions, providing a richer dataset for analysis and model training.

References

1. Al Mansoori, S., Salloum, S.A., Shaalan, K.: The impact of artificial intelligence and information technologies on the efficiency of knowledge management at modern organizations: a systematic review. In: Al-Emran, M., Shaalan, K., Hassanien, A. (eds.) Recent Advances in Intelligent Systems and Smart Applications. Studies in Systems, Decision and Control, vol. 295, pp. 163–182. Springer, Cham (2020). https://doi.org/10.1007/978-3-030-47411-9_9
2. Salloum, S.A., Al-Emran, M., Habes, M., Alghizzawi, M., Ghani, M.A., Shaalan, K.: What impacts the acceptance of E-learning through social media? An empirical study. In: Al-Emran, M., Shaalan, K. (eds.) Recent Advances in Technology Acceptance Models and Theories. SSDC, vol. 335, pp. 419–431. Springer, Cham (2021). https://doi.org/10.1007/978-3-030-64987-6_24
3. Kwong, T., Mui, L., Wong, E.Y.: Case study: a case study on online learning and digital assessment in times of crisis. World **7**, 44–49 (2020)
4. Kebritchi, M., Lipschuetz, A., Santiague, L.: Issues and challenges for teaching successful online courses in higher education: a literature review. J. Educ. Technol. Syst. **46**, 4–29 (2017)

5. Truong, H.M.: Integrating learning styles and adaptive e-learning system: current developments, problems and opportunities. Comput. Hum. Behav. **55**, 1185–1193 (2016). https://doi.org/10.1016/j.chb.2015.02.014
6. Dietz-Uhler, B., Hurn, J.E.: Using learning analytics to predict (and improve) student success: a faculty perspective. J. Interact. Online Learn. **12**, 17–26 (2013)
7. Biwer, F., Wiradhany, W., Oude Egbrink, M., et al.: Changes and adaptations: how university students self-regulate their online learning during the COVID-19 pandemic. Front. Psychol. **12**, 642593 (2021)
8. Nataliia, K., Antonina, D., Maksym, D., et al.: The higher education adaptability to the digital economy. Научный Журнал «Вестник Нан Рк» 294–306 (2020)
9. Azıonya, C.M., Nhedzı, A.: The digital divide and higher education challenge with emergency online learning: analysis of tweets in the wake of the COVID-19 lockdown. Turk. Online J. Distance Educ. **22**, 164–182 (2021)
10. El-Sabagh, H.A.: Adaptive e-learning environment based on learning styles and its impact on development students' engagement. Int. J. Educ. Technol. High. Educ. **18**, 53 (2021)
11. Students adaptability level in online education. In: Kaggle (2022). https://www.kaggle.com/datasets/mdmahmudulhasansuzan/students-adaptability-level-in-online-education
12. Chawla, N.V., Bowyer, K.W., Hall, L.O., Kegelmeyer, W.P.: SMOTE: synthetic minority over-sampling technique. J. Artif. Intell. Res. **16**, 321–357 (2002)
13. Breiman, L.: Random forests. Mach. Learn. **45**, 5–32 (2001)
14. Powers, D.M.W.: Evaluation: from precision, recall and F-measure to ROC, informedness, markedness and correlation. arXiv Prepr arXiv:201016061 (2020)

Predicting Student Retention in Higher Education Using Machine Learning

Said A. Salloum[1,2](✉), Azza Basiouni[3], Raghad Alfaisal[4], Ayham Salloum[5], and Khaled Shaalan[6]

[1] Health Economic and Financing Group, University of Sharjah, Sharjah, UAE
ssalloum@sharjah.ac.ae
[2] School of Science, Engineering, and Environment, University of Salford, Salford, United Kingdom
[3] Faculty of Information Technology, Liwa College, Abu Dhabi, UAE
azza.basiouni@lc.ac.ae
[4] Faculty of Computing and Meta-Technology, Universiti Pendidikan Sultan Idris, Perak, Malaysia
[5] College of Medicine, University of Sharjah, Sharjah, UAE
[6] Faculty of Engineering and IT, The British University in Dubai, Dubai, UAE
khaled.shaalan@buid.ac.ae

Abstract. Student retention is a critical concern for higher education institutions worldwide, impacting both institutional success and student outcomes. High dropout rates can lead to significant financial losses for universities and detrimental effects on students' personal and professional futures. Predicting student retention accurately enables institutions to proactively address factors leading to dropouts and implement targeted interventions to support at-risk students. This study addresses the problem of student retention prediction by leveraging advanced machine learning techniques. Specifically, we utilized a RandomForestClassifier to analyze a comprehensive dataset of student records, which includes various features related to demographics, academic performance, and other relevant factors influencing student retention. Our methodology involved several steps: data preprocessing to encode categorical variables and scale numerical features, hyperparameter tuning using GridSearchCV to optimize the model, and evaluation of the model's performance using metrics such as accuracy, precision, recall, F1-score, and ROC curves. Visualizations were generated to provide deeper insights into the model's performance and behavior. The results of our analysis indicate that the RandomForestClassifier can effectively predict student retention, achieving an accuracy score of 76.72%. This performance demonstrates the model's potential as a valuable tool for higher education institutions aiming to improve student retention rates. By integrating such predictive models into their student support systems, universities can identify at-risk students early and provide targeted support to enhance their chances of success. This proactive approach can lead to better academic outcomes for students and reduced financial losses for institutions due to dropouts. Future research could explore the integration of additional features and alternative machine learning models to further improve predictive accuracy and applicability in diverse educational contexts.

A. Basiouni and C. Frasson (Eds.): BBGI 2024, CCIS 2162, pp. 197–206, 2024.
https://doi.org/10.1007/978-3-031-65996-6_17

Keywords: Dropout · higher education · machine learning · predictive model · Random Forest Classifier · student retention

1 Introduction

Student retention is a critical concern for higher education institutions, impacting both institutional success and student outcomes. High dropout rates can lead to significant financial losses for universities and adverse effects on students' personal and professional futures. According to [1], student retention is influenced by a complex interplay of factors including academic performance, socioeconomic background, engagement with the university community, and personal circumstances. Early identification of at-risk students allows institutions to provide targeted interventions that can improve retention rates. For instance, academic support programs, counseling services, and financial aid can be strategically deployed to support students who are at risk of dropping out.

Despite the importance of student retention, many higher education institutions struggle to develop effective predictive models that can accurately identify students who are likely to drop out. Traditional methods often fail to capture the complexity of the factors involved and may not be adaptable to the unique contexts of different institutions. Astin [2] emphasizes that understanding what matters in college is crucial for improving retention rates. However, there is a need for more sophisticated approaches that can leverage the vast amounts of data available to institutions and provide actionable insights. This gap in the existing literature and practices highlights the necessity for innovative solutions in predicting student retention.

This study leverages advanced machine learning techniques to predict student retention. Specifically, we use a RandomForestClassifier to analyze a comprehensive dataset of student records. The dataset includes various features related to demographics, academic performance, and other relevant factors that influence retention. Our methodology involves several steps: data preprocessing to encode categorical variables and scale numerical features, hyperparameter tuning using GridSearchCV to optimize the model, and evaluation of the model's performance using metrics such as accuracy, precision, recall, F1-score, and ROC curves. Visualizations are generated to provide deeper insights into the model's behavior.

The primary contribution of this study is the development of a predictive model for student retention that can be used by higher education institutions to identify at-risk students early. By integrating such predictive models into their student support systems, universities can implement targeted interventions to enhance student success. This proactive approach can lead to better academic outcomes for students and reduced financial losses for institutions due to dropouts. Furthermore, the study provides a methodological framework that can be adapted and extended by other researchers and practitioners in the field. The remainder of this paper is structured as follows: Sect. 2 describes the dataset used in this study, Sect. 3 outlines the methodology, Sect. 4 presents the results, and Sect. 5 discusses the conclusions and suggests directions for future research.

2 Literature Review

Research has extensively studied the various factors influencing student retention in higher education. Tinto [1] identifies academic integration and social integration as critical components affecting a student's decision to stay or leave an institution. Academic integration refers to the extent to which students feel connected to their academic programs, while social integration pertains to their involvement in the campus community [3, 4]. Additionally, financial issues, family responsibilities, and personal challenges significantly impact retention rates. These findings suggest that retention strategies need to be multifaceted, addressing both academic and non-academic aspects of student life.

The advent of data analytics has brought new dimensions to predicting student retention. According to [5], traditional statistical models have been supplemented by machine learning algorithms, which can handle large datasets and identify complex patterns. Logistic regression, decision trees, and neural networks are among the models used to predict retention. Recent studies, such as those by [6], have demonstrated that machine learning models can achieve higher accuracy in predicting dropouts compared to traditional methods. These models consider a wide range of variables, from academic performance to extracurricular involvement, providing a more comprehensive analysis.

Machine learning techniques have proven effective in educational contexts due to their ability to analyze vast amounts of data and uncover hidden patterns. Random forests, support vector machines, and ensemble methods are popular choices for educational data mining. For instance, [7] found that ensemble methods combining multiple algorithms often outperform single models in predicting student outcomes. Furthermore, the flexibility of machine learning models allows them to be tailored to the specific characteristics of different institutions, enhancing their predictive power. However, these techniques also require careful tuning and validation to avoid overfitting and ensure generalizability.

Despite the advances in predictive modeling, several challenges and gaps remain. Many studies, including those by [8], highlight the need for more personalized and adaptive models that can accommodate the unique needs of individual students. There is also a call for integrating qualitative data, such as student feedback and engagement metrics, which are often overlooked in quantitative analyses. Moreover, most existing models focus on short-term predictions, while long-term retention strategies require continuous monitoring and adjustment. Addressing these gaps could lead to more effective and sustainable retention initiatives.

This study aims to fill these gaps by developing a predictive model that not only leverages advanced machine learning techniques but also incorporates a broad spectrum of variables, including demographic, academic, and engagement factors. By optimizing and validating the model using GridSearchCV, this research seeks to enhance its accuracy and applicability across different institutional contexts. The goal is to create a tool that higher education institutions can use to implement timely and targeted interventions, ultimately improving student retention rates.

3 Methodology

3.1 Data Source

The dataset used in this study is sourced from Kaggle [9]. It contains various features related to students' demographics, academic performance, and other relevant factors. The dataset includes columns such as Marital status, Application mode, Application order, Course, Daytime/evening attendance, Previous qualification, Nationality, Mother's qualification, Father's qualification, Mother's occupation, Father's occupation, and several others, ending with the target variable indicating whether a student is a "Dropout," "Graduate," or "Enrolled."

3.2 Data Preprocessing

Data preprocessing is a crucial step in preparing the data for machine learning algorithms. This involves handling missing values, encoding categorical variables, and scaling numerical features. In our study, we used LabelEncoder from the sklearn library to encode categorical variables, transforming them into numerical format suitable for machine learning models [10]. Numerical features were standardized using StandardScaler to ensure they have a mean of zero and a standard deviation of one, which helps improve the performance of the machine learning models by ensuring all features contribute equally to the model's learning process [11].

3.3 Model Selection

The Random Forest algorithm was selected for this study due to its robustness and effectiveness in handling both binary and multi-class classification problems. Random Forest operates by constructing a multitude of decision trees at training time and outputting the class that is the mode of the classes predicted by individual trees. This ensemble method is advantageous due to its ability to improve prediction accuracy and control over-fitting, making it highly reliable for complex classification tasks [12]. The One-vs-Rest (OvR) strategy was employed to adapt the Random Forest algorithm for multi-class classification tasks. In the OvR approach, a separate model is trained for each class to distinguish instances of that class from all other classes, which simplifies the multi-class problem into multiple binary classification problems. This method was chosen because of its scalability and ease of implementation, especially useful when dealing with a limited number of classes as in this dataset.

3.4 Feature Selection and Engineering

Feature selection and engineering are vital in enhancing the predictive power of the model. We explored various techniques to select the most relevant features that contribute significantly to the target variable. According to [13], feature selection helps reduce the dimensionality of the dataset, remove noise, and improve model performance. In this study, we initially included all features provided in the dataset, and later refined them based on their importance scores from the RandomForestClassifier. Feature engineering involved creating new features and transforming existing ones to capture more information that might improve the model's predictive accuracy.

3.5 Model Training and Evaluation

For model training, we employed the RandomForestClassifier, a robust ensemble learning method known for its high accuracy and ability to handle large datasets with numerous features [12]. Random forests operate by constructing multiple decision trees during training and outputting the mode of the classes (classification) or mean prediction (regression) of the individual trees. This method is effective in reducing overfitting and improving generalization.

Hyperparameter tuning is essential for optimizing the model's performance. We used GridSearchCV to systematically explore the hyperparameters of the RandomForestClassifier, including the number of trees in the forest (n_estimators), the maximum depth of the tree (max_depth), and the function to measure the quality of a split (criterion). GridSearchCV performs an exhaustive search over specified parameter values and uses cross-validation to ensure the model's performance is robust and not reliant on specific data splits [14].

The model's performance was evaluated using several metrics to provide a comprehensive understanding of its effectiveness. The confusion matrix, precision, recall, F1-score, and accuracy score were calculated to assess the classification performance. According to [15], these metrics offer insights into different aspects of the model's prediction capabilities, such as its ability to correctly identify true positives and avoid false positives.

Moreover, we plotted ROC (Receiver Operating Characteristic) curves and calculated the AUC (Area Under the Curve) to evaluate the model's discriminatory power. ROC curves are a graphical representation of a classifier's ability to distinguish between classes, and the AUC provides a single scalar value summarizing the performance [16]. Higher AUC values indicate better performance of the model in distinguishing between the classes.

3.6 Visualization and Interpretation

Visualizations were generated to interpret the model's performance and understand its behavior. We used seaborn and matplotlib libraries to create detailed plots of the confusion matrix, ROC curves, and the training and testing accuracy and loss curves. These visualizations help in diagnosing the model's strengths and weaknesses, providing a clearer picture of its predictive power and areas for improvement.

4 Results

4.1 Confusion Matrix

The confusion matrix (Fig. 1) provides a detailed breakdown of the model's performance in classifying the students into the three categories: Dropout (0), Enrolled (1), and Graduate (2). The matrix shows that the model correctly identified 241 Dropouts, 42 Enrolled, and 396 Graduates. However, there were also some misclassifications: 52 Dropouts were classified as Graduates, 72 Enrolled were classified as Graduates, and 14 Graduates were classified as Enrolled.

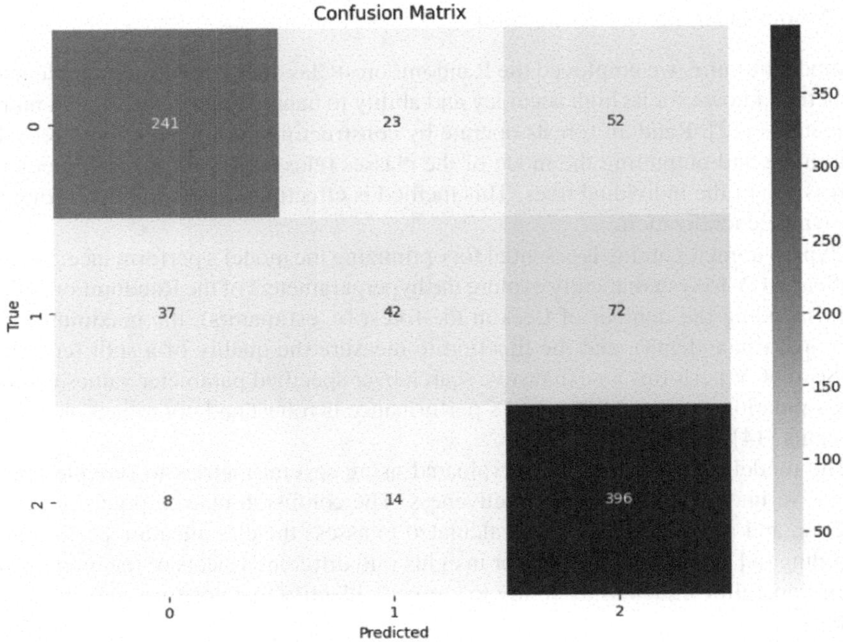

Fig. 1. The confusion matrix

4.2 ROC Curve

The Receiver Operating Characteristic (ROC) curve (Fig. 2) illustrates the true positive rate (sensitivity) against the false positive rate (1-specificity) for the RandomForestClassifier. The ROC curve is plotted for each class, and the area under the curve (AUC) is calculated to measure the model's ability to distinguish between the classes. The AUC values for Class 0 (Dropout) and Class 1 (Enrolled) are 0.91 and 0.79, respectively. These values indicate that the model performs well in differentiating between Dropouts and Graduates but has some difficulty distinguishing between Enrolled and the other two classes.

4.3 Training and Testing Loss/Accuracy Curves

The training and testing accuracy and loss curves (Fig. 3) provide insights into the model's learning process and performance across different hyperparameter combinations. The curves show that the model achieves high training accuracy, indicating that it fits well to the training data. However, there is a slight drop in testing accuracy, suggesting some degree of overfitting. The testing loss is higher than the training loss, which is expected in real-world scenarios where models typically perform better on training data.

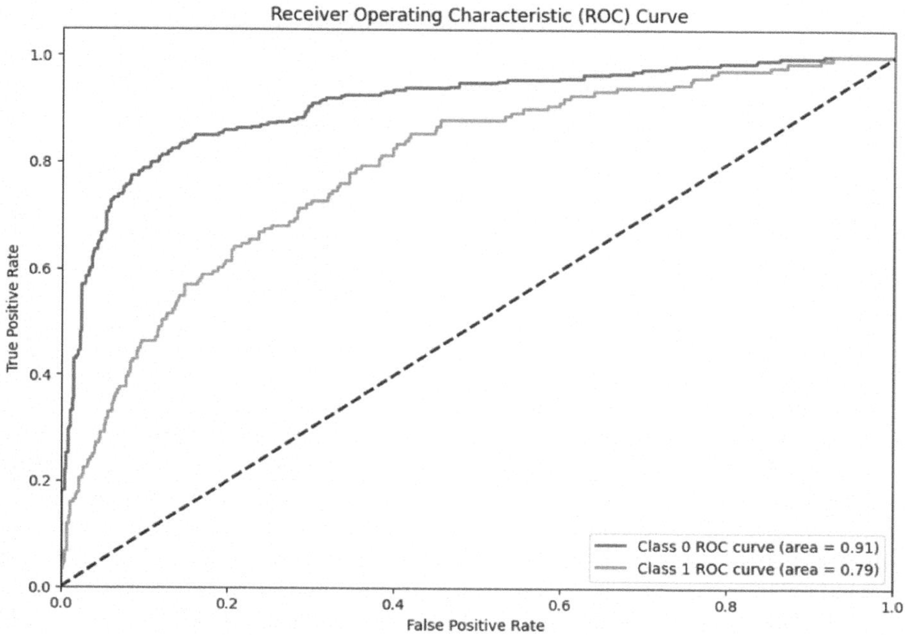

Fig. 2. ROC Curve

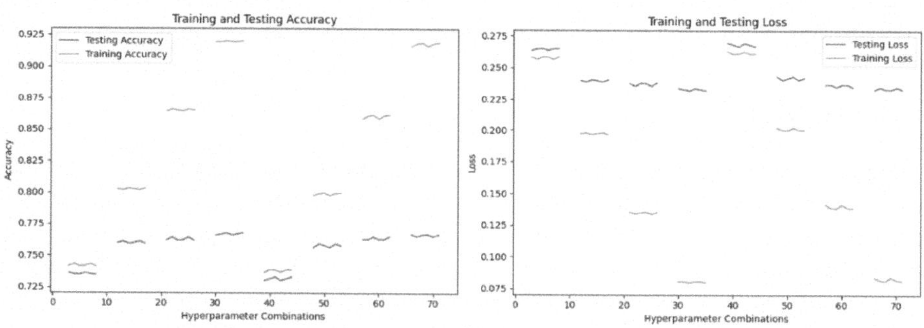

Fig. 3. The training and testing accuracy and loss curves

4.4 Classification Report

The classification report (Table 1) summarizes the precision, recall, and F1-score for each class. Precision measures the accuracy of the positive predictions, recall measures the ability to capture all positive instances, and the F1-score is the harmonic mean of precision and recall. The results indicate that the model performs best for the Graduate class (2), with a precision of 0.76, recall of 0.95, and F1-score of 0.84. The model performs moderately well for the Dropout class (0) with an F1-score of 0.80, but less effectively for the Enrolled class (1) with an F1-score of 0.37.

Table 1. Classification Report

Class	Precision	Recall	F1-score	Support
0	0.84	0.76	0.80	316
1	0.53	0.28	0.37	151
2	0.76	0.95	0.84	418
Macro avg.	0.71	0.66	0.67	855
Weighted avg.	0.75	0.77	0.75	855
Accuracy	0.76.7			885

The overall accuracy score of the RandomForestClassifier is 0.767, indicating that approximately 76.7% of the predictions made by the model are correct. This level of accuracy demonstrates the model's potential as a tool for predicting student retention in higher education. However, there is room for improvement, particularly in enhancing the model's ability to correctly classify Enrolled students. The results from the confusion matrix, ROC curve, and classification report collectively demonstrate that the RandomForestClassifier is effective in predicting student retention, with notable strengths in identifying Dropouts and Graduates. However, the model's performance is less robust for the Enrolled category, suggesting the need for further refinement and potential integration of additional features or alternative machine learning techniques to improve classification accuracy. The visualizations provide a clear and comprehensive understanding of the model's performance and areas for enhancement.

5 Conclusion

This study demonstrates the potential of using a RandomForestClassifier to predict student retention in higher education. By leveraging a comprehensive dataset that includes demographic, academic, and socio-economic factors, we were able to build a model that achieved an overall accuracy of 76.72%. The model's performance, particularly in accurately identifying Dropouts and Graduates, underscores its robustness and applicability in real-world educational settings. The detailed analysis provided by the confusion matrix revealed the model's strengths and areas for improvement. While the model performed well in classifying Dropouts and Graduates, it faced challenges in accurately identifying Enrolled students. The ROC curves and corresponding AUC values further highlighted these findings, showing strong performance for Dropouts and Graduates but a lower AUC for the Enrolled category. This indicates that while the model is effective in certain areas, there is room for refinement. The implications of these findings are significant for higher education institutions. Integrating predictive models like the RandomForestClassifier into student support systems can enable institutions to proactively identify and assist at-risk students. This proactive approach aligns with [1]'s framework, which emphasizes the importance of both academic and social integration in improving student retention. By identifying students who are likely to drop out, institutions can deploy targeted interventions such as academic support, counseling, and financial aid, thereby enhancing student success and retention rates. Furthermore, the insights gained from this study can inform the development of more effective retention strategies. Understanding the factors that contribute to student retention allows institutions to design policies and programs that address these issues directly. This can lead to more holistic support systems that not only help students academically but also address their social and personal needs. Despite its strengths, this study has several limitations. The model's lower performance in predicting Enrolled students suggests that additional features or alternative models may be needed to improve accuracy. The dataset, while comprehensive, may not capture all relevant factors influencing student retention. Future research could incorporate qualitative data, such as student surveys or engagement metrics, to provide a more holistic view of the factors affecting retention. Another limitation is the potential for bias in the dataset. If certain groups of students are underrepresented, the model's predictions may not be equally accurate across all demographics. Ensuring a diverse and representative dataset is crucial for developing fair and equitable predictive models [15]. Additionally, the study's reliance on historical data means that the model's predictions are based on past trends, which may not fully capture future changes in student behavior or institutional policies. There are several avenues for future research that could build on the findings of this study. Firstly, incorporating additional features, such as behavioral data from learning management systems or psychological factors, could enhance the model's predictive accuracy. Exploring other machine learning models, such as neural networks or gradient boosting machines, may also yield better performance, particularly for the Enrolled category [17]. Moreover, future studies should consider longitudinal data to assess the model's performance over time and its ability to adapt to changing student populations and institutional contexts. Longitudinal studies would provide insights into how retention predictors evolve and whether early interventions have long-term impacts on student success. Additionally, developing adaptive and personalized models that can provide individualized predictions and recommendations would be a valuable direction. Such models could continuously learn from new data and adjust predictions and interventions in real-time, offering more dynamic and responsive support to students. Finally, collaboration between researchers and educational institutions is essential to ensure that predictive models are practically applicable and aligned with the needs of the institutions. Engaging with stakeholders, including educators, administrators, and students, can provide valuable feedback and ensure that the models are used ethically and effectively. In conclusion, this study demonstrates the significant potential of using machine learning techniques to predict student retention in higher education. The RandomForestClassifier, with its robust performance and detailed insights, offers a valuable tool for institutions aiming to improve student retention rates. By continuing to refine and enhance these predictive models, higher education institutions can better understand and support their students, ultimately leading to improved academic outcomes and reduced dropout rates. The journey towards more effective retention strategies is ongoing, and this study provides a solid foundation for future research and practical applications.

References

1. Tinto, V.: Leaving College: Rethinking the Causes and Cures of Student Attrition, University of Chicago Press, Chicago (2012)
2. Astin, A.W.: What Matters in College: Four Critical Years Examined, Jossey-Bass, San Francisco (1997)
3. Tinto, V. Leaving College: Rethinking the Causes and Cures of Student Attrition, ERIC (1987)
4. Braxton, J.M.: Leaving college: rethinking the causes and cures of student attrition by Vincent Tinto. J. Coll. Stud. Dev. **60**, 129–134 (2019)
5. Herzog, S.: Estimating student retention and degree-completion time: decision trees and neural networks vis-à-vis regression. New Dir. Inst. Res. **131**, 17–33 (2006)
6. Aulck, L., Velagapudi, N., Blumenstock, J., West, J.: Predicting student dropout in higher education. arXiv Preprint arXiv:1606.06364 (2016)
7. Rahul, Katarya, R.A.: Systematic review on predicting the performance of students in higher education in offline mode using machine learning techniques. Wireless Pers. Commun. **133**(1), 1–32 (2024). https://doi.org/10.1007/s11277-023-10838-x
8. Braxton, J.M., Doyle, W.R., Hartley, H.V., III., et al.: Rethinking College Student Retention. Wiley (2013)
9. Predict students' dropout and academic success. In: Kaggle (2023). https://www.kaggle.com/datasets/thedevastator/higher-education-predictors-of-student-retention
10. Pedregosa, F., Varoquaux, G., Gramfort, A., et al.: Scikit-learn: machine learning in Python. J. Mach. Learn. Res. **12**, 2825–2830 (2011)
11. Bishop, C.M., Nasrabadi, N.M.: Pattern Recognition and Machine Learning. Springer (2006)
12. Breiman, L.: Random forests. Mach. Learn. **45**, 5–32 (2001)
13. Guyon, I., Elisseeff, A.: An introduction to variable and feature selection. J. Mach. Learn. Res. **3**, 1157–1182 (2003)
14. Bergstra, J., Bengio, Y.: Random search for hyper-parameter optimization. J. Mach. Learn. Res. **13**(2) (2012)
15. Sokolova, M., Lapalme, G.: A systematic analysis of performance measures for classification tasks. Inf. Process. Manag. **45**, 427–437 (2009)
16. Fawcett, T.: An introduction to ROC analysis. Pattern Recognit. Lett. **27**, 861–874 (2006)
17. Akmeşe, Ö.F., Kör, H., Erbay, H.: Use of machine learning techniques for the forecast of student achievement in higher education. Inf. Technol. Learn. Tools **82**, 297–311 (2021)

Building and Evaluating a Chatbot Using a University FAQs Dataset

Said A. Salloum[1,2](✉), Khaled Shalan[3], Azza Basiouni[4], Ayham Salloum[5], and Raghad Alfaisal[6]

[1] Health Economic and Financing Group, University of Sharjah, Sharjah, UAE
ssalloum@sharjah.ac.ae
[2] School of Science, Engineering, and Environment, University of Salford, Salford, England
[3] Faculty of Engineering and IT, The British University in Dubai, Dubai, UAE
khaled.shaalan@buid.ac.ae
[4] Faculty of Information Technology, Liwa College, Abu Dhabi, UAE
azza.basiouni@lc.ac.ae
[5] College of Medicine, University of Sharjah, Sharjah, UAE
[6] Faculty of Computing and Meta-Technology, Universiti Pendidikan Sultan Idris, Perak, Malaysia

Abstract. The integration of artificial intelligence in educational settings has increasingly shown potential to enhance the efficiency and accessibility of information. One such application is the development of chatbots that can provide instant responses to frequently asked questions, thereby alleviating the workload on administrative staff and improving user experience. This paper presents the development and evaluation of a chatbot designed to assist students and staff at a university by providing accurate responses to common queries. Using a dataset sourced from Kaggle, the chatbot is trained on various intents, including course information, fees, hostel facilities, and more. The dataset undergoes thorough preprocessing, including tokenization, lemmatization, and vectorization to ensure effective model training. The neural network model is built using TensorFlow and comprises multiple dense layers with ReLU activation functions and dropout layers to prevent overfitting. The model is trained over 200 epochs with a batch size of 5, utilizing the Adam optimizer and categorical cross-entropy loss function. The results demonstrate the chatbot's high accuracy and effectiveness, achieving an accuracy of 99.75%, precision of 99.76%, recall of 99.75%, and an F1 score of 99.75%. These metrics indicate the model's robustness in understanding and responding to user queries accurately. The implications of this study suggest that implementing such chatbots in educational institutions can significantly streamline information dissemination and improve user engagement.

Keywords: Artificial intelligence · chatbot · educational institutions · FAQs · machine learning · neural networks · text classification

A. Basiouni and C. Frasson (Eds.): BBGI 2024, CCIS 2162, pp. 207–218, 2024.
https://doi.org/10.1007/978-3-031-65996-6_18

1 Introduction

In recent years, educational institutions have increasingly turned to digital solutions to improve operational efficiency and enhance student engagement [1]. One significant trend is the deployment of chatbots, which are AI-driven systems designed to simulate human conversation and provide instant responses to user queries [2]. Chatbots have found applications in various domains, including customer service, healthcare, and education [3]. In the context of higher education, chatbots can play a critical role in addressing the diverse and frequent queries posed by students, staff, and prospective applicants. The ability of chatbots to provide automated, accurate, and instant responses makes them an invaluable tool for universities striving to improve their service delivery and overall user experience.

The demand for automated responses in educational settings is driven by several factors. First, the volume of inquiries related to admissions, course details, campus facilities, and administrative procedures can be overwhelming for university staff. Manual handling of these queries is not only time-consuming but also prone to human error. Studies have shown that chatbots can effectively manage high volumes of repetitive questions, thereby freeing up human resources for more complex and value-added tasks [4]. Furthermore, the availability of chatbots around the clock ensures that users can access information at any time, which is particularly beneficial for international students and stakeholders across different time zones.

The primary objective of this research is to develop and evaluate a chatbot using a dataset of frequently asked questions (FAQs) from a university. By leveraging natural language processing (NLP) techniques and machine learning algorithms, the chatbot aims to understand and respond to a wide range of queries accurately. The dataset used in this study, sourced from Kaggle, contains intents and responses typical of university FAQs, covering areas such as course information, fees, hostel facilities, and more. Through systematic data preprocessing and model training, this research seeks to create a robust and efficient chatbot capable of handling real-world inquiries from students and staff.

The significance of this research lies in its potential to enhance the efficiency of information dissemination within educational institutions. Effective information management is crucial for universities, as it directly impacts student satisfaction and operational effectiveness. Chatbots can streamline the process of providing information, reducing the burden on administrative staff and ensuring consistent and accurate communication. Previous studies have highlighted the positive impact of chatbots on user experience, noting improvements in satisfaction, engagement, and overall service quality [5]. By developing a specialized chatbot for university FAQs, this research aims to contribute to the growing body of knowledge on AI applications in education and demonstrate practical benefits for universities.

This paper is structured as follows: Sect. 2 reviews related work on chatbots and their applications in education. Section 3 provides a detailed description of the dataset used for training the chatbot. Section 4 outlines the methodology, including data preprocessing, model building, and training processes. Section 5 presents the results, including evaluation metrics and graphical analyses. Section 6 discusses the performance of the chatbot, compares it with existing systems, and addresses potential challenges and limitations. Finally, Sect. 7 concludes the paper with a summary of findings and suggestions for future work. The rationale behind this research is to address the inefficiencies in handling frequent and repetitive queries in educational institutions through the deployment of an AI-driven chatbot. By automating the response process, universities can improve their service delivery and enhance user satisfaction.

This research contributes to the field of AI in education by developing a chatbot specifically tailored to handle university FAQs. The high accuracy and efficiency demonstrated by the chatbot highlight its potential to be implemented in real-world university settings, providing a valuable tool for information dissemination and user engagement. The paper is structured to guide the reader through the entire process of chatbot development, from data collection and preprocessing to model training and evaluation. Each section provides detailed insights into the methodologies used and the results obtained, culminating in a comprehensive discussion of the chatbot's performance and potential applications.

2 Related Work

Chatbots, or conversational agents, have undergone significant evolution since their inception. The earliest chatbot, ELIZA, was developed in the 1960s by [6] at the MIT Artificial Intelligence Laboratory. ELIZA simulated conversation by using pattern matching and substitution methodology, allowing it to provide scripted responses to typed inputs. Following ELIZA, other chatbots such as PARRY, which simulated the behavior of a paranoid schizophrenic, and A.L.I.C.E., which used heuristic pattern matching, further explored the capabilities of conversational agents [7, 8]. The advent of machine learning and natural language processing (NLP) in the 21st century significantly advanced chatbot technology. Modern chatbots leverage deep learning techniques to understand and generate human-like responses, allowing them to handle complex queries and engage in more meaningful interactions [9].

The application of chatbots in educational settings has gained considerable attention in recent years. Educational chatbots serve various purposes, including assisting with administrative tasks, providing academic support, and enhancing student engagement. For instance, chatbots like "Jill Watson" at Georgia Tech help answer student questions in online forums, significantly reducing response times and improving student satisfaction [10]. Other chatbots, such as "EdTech," offer personalized tutoring by assessing students' knowledge levels and tailoring responses accordingly [11]. Additionally, chatbots have been deployed to support administrative functions such as admissions, registration, and providing information about campus facilities, thereby easing the workload on university staff and improving operational efficiency [12].

Several chatbot solutions have been developed specifically for universities, each aiming to address the unique needs of educational institutions. For example, "Unibuddy" is a chatbot platform that connects prospective students with current students to answer questions about university life, helping improve engagement and conversion rates for admissions [13]. Another solution, "Ivy," offers AI-driven support for a range of administrative tasks, including financial aid, course registration, and IT support, streamlining processes and providing 24/7 assistance to students [14]. "HubSpot" has also developed chatbots that integrate with university websites to provide instant responses to frequently asked questions, enhancing the user experience and ensuring that students and staff receive timely information [15].

While significant progress has been made in the development and deployment of chatbots in educational settings, several gaps remain. Most existing solutions are either highly specialized, focusing on specific tasks, or generalized, lacking the depth required for comprehensive university support. Additionally, many chatbots do not fully leverage the latest advancements in deep learning and NLP, limiting their ability to handle complex and nuanced queries. This research aims to address these gaps by developing a chatbot that combines the specificity of university-focused support with the sophistication of modern AI techniques. By training the chatbot on a diverse and comprehensive dataset of university FAQs, this study seeks to create a robust and versatile tool capable of providing accurate and instant responses to a wide range of queries.

3 Methodology

The development of the chatbot involves several key steps, including data preprocessing, model building, and training. This section details each step, providing insights into the techniques and methodologies used to ensure the chatbot's accuracy and effectiveness.

3.1 Data Source

The dataset used in this study is obtained from Kaggle, a well-known platform for data science and machine learning datasets. The specific dataset, titled "Chatbot Dataset," is created by Nirali Vaghani and is available at the following URL [16]. This dataset is designed to facilitate the development of chatbots by providing a structured set of user intents, input patterns, and corresponding responses.

The dataset is structured into several key components: intents, patterns, and responses. Each intent represents a specific category of user query, patterns are the various ways users might phrase their queries, and responses are the pre-defined answers the chatbot can provide.

- **Intents**: Intents are labels that categorize the types of user queries. Examples include "greeting," "goodbye," "course," and "fees."
- **Patterns**: Patterns are different phrases or sentences that users might use to express a particular intent. These are used to train the chatbot to recognize various ways a question can be asked.
- **Responses**: Responses are the replies that the chatbot provides when it detects a specific intent. These are designed to be informative and relevant to the user's query.

The dataset is stored in a JSON format, where each intent contains a list of patterns and corresponding responses.

3.2 Sample Data

To illustrate the content of the dataset, here are a few example entries from different intents:

i. **Greeting Intent**:

- **Patterns**: "Hi", "How are you?", "Is anyone there?", "Hello", "Good day", "What's up"
- **Responses**: "Hello!", "Good to see you again!", "Hi there, how can I help?"

ii. **Goodbye Intent**:

- **Patterns**: "cya", "see you", "bye bye", "See you later", "Goodbye", "I am Leaving", "Bye", "Have a Good day"
- **Responses**: "Sad to see you go:(", "Talk to you later", "Goodbye!", "Come back soon"

iii. **Course Intent**:

- **Patterns**: "list of courses", "courses offered", "what courses are available", "can you tell me about courses", "available courses"
- **Responses**: "Our university offers various courses including Information Technology, Computer Engineering, Mechanical Engineering, Chemical Engineering, and Civil Engineering."

iv. **Fees Intent**:

- **Patterns**: "information about fee", "college fee", "what is the fee per semester", "how much is the fee", "fee details"
- **Responses**: "For fee details, visit the official university website or contact the admissions office for the latest information."

These examples show the diversity of queries the chatbot can handle, from simple greetings to more complex questions about courses and fees. The structured format of the dataset allows for effective training of the chatbot, enabling it to provide accurate and contextually relevant responses.

3.3 Data Preprocessing

Data preprocessing is a crucial step in preparing the dataset for training the machine learning model. It involves several steps to clean, tokenize, lemmatize, and vectorize the text data.

- **Tokenization**: Tokenization is the process of splitting text into individual words or tokens. This step is essential for breaking down user input into manageable pieces that the model can analyze. Tokenization was performed using the Natural Language Toolkit (NLTK), a widely-used library in NLP [17]
- **Lemmatization**: Lemmatization involves converting words to their base or root forms. This helps in reducing inflected forms and grouping similar words together. NLTK's WordNetLemmatizer was used for this purpose [18]

- **Vectorization**: After tokenization and lemmatization, the text data is converted into numerical format using a bag-of-words model. This model creates a vector representation of the text by counting the occurrence of each word in the vocabulary [19].

3.4 Model Building

The neural network model for the chatbot was built using TensorFlow, an open-source machine learning library developed by Google [20]. The model architecture consists of multiple dense layers with ReLU activation functions and dropout layers to prevent overfitting.

3.5 Model Architecture

The architecture includes an input layer, two hidden layers with dropout for regularization, and an output layer with softmax activation for multi-class classification. The model was trained using the Adam optimizer, which is known for its efficiency in training deep learning models [21]. The loss function used is categorical cross-entropy, suitable for multi-class classification tasks.

The model training process involves feeding the preprocessed data into the neural network and iteratively adjusting the model weights to minimize the loss function. This section describes the key steps and considerations during the training process.

- **Training Data**: The training data consists of tokenized, lemmatized, and vectorized user input patterns and their corresponding intents. The dataset was divided into training and validation sets to monitor the model's performance and prevent overfitting.
- **Epochs and Batch Size**: The model was trained for 200 epochs with a batch size of 5. These parameters were chosen based on experimental tuning to balance training time and model performance.
- **Evaluation**: The model's performance was evaluated using several metrics, including accuracy, precision, recall, and F1 score. Additionally, a confusion matrix and ROC curves were generated to provide a comprehensive assessment of the model's classification capabilities [22]

4 Results

This section presents the evaluation results of the chatbot model, highlighting its performance across various metrics including accuracy, precision, recall, and F1 score. Additionally, visualizations such as the confusion matrix, accuracy and loss plots, and ROC curves are provided to offer a comprehensive assessment of the model's capabilities.

4.1 Evaluation Metrics

- The **Accuracy**: Accuracy is the ratio of correctly predicted instances to the total instances. The chatbot model achieved an impressive accuracy of 99.75%, indicating its high reliability in classifying user queries correctly.

- **Precision**: Precision is the ratio of true positive predictions to the total positive predictions. The model obtained a precision score of 99.76%, reflecting its effectiveness in minimizing false positives.
- **Recall**: Recall is the ratio of true positive predictions to the total actual positives. The model's recall score of 99.75% demonstrates its proficiency in identifying relevant instances among the actual positive cases.
- **F1 Score**: The F1 score is the harmonic mean of precision and recall. It provides a balanced measure of the model's performance, especially when dealing with imbalanced datasets. The model achieved an F1 score of 99.75%, underscoring its overall accuracy and consistency.

These metrics collectively validate the high performance and robustness of the chatbot model in understanding and responding to user queries accurately.

4.2 Graphical Analysis

The following figures provide a detailed visual analysis of the model's performance:

- **Confusion Matrix**: The confusion matrix (Fig. 1) illustrates the model's performance in classifying each intent. It shows the number of correct and incorrect predictions

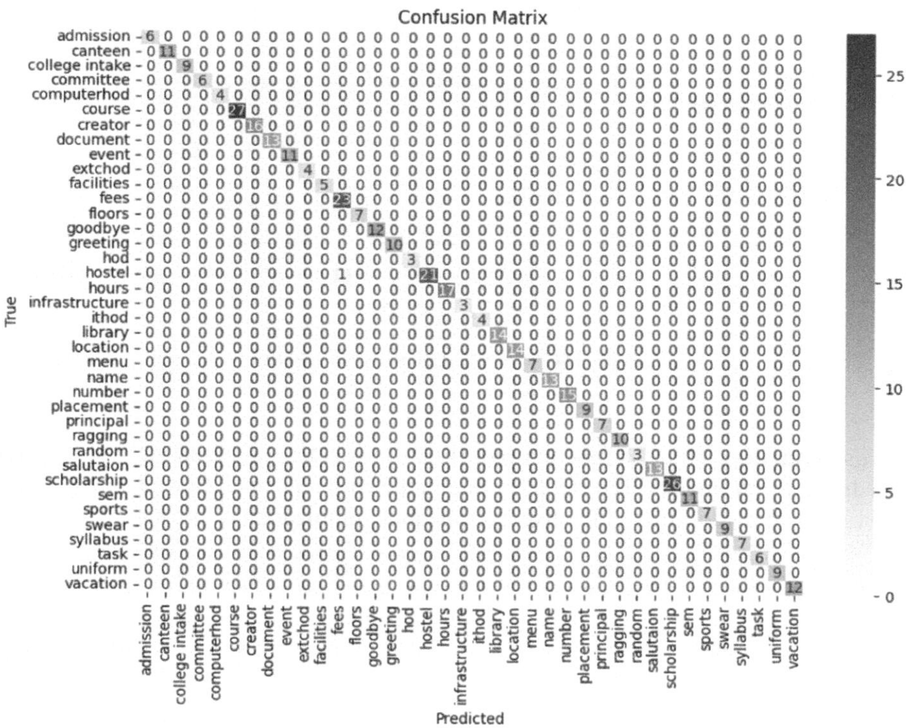

Fig. 1. The confusion matrix

for each class, allowing for a detailed examination of the model's strengths and weaknesses.

- **Accuracy and Loss over Epochs**: The accuracy and loss plots (Fig. 2) depict the model's training progress over 200 epochs. The accuracy plot shows a steady increase, reaching a plateau around the 100th epoch, indicating the model's convergence. The loss plot shows a consistent decrease, further confirming the model's learning process.

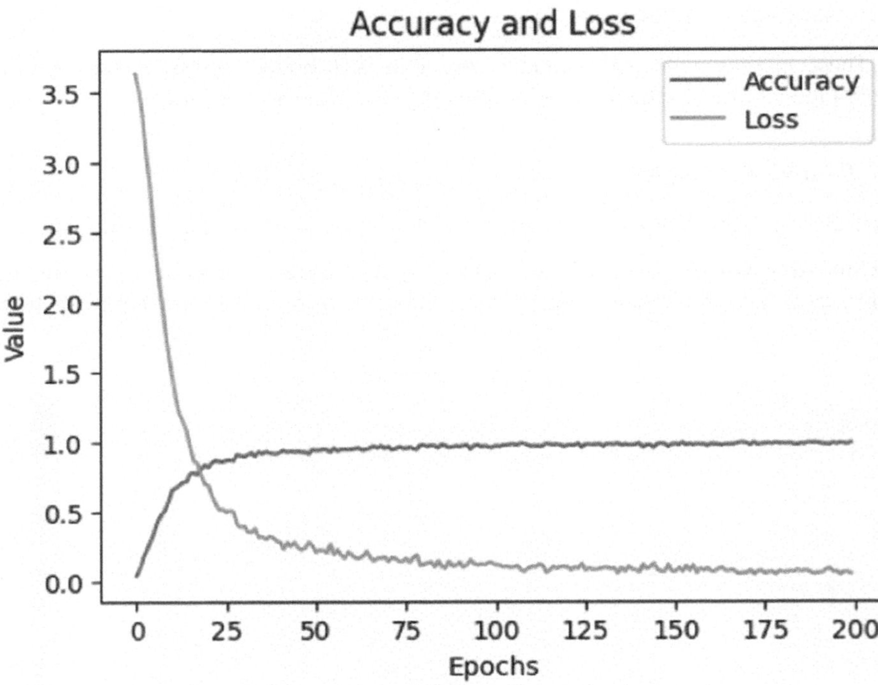

Fig. 2. The accuracy and loss over epochs

- **Loss Function**: The loss function plot (Fig. 3) provides a focused view of the loss reduction over epochs. The steep decline in the early epochs followed by a gradual leveling off demonstrates effective learning and optimization of the model.

- **ROC Curves**: The ROC curves (Fig. 4) for each class illustrate the true positive rate versus the false positive rate, providing insights into the model's discriminative ability. The areas under the ROC curves (AUC) for all classes are 1.00, indicating perfect classification performance .

These visualizations collectively confirm the model's high performance, with the confusion matrix highlighting its accuracy across different intents, the accuracy and loss

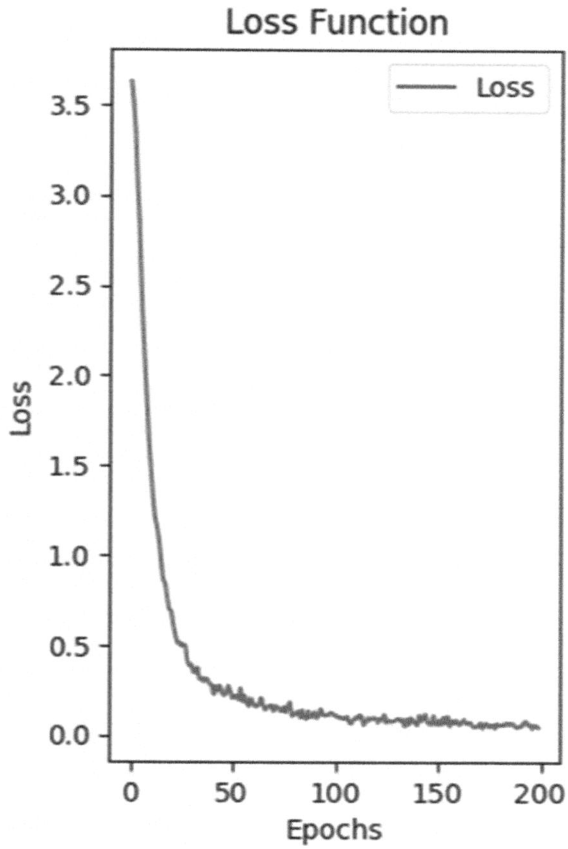

Fig. 3. The loss function

plots showing effective training, and the ROC curves demonstrating excellent classification capabilities. The high values of accuracy, precision, recall, and F1 score indicate that the chatbot model performs exceptionally well in classifying user intents. The confusion matrix reveals that the model has minimal misclassifications, demonstrating its ability to handle a diverse set of queries accurately. The ROC curves further validate the model's robustness, showing perfect separation between classes. The results underscore the effectiveness of the data preprocessing and model training methodologies employed in this study. The use of tokenization, lemmatization, and vectorization ensured that the input data was well-prepared for training, while the neural network architecture with dropout layers effectively prevented overfitting.

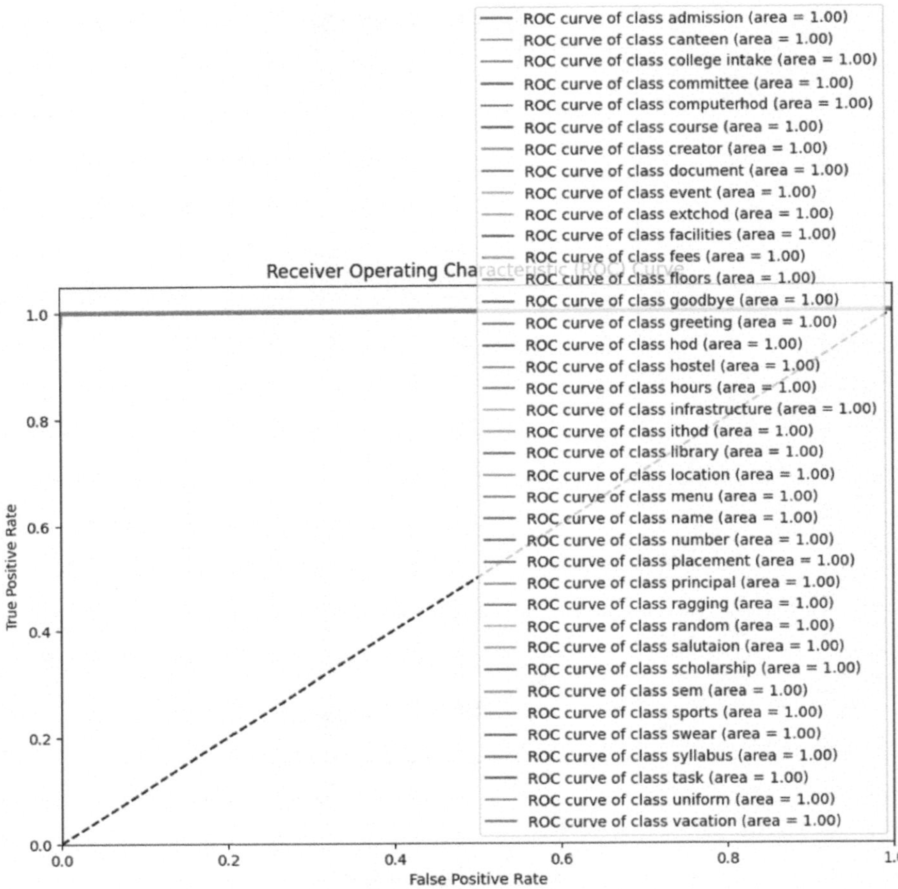

Fig. 4. ROC Curve Comparison

5 Conclusion

This research aimed to develop and evaluate a chatbot using a dataset of frequently asked questions (FAQs) from a university setting. The results indicate that the chatbot model, trained using modern machine learning techniques, performs exceptionally well in understanding and responding to user queries. This conclusion section summarizes the key findings, discusses the implications of the results, and suggests directions for future work. The primary objective of this study was to create a chatbot capable of accurately and efficiently handling a variety of queries typically encountered in a university environment. Using a comprehensive dataset sourced from Kaggle, the chatbot was trained to recognize different intents and provide appropriate responses. The methodology involved thorough data preprocessing, including tokenization, lemmatization, and vectorization, followed by training a neural network model using TensorFlow. The evaluation of the model yielded impressive results, with an accuracy of 99.75%, precision of 99.76%, recall of 99.75%, and an F1 score of 99.75%. These metrics demonstrate the model's high reliability and effectiveness in classifying user intents. Additionally, the visualizations, including the confusion matrix, accuracy and loss plots, and ROC curves, further validated the model's robust performance. The high performance of the chatbot model has several significant implications for educational institutions. Firstly, the deployment of such a chatbot can greatly enhance the efficiency of information dissemination. By providing instant and accurate responses to common queries, the chatbot can alleviate the workload on administrative staff, allowing them to focus on more complex and critical tasks. Furthermore, the availability of a chatbot can improve the overall user experience for students, staff, and prospective applicants. Users can access information at any time, without the need to wait for office hours or human intervention. This 24/7 availability is particularly beneficial for international students and stakeholders in different time zones. The success of this chatbot also highlights the potential for further applications of AI in educational settings. Beyond answering FAQs, chatbots can be integrated with other university systems to provide personalized support, assist with course registration, monitor student progress, and more. The scalability and flexibility of AI-driven chatbots make them a valuable tool for modernizing educational administration and support services. While the results of this study are promising, there are several areas for future research and development. One potential direction is to expand the dataset to include a broader range of queries and more detailed responses. This expansion can help the chatbot handle even more diverse and complex user interactions. Additionally, integrating advanced natural language processing techniques, such as transformer models (e.g., BERT, GPT-3), could further enhance the chatbot's understanding and generation of human-like responses. These models have shown remarkable performance in various NLP tasks and could significantly improve the chatbot's conversational abilities. Another area for future work is the deployment and testing of the chatbot in a real-world university setting. This deployment would provide valuable insights into the chatbot's practical utility, user satisfaction, and areas needing improvement. Continuous monitoring and iterative refinement based on user feedback would ensure the chatbot remains effective and relevant. Finally, exploring the ethical and privacy implications of deploying chatbots in educational environments is crucial. Ensuring that the chatbot adheres to data protection regulations and maintains user confidentiality is essential for gaining trust and widespread adoption. In conclusion, this study successfully developed and evaluated a highly effective chatbot for handling university FAQs. The impressive performance metrics and visualizations confirm the model's robustness and accuracy. The deployment of such chatbots in educational institutions holds great potential for improving efficiency, user experience, and overall service quality. Future research and development can further enhance the capabilities and applications of chatbots, making them an integral part of modern educational ecosystems.

References

1. Al Mansoori, S., Salloum, S.A., Shaalan, K.: The impact of artificial intelligence and information technologies on the efficiency of knowledge management at modern organizations: a systematic review. In: Al-Emran, M., Shaalan, K., Ella Hassanien, A. (eds.) Recent Advances in Intelligent Systems and Smart Applications. SSDC, vol. 295, pp. 163–182. Springer, Cham (2021). https://doi.org/10.1007/978-3-030-47411-9_9
2. Salloum, S.A., Shwedeh, F., Alfaisal, A.M., et al.: Understanding and forecasting chatbot adoption: an sem-ann methodology. Migr Lett **20**, 652–668 (2023)
3. Salloum, S.A., Almarzouqi, A., Aburayya, A., Alfaisal, R.: Adoption of Chatbots for University Students. In: Artificial Intelligence in Education: The Power and Dangers of ChatGPT in the Classroom. Springer, pp 233–246 (2024). https://doi.org/10.1007/978-3-031-52280-2_15
4. El Bakkouri, B., Raki, S., Belgnaoui, T.: The role of chatbots in enhancing customer experience: literature review. Procedia Comput Sci **203**, 432–437 (2022)
5. Følstad, A., Brandtzæg, P.B.: Chatbots and the new world of HCI. Interactions **24**(4), 38–42 (2017). https://doi.org/10.1145/3085558
6. Weizenbaum, J.: ELIZA—a computer program for the study of natural language communication between man and machine. Commun. ACM **9**, 36–45 (1966)
7. Colby, K.M.: Artificial paranoia: A computer simulation of paranoid processes, Elsevier (2013)
8. Wallace, R.S.: The anatomy of ALICE. Springer https://doi.org/10.1007/978-1-4020-6710-5_13(2009)
9. Serban, I., et al.: Building end-to-end dialogue systems using generative hierarchical neural network models. In: Proceedings of the AAAI Conference on Artificial Intelligence (2016)
10. Goel, A.K., Polepeddi, L.: Jill Watson: a virtual teaching assistant for online education. In: Learning Engineering for Online Education. Routledge, pp 120–143 (2018)
11. Kerlyl, A., Hall, P., Bull, S.: Bringing chatbots into education: towards natural language negotiation of open learner models. In: International conference On Innovative Techniques and Applications of Artificial Intelligence. Springer, pp 179–192 (2006) https://doi.org/10.1007/978-1-84628-666-7_14
12. Bii, P.: Chatbot technology: a possible means of unlocking student potential to learn how to learn. Educ. Res. **4**, 218–221 (2013)
13. Stigmar, M.: Peer-to-peer teaching in higher education: a critical literature review. Mentor Tutoring Partnersh Learn **24**, 124–136 (2016)
14. Srinivasa, K.G., Kurni, M., Saritha, K.: Harnessing the power of AI to education. In: Learning, Teaching, and Assessment Methods for Contemporary Learners: Pedagogy for the Digital Generation. Springer, pp 311–342 (2022) https://doi.org/10.1007/978-981-19-6734-4_13
15. HubSpotResearch Speed of response in customer support. https://www.hubspot.com/statistics/customer-service. (2020)
16. Chatbot dataset. In: Kaggle. https://www.kaggle.com/datasets/niraliivaghani/chatbot-dataset. (2023)
17. Bird, S., Klein, E., Loper, E.: Natural language processing with Python: analyzing text with the natural language toolkit. O'Reilly Media, Inc. (2009)
18. Miller, G.A.: WordNet: a lexical database for English. Commun. ACM **38**, 39–41 (1995)
19. Harris, Z.S.: Distributional structure. Word **10**, 146–162 (1954)
20. Abadi, M., et al.: {TensorFlow}: a system for {Large-Scale} machine learning. In: 12th USENIX Symposium on Operating Systems Design and Implementation (OSDI 16), pp 265–283 (2016)
21. Kingma, D.P., Ba, J.: Adam: A method for stochastic optimization. arXiv Prepr arXiv14126980 (2014)
22. Saito, T., Rehmsmeier, M.: The precision-recall plot is more informative than the ROC plot when evaluating binary classifiers on imbalanced datasets. PLoS ONE **10**, e0118432 (2015)

Comparative Analysis of Classical Machine Learning Techniques for Predicting Students' Exam Performance

Said A. Salloum[1,2](✉), Ayham Salloum[3], Khaled Shaalan[4], Raghad Alfaisal[5], and Azza Basiouni[6]

[1] Health Economic and Financing Group, University of Sharjah, Sharjah, UAE
ssalloum@sharjah.ac.ae

[2] School of Science, Engineering, and Environment, University of Salford, Salford, United Kingdom

[3] College of Medicine, University of Sharjah, Sharjah, UAE

[4] Faculty of Engineering and IT, The British University in Dubai, Dubai, UAE
khaled.shaalan@buid.ac.ae

[5] Faculty of Computing and Meta-Technology, Universiti Pendidikan Sultan Idris, Perak, Malaysia

[6] Faculty of Information Technology, Liwa College, Abu Dhabi, UAE
azza.basiouni@lc.ac.ae

Abstract. The prediction of student performance is a critical area of research in educational data mining, aiming to identify factors that contribute to academic success or failure. Accurate prediction models can help educators and policymakers develop interventions to improve student outcomes. Despite the availability of various machine learning techniques, there remains a need for a comprehensive comparison of these methods applied to a single dataset. This study addresses this gap by applying several classical machine learning algorithms, including Logistic Regression, Decision Tree, Random Forest, Support Vector Machine, K-Nearest Neighbors, Naive Bayes, and Gradient Boosting, to predict student performance using a publicly available dataset from Kaggle. The dataset includes demographic and educational attributes such as gender, race/ethnicity, parental level of education, lunch type, and test preparation course. The models were evaluated based on accuracy, precision, recall, F1 score, and ROC curves. Logistic Regression emerged as the top-performing model with an AUC of 0.72, accuracy of 0.71, and F1 score of 0.81, indicating robust predictive capability and high interpretability. Naive Bayes also performed competitively, highlighting the effectiveness of simple probabilistic models. These findings provide valuable insights for educators and policymakers, emphasizing the importance of machine learning in early identification of students at risk of underperforming, thereby enabling timely interventions. Future research should explore advanced techniques such as deep learning, feature engineering, and longitudinal data analysis to further enhance predictive accuracy. Additionally, the interpretability and ethical implications of deploying these models in educational settings must be considered to ensure responsible usage.

A. Basiouni and C. Frasson (Eds.): BBGI 2024, CCIS 2162, pp. 219–227, 2024.
https://doi.org/10.1007/978-3-031-65996-6_19

Keywords: Artificial intelligence · Educational data · machine learning · students' exam performance

1 Introduction

Student performance prediction is a critical area of research in educational data mining [1, 2], aimed at identifying factors that contribute to academic success or failure [3]. Over the past few decades, various factors influencing student performance have been identified, ranging from individual attributes such as motivation and study habits to broader contextual factors like socioeconomic status and school resources [2]. By accurately predicting student performance, educators and policymakers can develop targeted interventions to support students who are at risk of underperforming, thereby enhancing overall educational outcomes. For instance, early identification of students who may struggle academically allows for timely support and resource allocation, which can mitigate the risk of dropout and improve retention rates [4].

Machine learning techniques have been increasingly applied to educational data mining due to their ability to handle large datasets and uncover complex patterns [5, 6]. Classical machine learning algorithms such as Logistic Regression, Decision Trees, Random Forests, Support Vector Machines (SVMs), K-Nearest Neighbors (KNN), and Naive Bayes classifiers have demonstrated effectiveness in various prediction tasks. These algorithms offer different strengths: Logistic Regression provides interpretability, Decision Trees offer simplicity and visual insights, Random Forests combine multiple trees to improve accuracy, SVMs handle high-dimensional spaces effectively, KNN is intuitive and easy to implement, and Naive Bayes works well with small datasets despite its simplicity [7].

Despite the advancements in machine learning applications, challenges remain in predicting student performance accurately. Factors such as data quality, feature selection, and model selection significantly impact the performance of predictive models [8]. Moreover, educational data often include a mix of numerical and categorical variables, necessitating robust preprocessing techniques [9]. Additionally, the interpretability of machine learning models is crucial in the educational context, as educators and policymakers need to understand the reasoning behind predictions to trust and act upon them [8]. This study seeks to address these challenges by applying a comprehensive set of classical machine learning algorithms to a publicly available dataset of student performance and comparing their effectiveness in predicting academic success.

The dataset used in this study, sourced from Kaggle [10], includes information on marks secured by students in various subjects, along with demographic and educational attributes such as gender, race/ethnicity, parental level of education, lunch type, and test preparation course. The primary contributions of this study are twofold. First, we provide a detailed comparative analysis of several classical machine learning algorithms applied to the task of predicting student performance in exams. By evaluating these algorithms based on key metrics such as accuracy, precision, recall, F1 score, and ROC curves, we identify the most effective models for this task. Second, we highlight the practical implications of our findings for educators and policymakers, demonstrating how machine learning models can be leveraged to improve educational interventions and outcomes. By sharing our methodology and results, we aim to contribute to the broader field of educational data mining and support future research efforts in this domain.

The structure of this paper is as follows: Sect. 2 describes the methodology, including data preprocessing, feature selection, and the machine learning models used. Section 3 presents the results, including the performance metrics for each model and a comparative analysis. Section 4 discusses the findings, their implications, and potential limitations of the study. Finally, Sect. 5 concludes the paper, summarizing the key insights and suggesting directions for future research.

2 Related Work

The prediction of student performance using machine learning techniques has been widely studied in the field of educational data mining. Romero and Ventura [3] provided a comprehensive review of the state of the art in educational data mining, highlighting various techniques and their applications. They noted that early studies primarily focused on using decision trees and association rule mining to identify patterns in student data.

Baker and Inventado [4] discussed the evolution of educational data mining and learning analytics, emphasizing the role of machine learning in understanding and improving educational processes. They pointed out that machine learning algorithms such as logistic regression, support vector machines, and neural networks have been used to predict student performance with varying degrees of success. Their work underscored the importance of feature selection and preprocessing in enhancing the accuracy of these models.

In recent years, the application of ensemble methods has gained traction. Kotsiantis [8] reviewed various classification techniques and highlighted the superior performance of ensemble methods like Random Forests and Gradient Boosting in predictive tasks. He emphasized that these methods often outperform single classifiers by combining multiple models to reduce overfitting and improve generalization.

Several studies have focused on specific algorithms for predicting student performance. For example, [5] applied logistic regression and decision tree algorithms to a dataset of student grades, finding that logistic regression provided better interpretability while decision trees offered higher accuracy for complex interactions between variables. Similarly, [7] used the Naive Bayes classifier on educational data and found it to be effective despite its simplicity, particularly when combined with feature selection techniques to handle the assumption of feature independence.

Lantz [9] explored the application of K-Nearest Neighbors (KNN) and Support Vector Machines (SVM) to educational datasets. His findings indicated that while KNN is straightforward and easy to implement, it can be sensitive to the choice of distance metric and the number of neighbors. On the other hand, SVMs demonstrated robust performance in high-dimensional spaces but required careful tuning of hyperparameters to achieve optimal results.

Despite these advancements, challenges remain in accurately predicting student performance. One significant issue is the variability in data quality and the need for effective preprocessing techniques to handle missing values, categorical variables, and outliers.

Additionally, many studies have highlighted the importance of interpretability in educational contexts, as educators and policymakers need to understand the factors driving predictions to make informed decisions.

However, a notable gap in the literature is the lack of comprehensive comparative studies that evaluate the performance of a wide range of classical machine learning algorithms on a single dataset of student performance. While individual algorithms have been studied extensively, there is a need for a systematic comparison that considers multiple performance metrics and provides insights into the strengths and weaknesses of each method. This study aims to fill this gap by applying several classical machine learning algorithms to a dataset of student performance in exams. By evaluating these models based on accuracy, precision, recall, F1 score, and ROC curves, we seek to identify the most effective techniques for predicting student success. Our work contributes to the field by providing a detailed comparative analysis and highlighting practical implications for educational interventions.

3 Methodology

The methodology for this study involves several steps: data preprocessing, feature selection, model training, and evaluation. The process is designed to ensure that the models are trained on high-quality data and evaluated using robust metrics to determine their effectiveness in predicting student performance. Each step is detailed below.

3.1 Data Preprocessing

Data preprocessing is a critical step in machine learning, as it transforms raw data into a suitable format for analysis. The dataset used in this study, sourced from Kaggle [10], includes various features such as gender, race/ethnicity, parental level of education, lunch type, and test preparation course. The target variable is the average score of students in math, reading, and writing exams.

- **Categorical Encoding:** Categorical variables are encoded using Label Encoding to convert them into numerical values. Label encoding assigns a unique integer to each category, allowing the algorithms to process these variables [11].
- **Feature Standardization:** Standardizing features by removing the mean and scaling to unit variance is a common preprocessing step that ensures that each feature contributes equally to the analysis. This is particularly important for algorithms that rely on distance calculations, such as K-Nearest Neighbors and Support Vector Machines [9].
- **Binarization of Target Variable:** The target variable, representing the average score, is binarized into two classes: Pass (average score ≥ 60) and Fail (average score < 60). This binarization facilitates the application of binary classification algorithms.

3.2 Feature Selection

Feature selection involves identifying the most relevant features for the predictive model. This step is essential to improve model performance and reduce overfitting by eliminating irrelevant or redundant features. In this study, all available features are used, given their direct relevance to student performance [12].

3.3 Model Training

Several classical machine learning algorithms are employed to predict student performance. These algorithms are chosen for their diverse approaches to classification tasks, providing a comprehensive comparison.

- **Logistic Regression:** Logistic regression is a linear model for binary classification that estimates the probability of a binary response based on one or more predictor variables. It is widely used for its simplicity and interpretability [13].
- **Decision Tree:** A decision tree classifier is a non-parametric model that splits the data into subsets based on the value of input features. Decision trees are easy to interpret and visualize, making them popular for educational data mining [14].
- **Random Forest:** Random Forest is an ensemble method that builds multiple decision trees and merges them to obtain a more accurate and stable prediction. It is known for its high accuracy and robustness against overfitting [15].
- **Support Vector Machine (SVM):** SVM is a powerful classification algorithm that finds the hyperplane that best separates the data into classes. It is particularly effective in high-dimensional spaces and with clear margin of separation [16].
- **K-Nearest Neighbors (KNN):** KNN is a simple, instance-based learning algorithm that assigns class labels based on the majority class among the k-nearest neighbors of a point. Despite its simplicity, KNN can perform well with the right choice of k and distance metric [17].
- **Naive Bayes:** Naive Bayes is a probabilistic classifier based on Bayes' theorem with strong (naive) independence assumptions between features. It is efficient and works well with small datasets and categorical features [18].

3.4 Model Evaluation

The models are evaluated using several metrics to provide a comprehensive assessment of their performance:

- **Accuracy:** The proportion of correctly classified instances among the total instances. It is a basic metric but can be misleading if the classes are imbalanced [19].
- **Precision:** The proportion of true positive predictions among all positive predictions. Precision is crucial when the cost of false positives is high [19].
- **Recall:** The proportion of true positive predictions among all actual positives. Recall is important when the cost of false negatives is high [19].
- **F1 Score:** The harmonic mean of precision and recall. It provides a single metric that balances both concerns [19].
- **ROC Curve and AUC:** The ROC curve plots the true positive rate against the false positive rate at various threshold settings. The Area Under the ROC Curve (AUC) provides a single value to compare model performance across different threshold settings [20].

The dataset is split into training (70%) and testing (30%) sets. Each model is trained on the training set and evaluated on the testing set. The metrics for each model are calculated and compared to determine the most effective algorithm for predicting student performance.

4 Results

This section presents the performance evaluation of the classical machine learning algorithms applied to the dataset. The algorithms are evaluated based on accuracy, precision, recall, F1 score, and ROC curves. Table 1 summarizes the performance metrics for each classifier, while Fig. 1 shows the ROC curves for all classifiers.

4.1 Performance Metrics

The evaluation metrics for each classifier are shown in Table 1. These metrics provide insights into the effectiveness of each model in predicting student performance.

Table 1. Model Performance Metrics

Classifier	Accuracy	Precision	Recall	F1 Score
Logistic Regression	**0.707**	**0.743**	**0.908**	**0.810**
Decision Tree	0.623	0.722	0.733	0.728
Random Forest	0.620	0.700	0.782	0.739
Support Vector Machine	0.690	0.718	0.903	0.800
K-Nearest Neighbors	0.683	0.728	0.860	0.788
Naive Bayes	0.700	0.740	0.869	0.800
Gradient Boosting	0.687	0.741	0.830	0.784

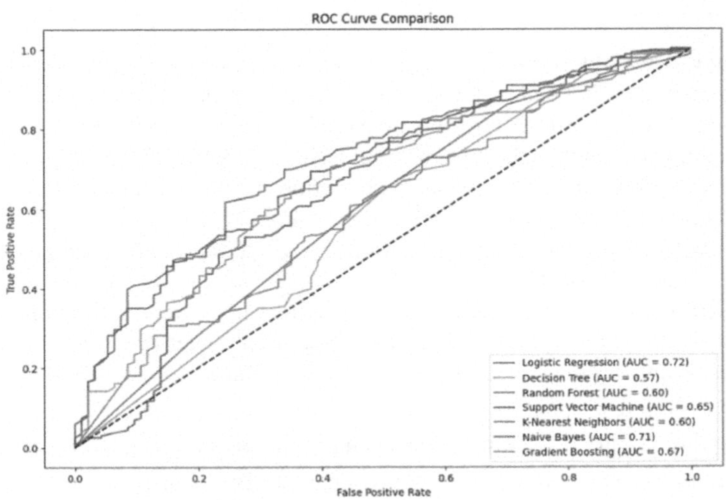

Fig. 1. ROC Curve Comparison

4.2 ROC Curve

The ROC curves for the classifiers are presented in Fig. 1. The ROC curve plots the true positive rate against the false positive rate at various threshold settings, providing a comprehensive view of the classifier's performance. The Area Under the ROC Curve (AUC) is also reported for each classifier, offering a single value to compare model performance.

4.3 Detailed Analysis

- **Logistic Regression**: The Logistic Regression model achieved the highest AUC score of 0.72, indicating a good balance between sensitivity and specificity. With an accuracy of 0.71 and an F1 score of 0.81, this model is highly effective in predicting student performance. The high recall of 0.91 suggests that Logistic Regression is particularly good at identifying students who pass.
- **Decision Tree**: The Decision Tree classifier demonstrated an accuracy of 0.62 and an F1 score of 0.73. Despite its simplicity and ease of interpretation, the Decision Tree model had the lowest AUC of 0.57, indicating lower discriminative power compared to other models.
- **Random Forest**: The Random Forest classifier achieved an accuracy of 0.62 and an F1 score of 0.74, with an AUC of 0.60. While it performed better than the Decision Tree, its performance was still lower than expected for this type of model, suggesting possible overfitting or the need for hyperparameter tuning.
- **Support Vector Machine (SVM)**: The SVM model achieved an accuracy of 0.69, an F1 score of 0.80, and an AUC of 0.65. The SVM showed strong performance, particularly in terms of recall (0.90), indicating its effectiveness in correctly identifying students who pass.
- **K-Nearest Neighbors (KNN)**: The KNN classifier had an accuracy of 0.68, an F1 score of 0.79, and an AUC of 0.60. KNN's performance was comparable to SVM and Naive Bayes, demonstrating its viability as a simple, yet effective classifier.
- **Naive Bayes**: The Naive Bayes classifier achieved an accuracy of 0.70, an F1 score of 0.80, and an AUC of 0.71. Despite its simplistic assumptions, Naive Bayes performed competitively, particularly in terms of precision (0.74).
- **Gradient Boosting**: The Gradient Boosting classifier achieved an accuracy of 0.69, an F1 score of 0.78, and an AUC of 0.67. This model performed well, leveraging its ability to correct errors iteratively, resulting in a strong balance of precision and recall.

Overall, Logistic Regression emerged as the top performer in terms of AUC, accuracy, and F1 score, followed closely by Naive Bayes and Support Vector Machine. Decision Tree and Random Forest showed lower performance, possibly due to overfitting or inadequate hyperparameter tuning. The Gradient Boosting model also demonstrated strong performance, validating the effectiveness of ensemble methods. These results provide valuable insights into the applicability of classical machine learning algorithms for predicting student performance and highlight the potential for further optimization and refinement.

5 Conclusion

This study aimed to predict student performance using various classical machine learning algorithms and to evaluate their effectiveness through a comprehensive set of metrics. Utilizing a dataset from Kaggle, which includes demographic and educational attributes such as gender, race/ethnicity, parental level of education, lunch type, and test preparation course, we assessed the performance of Logistic Regression, Decision Tree, Random Forest, Support Vector Machine (SVM), K-Nearest Neighbors (KNN), Naive Bayes, and Gradient Boosting. The evaluation was based on accuracy, precision, recall, F1 score, and ROC curves. Logistic Regression emerged as the top-performing model with the highest AUC of 0.72, accuracy of 0.71, and F1 score of 0.81, indicating its robust predictive capability and high interpretability. Naive Bayes also performed competitively, showcasing the effectiveness of simple probabilistic models. SVM demonstrated strong recall, making it suitable for identifying students who are likely to pass. Ensemble methods like Gradient Boosting also showed promise, validating the potential of iterative error correction techniques. The lower performance of Decision Tree and Random Forest models suggests a need for better hyperparameter tuning to prevent overfitting. These findings provide valuable insights for educators and policymakers, emphasizing the importance of machine learning in early identification of students at risk of underperforming, thereby enabling timely interventions. Future research should explore advanced techniques such as deep learning, feature engineering, and longitudinal data analysis to further enhance predictive accuracy. Additionally, the interpretability and ethical implications of deploying these models in educational settings must be considered to ensure responsible usage. This study contributes to the field of educational data mining by offering a detailed comparative analysis of classical machine learning algorithms and highlighting their practical applications in improving student outcomes.

References

1. Alsharhan, A.M., Salloum, S. (2022). Precision education approaches to education data mining and analytics: a review. In: Hassanien, A.E., Rizk, R.Y., Snášel, V., Abdel-Kader, R.F. (eds) The 8th International Conference on Advanced Machine Learning and Technologies and Applications (AMLTA2022). AMLTA 2022. Lecture Notes on Data Engineering and Communications Technologies, vol 113, pp 337–356. Springer, Cham (2022).https://doi.org/10.1007/978-3-031-03918-8_30
2. Salloum, S.A., Alshurideh, M., Elnagar, A., Shaalan, K. (2020). Mining in educational data: review and future directions. In: Hassanien, AE., Azar, A., Gaber, T., Oliva, D., Tolba, F. (eds) Proceedings of the International Conference on Artificial Intelligence and Computer Vision (AICV2020). AICV 2020. Advances in Intelligent Systems and Computing, vol 1153, pp 92–102. Springer, Cham (2020). https://doi.org/10.1007/978-3-030-44289-7_9
3. Romero, C., Ventura, S.: Educational data mining: a review of the state of the art. IEEE Trans. Syst. Man Cybern. Part C Appl. Rev. **40**(6), 601–618. (2010)
4. de Baker, R.S.J., Inventado, P.S.: Chapter 4: educational data mining and learning analytics. Comput. Sci. **7**, 1–16 (2014)
5. Marsland, S.: Machine Learning: An Algorithmic Perspective, Chapman and Hall/CRC, New York (2011)

6. Al Mansoori, S., Salloum, S.A., Shaalan, K.: The impact of artificial intelligence and information technologies on the efficiency of knowledge management at modern organizations: a systematic review. In: Al-Emran, M., Shaalan, K., Hassanien, A. (eds.) Recent Advances in Intelligent Systems and Smart Applications. SSDC, vol. 295, pp. 163–182. Springer, Cham (2021). https://doi.org/10.1007/978-3-030-47411-9_9
7. Witten, I.H., Frank, E., Hall, M., Pal, C.: Data Mining: Practical Machine Learning Tools and Techniques. Morgan Kaufmann, United States (2016)
8. Kotsiantis, S.B., Zaharakis, I., Pintelas, P.: Supervised machine learning: a review of classification techniques. Emerg. Artif. Intell. Appl. Comput. Eng. **160**, 3–24 (2007)
9. Lantz, B.: Machine Learning with R: Expert Techniques for Predictive Modeling, Packt Publishing Ltd (2019)
10. Students Performance in exams. In: Kaggle (2018). https://www.kaggle.com/datasets/spscientist/students-performance-in-exams
11. Pedregosa, F., Varoquaux, G., Gramfort, A., et al.: Scikit-learn: machine learning in Python. J. Mach. Learn. Res. **12**, 2825–2830 (2011)
12. Guyon, I., Elisseeff, A.: An introduction to variable and feature selection. J. Mach. Learn. Res. **3**, 1157–1182 (2003)
13. Jr Hosmer, D.W., Lemeshow, S., Sturdivant, R.X.: Applied Logistic Regression. Wiley (2013)
14. Breiman, L.: Classification and Regression Trees. Routledge (2017)
15. Breiman, L.: Random forests. Mach. Learn. **45**, 5–32 (2001)
16. Cortes, C., Vapnik, V.: Support-vector networks. Mach. Learn. **20**, 273–297 (1995)
17. Cover, T., Hart, P.: Nearest neighbor pattern classification. IEEE Trans. Inf. theory **13**, 21–27 (1967)
18. Rish, I.: An empirical study of the naive Bayes classifier. In: IJCAI 2001 Workshop on Empirical Methods in Artificial Intelligence. Citeseer, pp 41–46 (2001)
19. Powers, D.M.W.: Evaluation: from precision, recall and F-measure to ROC, informedness, markedness and correlation. arXiv Preprint arXiv:2010.16061 (2020)
20. Fawcett, T.: An introduction to ROC analysis. Pattern Recognit. Lett. **27**, 861–874 (2006)

Exploring Machine Learning's Role in Education: A Comprehensive Review and Academic Implications

Maha Salem(✉) and Khaled Shaalan

Faculty of Engineering and IT, The British University in Dubai, 345015 Dubai, UAE
mahasalim2021@gmail.com, Khaled.shaalan@buid.ac.ae

Abstract. Behind the academic institution, it is a competitive environment in which there is a question of how to best represent the quality of education produced, what system of evaluation of students' productivity best suited, and how to best predict future education needs. With the recent developments in the computerization of along with other methods data management, the rapidly expanding educational field is becoming more and more interested in finding the novel machine learning (ML) applications into educational Data Analysis. The purpose of this review is to in-depth critically assess the existing literature on the ML application to the educational field. The target is to search for the trend in this field and to define which way tends to give better results. The review focuses on the ML algorithms, examining their effectiveness in predicting academic performance, creating space for adaptive learning formats, and impacting other educational variables. The major objectives include better understanding of the existing gaps in research and opportunities to suggest relevant questions on the subject in the directions of future ML implementation development in education. Four main research questions include different ML approaches and algorithms used in educational data analyses, the role of features in ML modeling, types of educational data often considered in the study, the educational outcomes and changes associated with ML integration. By providing the thorough examination of those areas, the review is designed to present valuable implications for academic, student, and administrative practice, offering guidance for possible further studies in the field.

Keywords: Machine learning (ML) · Educational Data · Educational Data mining · Academic Performance

1 Introduction

In recent times, the surge in educational data has spotlighted the importance of data mining techniques in education [1]. Educational institutions now hold vast amounts of both personal and academic data related to students, faculty, and curricula [2]. Sophisticated analytics are employed on these large data sets to unearth patterns, trends, and insights that might otherwise go unnoticed by conventional methods [32]. Educational institutions leverage data mining to improve the learning and teaching

A. Basiouni and C. Frasson (Eds.): BBGI 2024, CCIS 2162, pp. 228–241, 2024.
https://doi.org/10.1007/978-3-031-65996-6_20

environments [4, 5]. Machine Learning, as a pivotal aspect of educational data mining, utilizes complex algorithms and statistical techniques to derive significant insights from extensive data pools [4].

Educational institutions face intense competition and elevated expectations. They encounter challenges in delivering quality education, devising ways to evaluate student performance effectively, and planning for future educational needs [3, 6]. Academic scholars from diverse fields dedicate their research to pinpointing key factors that influence educational outcomes and effective teaching strategies. Their goal is to assist administrators in creating the most conducive learning environments for their students [7].

ML technologies are increasingly being used in the field of education to forecast student outcomes, discern learning behaviors, and customize educational experiences. ML algorithms analyze large data sets to detect patterns related to student activities and achievements [8]. It is crucial for educators and policymakers to understand the impact of various ML methods on refining educational tactics and curriculum design [9]. The development and implementation of ML models in education primarily focus on the accuracy of model predictions. However, in educational settings, high predictive accuracy across the whole student body may not always be adequate. There is a strong focus on both accuracy and fairness in educational ML models, underlining a commitment to maintaining equitable learning opportunities for all students [10]. Thus, a thorough grasp of the capabilities and drawbacks of different ML models is vital in helping educational institutions choose technologies that best match their specific objectives and ethical standards.

The main goal of this review is to critically assess and integrate existing research on the application of machine learning within educational settings, focusing on uncovering key trends and effective strategies. This review aims to deliver valuable insights into the effectiveness of ML algorithms in predicting student performance, facilitating personalized learning, and improving educational results. Moreover, it aims to pinpoint research gaps and propose directions for future research to enhance the use of machine learning in educational environments. To achieve these aims, we have formulated the following research questions for this review:

RQ1: Which ML techniques and algorithms are frequently employed in analyzing educational data, and in what ways do they enhance educational results?
RQ2: Which attributes are found to be significant predictors in ML models within the educational sector?
RQ3: What kinds of educational data are commonly utilized in studies, and which primary institutions provide these data?
RQ4: What improvements and outcomes in education have been observed following the deployment of ML solutions?

2 Background of the Study

Machine Learning (ML) has emerged as a pivotal tool in predictive analytics, aiding decision-making across various sectors like finance, operations, and risk management [11]. Over the last ten years, ML techniques have increasingly addressed various predictive challenges within the education sector [10].

In the evolving landscape of education, employing data mining techniques alongside ML algorithms is crucial for deciphering complexities in student performance and outcomes. Numerous studies utilize sophisticated computational methods to tackle a broad range of educational issues. These include predicting academic success from past performance [1, 2, 4, 9, 12–17], enhancing engagement in digital learning spaces, and exploring factors that influence student success [17–19]. Each study contributes unique insights to the rapidly evolving field of educational data mining and ML.

ML also enables the personalization of educational experiences, such as tailoring assessments dynamically through predictive modeling [12], predicting student dropouts and identifying at-risk students early [20, 21], detecting cheating by analyzing assessment logs [18], and creating customized course recommendations based on student preferences [22]. Thus, ML's integration continues to transform and redefine educational methodologies.

The capability of educational institutions to predict student performance, categorize students based on their skills, and enhance their future exam results is of paramount importance [4]. Effective prediction of student performance often involves analyzing their past academic achievements, as these are indicative of the relationship between a student's interests and their academic success. This approach enables educators to pinpoint and support students who might need additional guidance [4].

Three types of machine learning are used in education: analogical learning, which applies specific instances and logical reasoning to derive partial rules and apply them to new situations; inductive learning, which involves incomplete induction and causal reasoning; and deductive learning, which forms conclusions using inference rules.

The application of ML in educational data analysis requires a cross-disciplinary knowledge base encompassing computer science, education, statistics, and cognitive science [22]. A variety of ML algorithms are available to tackle diverse educational tasks and challenges.

The logistic regression method is widely utilized to examine the connections among multiple independent variables, which may be binary, categorical, or continuous [24, 25]. Decision Trees are favored for their transparency and simplicity in managing both small and extensive datasets, operating through a logic similar to IF-THEN rules, which aids in demystifying this approach [11]. An Artificial Neural Network (ANN) excels at detecting interactions among independent variables, proving its efficacy in mining educational data [26]. The Naïve Bayes classifier, based on Bayes' theorem, is a probabilistic method that calculates the likelihood of a hypothesis with pre-existing knowledge and evidence, determining the joint probability of features within a class by multiplying their conditional probabilities [18]. The K-Nearest Neighbors (KNN) algorithm classifies a data point by the majority class within its closest neighbors, using multivariate attributes for classification [25]. Support Vector Machine (SVM) is a supervised learning model that separates data points using an N-dimensional hyperplane, where N represents the number of features defining each point [27]. Gradient Boosting (XGBoost) applies gradient tree boosting to optimize predictions by minimizing a loss function during training [28].

Several ML algorithms have been extensively used across different studies to tackle tasks and challenges within the realm of education. Logistic Regression (LR) has been frequently cited in research for its effectiveness [12, 13, 18, 20, 23]. Decision Trees are noted for their utility in multiple studies [5, 13, 20]. The ANN is highlighted in recent analyses [16, 29], while the Naive Bayes approach is well-documented for its probabilistic processing [4, 13, 18]. KNN application is acknowledged for its simplicity and effectiveness [18]. SVM have been applied to discern complex patterns [17, 18] and XGBoost is recognized for its performance in gradient boosting [20, 30, 31] along with other methods contributing valuable insights to the field.

3 Research Methodology

The research methodology for this study entailed a thorough review of literature published from 2020 to 2024. A systematic approach was utilized to assess a broad spectrum of scholarly articles, drawing from established databases like IEEE Xplore, ScienceDirect, Emerald, and Springer. The review was conducted by filtering studies that matched the designated timeframe. The search strategy was formulated using the query: ("ML" OR "predictive modeling") AND "education" AND ("student performance" OR "academic achievement" OR "learning outcomes" OR "Learning Patterns").

A thorough screening procedure was carried out once the articles had been collected from various digital sources. We took into consideration just those papers that had directly related on using machine learning in educational settings. Table 1. of the primary study provides specific inclusion and exclusion criteria that influenced the selection of articles. PRISMA principles were followed in the systematic review, and the search approach is

Table 1. The inclusion and exclusion criteria.

Inclusion criteria	Exclusion criteria
Studies must specifically engage with ML techniques within an educational framework	Studies irrelevant to ML applications in educational contexts are excluded
The research must focus on educational settings, covering themes like student performance	Excluded are studies that do not address important educational issues like academic performance, learning outcomes, performance of pupils, or patterns of learning
Only articles published between 2020 and 2024 are included	Not included are articles published after 2020 and up to 2024
Research articles must be available in English	Articles not written in English are excluded

shown in the PRISMA flow diagrams in Fig. 1. Figure 2show that most of the papers that are relevant were published in 2023.

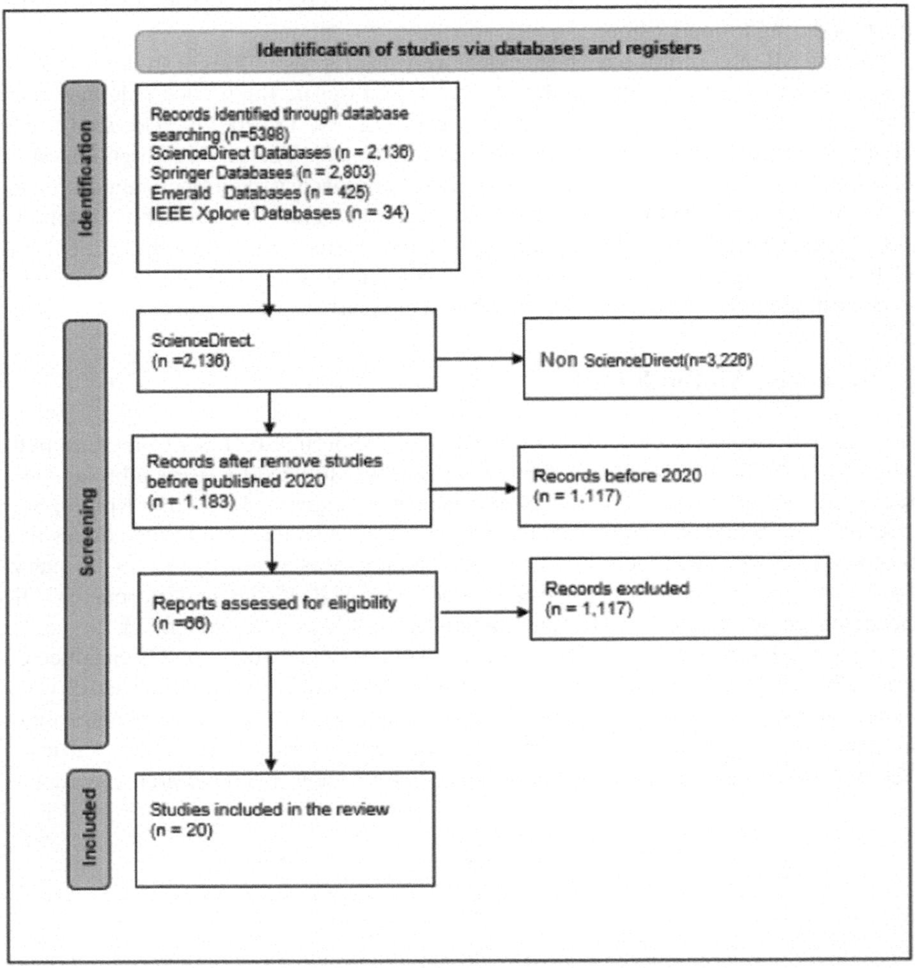

Fig 1. PRISMA flowchart

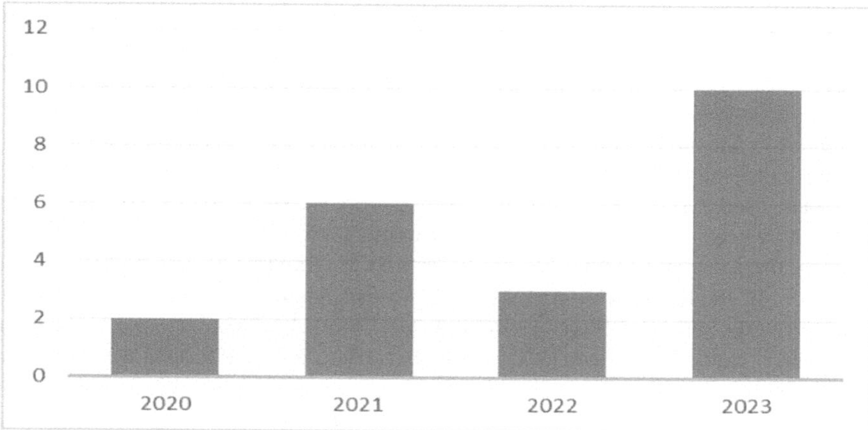

Fig 2. Selected articles categorized based on the year of publication

4 Results

In educational settings, ML signifies a transformative shift, introducing revolutionary capabilities that extend far beyond conventional teaching methodologies. As educators and researchers explore innovative ways to enhance teaching and learning experiences, educational environments have become prime venues for integrating ML algorithms. The outcomes of this study will be presented in relation to specific research questions, following a review of chosen research publications that focus on ML within educational contexts.

4.1 RQ1: Frequently Used Machine Learning Techniques and Algorithms in Educa.

In educational settings, machine learning (ML) techniques are essential for providing predictive modeling, clustering, recommendation systems, natural language processing, and other features. Scholars employ diverse machine learning models, with a primary focus on classification algorithms, to predict and analyze a range of educational outcomes. This includes predicting student performance based on historical academic data [4, 11–14], assessing academic achievements through online engagement, and adaptively forecasting results in online education settings [17]. Noteworthy is the use of both supervised and unsupervised learning methods in crafting intelligent recommendation systems, as demonstrated by [19] which tailor content recommendations for smart educational platforms.

Furthermore, the research explores a wide range of classification applications, such as categorizing forum posts, analyzing legal assignments, predicting student dropouts, and forecasting career paths [10]. Additionally, [23] analyzed secondary data from the Spanish cohort of PISA 2015, employing classification models to identify high- and low-effectiveness schools. Their goal was to pinpoint process variables that significantly improve the accuracy of predictions in distinguishing between these schools.

In machine learning for education, clustering is the process of assembling pupils that are similar to each other based on particular traits.[18] Used this method to create a model by analyzing assessment log files, with the aim of identifying and clustering instances of Internet cheating.

The use of ML algorithms to forecast and enhance student performance has been a recurring theme in many studies. Twelve research demonstrate how machine learning (ML) can be used to predict performance in educational settings, while two more studies look into techniques for predicting student dropout. Table 2. lists the algorithms that are frequently used in these studies: Naive Bayes, SVM, Random Forest, Decision Trees (C4.5, ID3), ANN, KNN, XGBoost, Long Short-term Memory (LSTM), Convolutional Neural Networks and Long Short-Term Memory (CONV-LSTM), Deep Belief Network (DBN), and Logistic Regression (LR). These algorithms are used for a number of different tasks, including regression, pattern recognition, prediction, and classification. The range of machine learning algorithms employed in the various investigations is shown in Fig. 3.

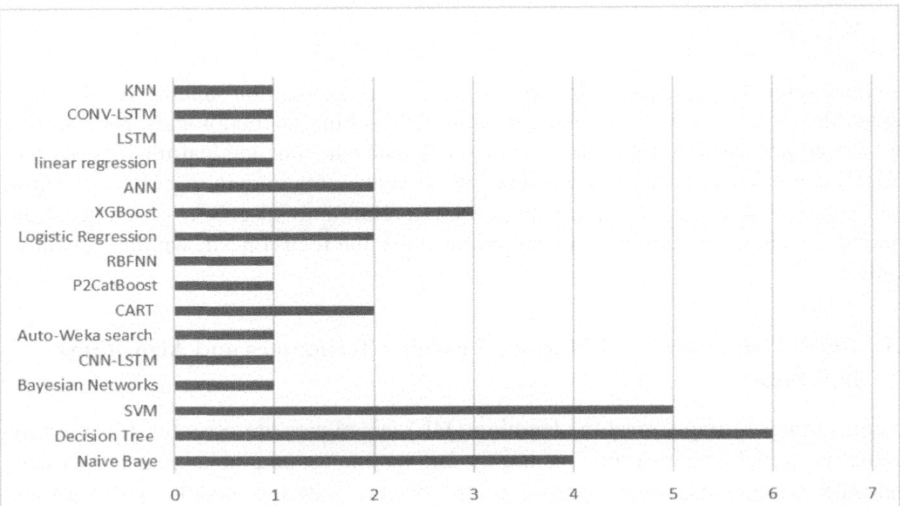

Fig 3. Distribution of ML algorithms used across the analyzed Studies

4.2 RQ2: Significant Predictive Features in ML Models

Research has identified a variety of factors that influence the accuracy of ML models in educational settings. These factors encompass demographic details, historical academic performance, learning habits, self-efficacy, motivation, social support, and other elements pertinent to educational contexts [19]. [13] detail the method for defining the dependent (target) variable in scenarios lacking final grades. Student performance is assessed using grades from assignments uploaded to the Learning Management System

(LMS). To prevent bias, this dependent variable is calculated by aggregating scores from both compulsory and optional assignments.

In terms of attributes utilized across various studies, demographic information is employed in nine studies, while academic performance data is used in eight. These attributes are categorized into seven groups, as outlined in Table 3.

Table 2. Commonly Used Attributes in ML Algorithms for Educational Data Analysis

Attributes	Description	References
Demographic information	Gender, age, educational institution, home address, educational background of parents, father's occupation, guardian details, number of family members, motivation for selecting the school, and commute time to school	[2, 9, 14, 16, 17, 19, 22, 30]
Academic Performance	Cumulative Grade Point Averages, Probations, Warnings, Participation in the classroom, extracurricular activities, academic standing, educational stage information, and dropout status	[10, 11, 15, 16, 19, 20, 29, 30, 31]
Behavioral Factors	Learning behaviors, self-efficacy levels, motivation, social support networks, students' emotional states, and personality traits, such as neuroticism and achievement striving	[11, 14, 19, 20]
Participation and Engagement	Engagement in academic and extracurricular activities, interactions with faculty members, time dedicated to social media and watching movies, and involvement in sports or club activities	[10, 16, 18, 21, 22]
Financial and Socioeconomic Factors	Family Income, Financial Situation and Fees, Parent Income	[12, 20, 30]
Educational Goals and Career Aspirations	Motivations for enrolling in the academic program, career aspirations	[2, 30]
Online Learning Behaviors	Viewing patterns for educational videos, performance on assignments and tests, engagement in discussion forums, navigation data, and types of courses registered	[10, 16, 18, 21]

4.3 RQ3: Types of Educational Data Utilized in Research

The educational data employed in the reviewed studies originate from a variety of sources and are gathered through different methodologies. Significant datasets provided by educational institutions exemplify a collaborative spirit within the academic community and are highlighted in multiple studies [4, 9, 11, 15]. Another critical source is data derived from online training platforms and Learning Management System (LMS) logs, which capture the digital interactions of students engaged in educational activities [19, 27, 29].

Data from Kaggle, a well-known platform for data science challenges, includes datasets focusing on students' adaptability in online learning environments [27]. These studies also utilize rigorously tested models known for their benchmark prediction accuracy, ensuring the reliability and consistency of the research findings [10].

Survey data also plays a pivotal role, offering insights from a diverse array of students and capturing their subjective experiences and perspectives within educational frameworks [2]. Additionally, repositories of raw academic scores and teacher evaluations provide a longitudinal perspective on student performance over time [15].

Moreover, national studies offer datasets that expand the research scope, providing a broader understanding of educational systems [30]. The global aspect of educational research is further enriched by panel data from international assessments, which offer comparative insights across different educational systems.

This comprehensive data collection approach enables researchers to analyze a broad spectrum of educational phenomena and contributes significantly to the field of educational data analysis.

4.4 RQ4: Educational Outcomes and Improvements Identified with ML Solutions.

The studies reviewed demonstrate a broad spectrum of positive impacts from the deployment of ML solutions in education. These applications span from utilizing historical data to predict student performance to using online engagement metrics for forecasting academic achievements, embodying a proactive and personalized educational approach.

A major focus of these applications is the prediction and enhancement of student performance across various educational levels, with 14 studies emphasizing this aspect. Using ML to predict student outcomes based on past success in similar courses is a recurring theme. The adaptive prediction of results in online education settings [19] and tailoring content recommendations to individual learner preferences [22] emphasize how these ML applications are dynamic and individualized.

Using classification approaches to predict student performance has been investigated in ten research and has proven to be accurate and reliable. These studies also explore other facets of the students' academic journeys, like earlyz detection of dropout concerns. [20, 30predicting performance in secondary school and university, and examining factors that affect future GPAs [30].

Moreover, the research tackles challenges like detecting cheating in online environments [18], assessing students' knowledge levels [12], measuring undergraduate program final year academic performance and predicting results for Massive Open Online Courses (MOOCs) [21]. The identification of key variables for distinguishing highly effective from less effective schools illustrates how ML can enhance educational policy and practice [23].

Overall, the use of ML in education is proving to be extremely promising, significantly improving educational outcomes and providing customized support to students, thereby enhancing the efficiency and effectiveness of educational practices (Fig. 4).

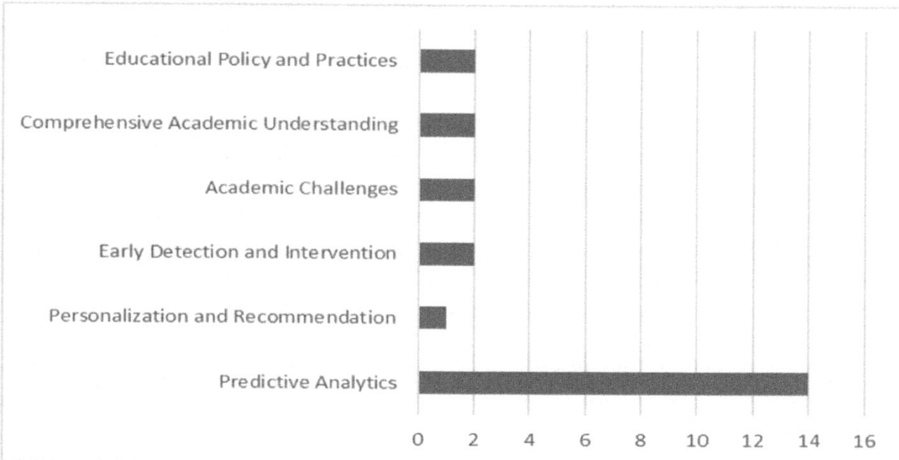

Fig 4. Distribution of studies by educational applications

5 Discussion

A wide range of research on ML in education is examined in 20 papers, revealing several important subjects. These include predicting success through online engagement, predicting adaptability in online learning environments, and creating individualized learning experiences. They also include predictive modeling of academic performance utilizing different algorithms. The research also focusses on early identification of underperforming students and address biases in prediction tasks and factors influencing student performance.

ML applications further include predicting dropout rates, detecting cheating in online assessments, and developing sophisticated ensemble models. Additionally, the research contributes to a better understanding of the effectiveness of a growth mindset, employs automated ML for precise predictions, and utilizes advanced deep learning techniques for success prediction. These broad themes together illustrate the complex and evolving nature of ML applications in educational contexts.

The variety of algorithms employed shows how adaptable ML approaches are to different teaching scenarios. The discipline investigates a wide range of instruments, from traditional algorithms like Naive Bayes and decision trees to sophisticated models like CNN-LSTM and BERT. The goal of incorporating hybrid methodologies, optimization techniques, and ensemble models is to increase prediction efficiency and accuracy.

This multidisciplinary approach demonstrates a dedication to finding the best ways to anticipate academic achievement, adjust to virtual learning environments, and customize educational experiences.

Furthermore, [4] examine algorithms according to fundamental characteristics, with a focus on accuracy and error rate. According to their research, SVM is the most accurate technique for categorizing datasets pertaining to student performance, suggesting that SVM may be the most popular choice for accurately classifying and forecasting student outcomes. SVM is a strong predictor of academic success that outperforms other algorithms like KNN and Decision Trees, including Naive Bayes, in terms of accuracy [17].

This demonstrates that SVM is particularly effective in predicting student outcomes, which can significantly enhance educational strategies and interventions aimed at improving student performance.

The proposed Stacking Ensemble Learning model stands out by achieving the highest accuracy of 93.96% when compared with other algorithms such as Bayesian networks, Random Forest, and CART [22]. This result underscores the effectiveness of the ensemble approach in delivering superior predictive performance for the specific dataset or task under review.

The model leverages the Particle Swarm Optimization (PSO) algorithm, which enhances the deep learning process by optimizing feature extraction and learning. This integration aligns with the broader goal of using ML for personalized education, facilitating tailored content recommendations based on learners' preferences via a smart education big data platform [22].

Additionally, the P2CatBoost model [9] demonstrates remarkable accuracy, hitting 96.62% and 94.45% for final math and Portuguese course grade predictions respectively. This highlights the capability of advanced ML models to provide highly accurate predictions, significantly aiding personalized educational strategies and interventions.

A method proposed by [18] has been effective in identifying various patterns crucial for understanding student cheating behaviors. Beyond its descriptive value, the study offers significant implications for online educators, particularly in creating assessments that are harder to cheat on. By highlighting patterns of cheating behavior, the study provides insights that can help in developing strategies to design more secure assessments. This is crucial for enhancing the integrity of online evaluations and combating academic dishonesty in digital learning environments.

Additionally, the work by [13] on identifying distinct clusters based on student interactions with Learning LMS provide insightful data on the intricate structure of student behavior. In addition to highlighting the variety of interactions that occur in the classroom, this classification helps to clarify the patterns of student participation.

In order to identify the elements that contribute to secondary school effectiveness, [23] made use of the PISA dataset and multilevel models. The study's legitimacy and usefulness are increased by this strong analytical methodology, which offers insightful information on the mechanisms that distinguish high-performing institutions from less successful ones.

Various studies demonstrate ML's practical applications, such as reducing dropout rates through targeted interventions [20], improving academic performance via personalized learning plans [22], and decreasing cheating incidents by redesigning assessments based on cheating patterns [18]. Additionally, ML-enhanced student engagement in online courses by helping instructors create more interactive materials [13] and providing targeted academic support based on online participation predictions [19]. These examples underscore ML's transformative potential in education, driving personalized and effective strategies that significantly improve student outcomes.

6 Conclusion Limitations and future work

This comprehensive analysis of machine learning (ML) applications and educational data reveals a dynamic research environment enhanced by a variety of technology interventions. The compilation of numerous studies demonstrates the broad use of machine learning (ML) in educational settings, encompassing personalized content recommendations, adaptive learning, predictive modeling of academic achievement, and the discovery of critical variables impacting student results. The paper emphasizes how important machine learning (ML) is to early warning systems, dropout prediction, and improving teaching and learning procedures. With ongoing technological advancements, ML's potential to significantly improve educational practices continues to grow. This review serves as a foundation for future research and innovation at the nexus of ML and education.

It's crucial to understand this review's limits, though. The amount of literature and resources available may limit the scope, which could result in gaps in the coverage of ML applications and educational data. Furthermore, the review's comprehensiveness may be compromised by inherent biases in the selection of the studies.

The integration of ML into education has advanced significantly, however there are still research gaps that require investigation. Future research might take advantage of these gaps to improve methods, look further into particular areas, and improve our understanding of ML application in education. A detailed examination of the ethical consequences of ML in education, an exploration of various demographic scenarios, and the long-term effects of ML interventions in educational settings are all crucial areas for future research. Moreover, standardizing frameworks for assessing ML applications' efficacy and creating rules for their morally and responsibly implementation are urgently needed.

Acknowledgments. This work is a part of a project undertaken at the British University in Dubai. Exploiting AI's Potential in Knowledge Management.

References

1. Hussain, A., Khan, M., Ullah, K.: Student's performance prediction model and affecting factors using classification techniques. Educ. Inf. Technol. **27**(6), 8841–8858 (2022). https://doi.org/10.1007/s10639-022-10988-8
2. Dabhade, P., Agarwal, R., Alameen, K.P., Fathima, A.T., Sridharan, R., Gopakumar, G.: Educational data mining for predicting students' academic performance using machine learning algorithms. Mater. Today Proc. **47**, 5260–5267 (2021). https://doi.org/10.1016/j.matpr.2021.05.646
3. Assayed, S.K., Alkhatib, M., Shaalan, K.: Enhancing student services: machine learning Chatbot intent recognition for high school inquiries. BUiD Doct. Res. Conf. **2023**, 243–254 (2024). https://doi.org/10.1007/978-3-031-56121-4_24
4. Pallathadka, H., Wenda, A., Ramirez-Asís, E., Asís-López, M., Flores-Albornoz, J., Phasinam, K.: Classification and prediction of student performance data using various machine learning algorithms. Mater. Today: Proc. **80**, 3782–3785 (2023). https://doi.org/10.1016/j.matpr.2021.07.382
5. Saa, A.A.: Educational data mining and students' performance prediction. IJACSA **7**(5) (2016). www.ijacsa.thesai.org
6. Albreiki, B., Zaki, N., Alashwal, H.: A systematic literature review of student' performance prediction using machine learning techniques. Educ. Sci. **11**(9), 552 (2021). https://doi.org/10.3390/educsci11090552
7. Enughwure, A.A., Ogbise, M.E.: Application of machine learning methods to predict student performance: a systematic literature review. IRJET (2020). www.irjet.net
8. Kotsiantis, S.B.: Use of machine learning techniques for educational proposes: a decision support system for forecasting students' grades. Artif. Intell. Rev. **37**(4), 331–344 (2012). https://doi.org/10.1007/s10462-011-9234-x
9. Fan, Z., Gou, J., Wang, C.: Predicting secondary school student performance using a double particle swarm optimization-based categorical boosting model. Eng. Appl. Artif. Intell. **124**, 106649 (2023). https://doi.org/10.1016/j.engappai.2023.106649
10. Sha, L., Gašević, D., Chen, G.: Lessons from debiasing data for fair and accurate predictive modeling in education. Expert Syst. Appl. **228**, 120323 (2023). https://doi.org/10.1016/j.eswa.2023.120323
11. Zeineddine, H., Braendle, U., Farah, A.: Enhancing prediction of student success: automated machine learning approach. Comput. Electr. Eng. **89**, 106903 (2021). https://doi.org/10.1016/j.compeleceng.2020.106903
12. Matzavela, V., Alepis, E.: Decision tree learning through a predictive model for student academic performance in intelligent M-learning environments. Comput. Educ. Artif. Intell. **2**, 100035 (2021). https://doi.org/10.1016/j.caeai.2021.100035
13. Riestra-González, M., del Puerto Paule-Ruíz, M., Ortin, F.: Massive LMS log data analysis for the early prediction of course-agnostic student performance. Comput. Educ. **163**, 104108 (2021). https://doi.org/10.1016/j.compedu.2020.104108
14. Deeva, G., De Smedt, J., Saint-Pierre, C., Weber, R., De Weerdt, J.: Predicting student performance using sequence classification with time-based windows. Expert Syst. Appl. **209**, 118182 (2022). https://doi.org/10.1016/j.eswa.2022.118182
15. Olabanjo, O.A., Wusu, A.S.: A machine learning prediction of academic performance of secondary school students using radial basis function neural network. Trends Neurosci. Educ. **29**, 100190 (2022). https://doi.org/10.20944/preprints202207.0088.v1
16. Al-Azazi FA, Ghurab M. ANN-LSTM: A deep learning model for early student performance prediction in MOOC. Heliyon **9**(4) (2023). https://doi.org/10.1016/j.heliyon.2023.e15382

17. Alsubaie, M.N.: Predicting student performance using machine learning to enhance the quality assurance of online training via Maharat platform. Alex. Eng. J. **69**, 323–339 (2023). https://doi.org/10.1016/j.aej.2023.02.004
18. Garg, M., Goel, A.: Preserving integrity in online assessment using feature engineering and machine learning. Expert Syst. Appl. **225** (2023). https://doi.org/10.1016/j.eswa.2023.120111
19. Malik, A. et al: Forecasting students' adaptability in online entrepreneurship education using modified ensemble machine learning model. Array **19** (2023). https://doi.org/10.1016/j.array.2023.100303
20. Krüger, J.G.C., de Souza Britto Jr, A., Barddal, J.P.: An explainable machine learning approach for student dropout prediction. Expert Syst. Appl. **233** (2023). https://doi.org/10.1016/j.eswa.2023.120933
21. Mubarak, A.A., Cao, H., Hezam, I.M.: Deep analytic model for student dropout prediction in massive open online courses. Comput. Electr. Eng. **93**https://doi.org/10.1016/j.compeleceng.2021.107271
22. Zheng, L., Wang, C., Chen, X., Song, Y., Meng, Z. Zhang, R.: Evolutionary machine learning builds smart education big data platform: data-driven higher education. Appl. Soft Comput. **136** (2023). https://doi.org/10.1016/j.asoc.2023.110114
23. Martínez-Abad, F., Gamazo, A., Rodriguez-Conde, M.J.: Educational data mining: identification of factors associated with school effectiveness in PISA assessment. Stud. Educ. Eval. **66** (2020). https://doi.org/10.1016/j.stueduc.2020.100875
24. Hoffait, A.-S., Schyns, M.: Early detection of university students with potential difficulties. Decis. Support. Syst. **101**, 1–11 (2017). https://doi.org/10.1016/j.dss.2017.05.003
25. Marbouti, F., Diefes-Dux, H.A., Madhavan, K.: Models for early prediction of at-risk students in a course using standards-based grading. Comput. Educ. **103**, 1–15 (2016). https://doi.org/10.1016/j.compedu.2016.09.005
26. Issah, I., Appiah, O., Appiahene, P., Inusah, F.: A systematic review of the literature on machine learning application of determining the attributes influencing academic performance. Decis. Anal. J. **7**, 100204 (2023). https://doi.org/10.1016/j.dajour.2023.100204
27. Jokhan, A., Sharma, B., Singh, S.: Early warning system as a predictor for student performance in higher education blended courses. Stud. High. Educ. **44**(11), 1900–1911 (2019). https://doi.org/10.1080/03075079.2018.1466872
28. Chen, T., Guestrin, C.: XGBoost: a scalable tree boosting system. In: Proceedings of the 22nd ACM SIGKDD International Conference on Knowledge Discovery and Data Mining, 785–794. https://doi.org/10.1145/2939672.2939785
29. Waheed, H., Hassan, S.U., Nawaz, R., Aljohani, N.R., Chen, G., Gasevic, D.: Early prediction of learners at risk in self-paced education: a neural network approach. Expert Syst. Appl. 213 (2023). https://doi.org/10.1016/j.eswa.2022.118868
30. Bosch, N.: Identifying supportive student factors for mindset interventions: a two-model machine learning approach. Comput. Educ. **167** (2021). https://doi.org/10.1016/j.compedu.2021.104190
31. Niyogisubizo, J., Liao, L., Nziyumva, E., Murwanashyaka, E., Nshimyumukiza, P.C.: Predicting student's dropout in university classes using two-layer ensemble machine learning approach: a novel stacked generalization. Comput. Educ. Artif. Intell. **3** (2022). https://doi.org/10.1016/j.caeai.2022.100066
32. Romero, C., Ventura, S.: Educational data mining and learning analytics: an updated survey. Wiley Interdisc. Rev. Data Min. Knowl. Discovery **10**(3) (2020). https://doi.org/10.1002/widm.1355

Author Index

A. Basiouni and C. Frasson (Eds.): BBGI 2024, CCIS 2162, p. 243, 2024.
https://doi.org/10.1007/978-3-031-65996-6

The manufacturer's authorised representative in the EU is Springer Nature Customer Service Centre GmbH, Europaplatz 3, 69115 Heidelberg, Germany. If you have any concerns regarding our products, please contact ProductSafety@springernature.com

Printed and bound by CPI Group (UK) Ltd, Croydon, CR0 4YY
30/09/2026
02225560-0005